COPING WIT

COPING WITH ADVERSITY

Regional Economic Resilience
and Public Policy

**Harold Wolman, Howard Wial,
Travis St. Clair, and Edward Hill**

CORNELL UNIVERSITY PRESS ITHACA AND LONDON

First published 2017 by Cornell University Press

Printed in the United States of America

Library of Congress Cataloging-in-Publication Data

Names: Wolman, Harold, author. | Wial, Howard, author. | St. Clair, Travis, author. | Hill, Edward W., author.
Title: Coping with adversity : regional economic resilience and public policy / Harold (Hal) Wolman, Howard Wial, Travis St. Clair, and Edward (Ned) Hill.
Description: Ithaca : Cornell University Press, 2017. | Includes bibliographical references and index.
Identifiers: LCCN 2017019556 (print) | LCCN 2017022715 (ebook) | ISBN 9781501712135 (epub/mobi) | ISBN 9781501709494 (pdf) | ISBN 9780801451690 (cloth : alk. paper) | ISBN 9780801478543 (pbk. : alk. paper)
Subjects: LCSH: United States—Economic conditions—20th century—Regional disparities. | United States—Economic conditions—21st century—Regional disparities. | United States—Economic policy—20th century. | United States—Economic policy—21st century. | Financial crises—United States. | Urban policy—United States.
Classification: LCC HC110.D5 (ebook) | LCC HC110.D5 W65 2017 (print) | DDC 330.973—dc23
LC record available at https://lccn.loc.gov/2017019556

Cornell University Press strives to use environmentally responsible suppliers and materials to the fullest extent possible in the publishing of its books. Such materials include vegetable-based, low-VOC inks and acid-free papers that are recycled, totally chlorine-free, or partly composed of nonwood fibers. For further information, visit our website at cornellpress.cornell.edu.

Contents

Acknowledgments

On the title page, the authors are listed in reverse alphabetical order. Each of the authors made distinct and important contributions.

The authors would like to acknowledge and thank the following individuals who contributed to the writing of and research for this book: Patricia Atkins, Pamela Blumenthal, Diana Hincapie, Sarah Ficenec, and Rosa (Hung Kyong) Lee, all of whom were staff members of the George Washington Institute of Public Policy at The George Washington University; Alec Friedhoff, Alex Gold, Tara Kotagal, Howard Lempel, and Chad Shearer, all of whom were staff members at the Brookings Institution; and Kelly Kinahan and Fran Stewart who were at Cleveland State University.

The authors would also like to thank the MacArthur Foundation for providing funding for the research on this project through the Regional Resilience Program, which was administered by Margaret Weir through the University of California-Berkeley.

COPING WITH ADVERSITY

INTRODUCTION

Metropolitan economies sometimes experience economic adversity, with resulting serious impacts on the area's residents and institutions. The causes, nature, and length of these regional economic problems vary. Although the most visible adversity stems from natural disasters such as Hurricane Katrina in New Orleans or from man-made disasters such as the 9/11 terrorist attack in New York, they more commonly occur as a result of national economic downturns. These include those that affected Detroit during major recessions, the steady decline of a region's dominant export industry that affected Charlotte's textile industry in the 1970s and 1980s, and national and international forces that erode the region's prior economic competitiveness, as seen in Cleveland, Detroit, and Hartford over the past three decades.

The question we address in this book is why some regions are resilient in the face of economic adversity, while others are not. In particular, we examine the role of public policy and intentional activity in achieving resiliency: what strategies and policies can regions pursue to help bring about economic resilience and long-term economic health and what are the implications for economic development policymakers and practitioners? Our analysis covers the period from 1978 to 2014. We separate out the Great Recession years and their aftermath (2007–2014) in order to assess the effect of this severe and prolonged shock on metropolitan area economic adversity and resilience.

Economic Adversity

We focus on two different, though not necessarily unrelated, forms of regional economic adversity: adverse effects from sudden shocks to the regional economy and long-term regional economic stagnation or chronic distress. Based on our findings, we argue that the determinants of both types of economic adversity and of resilience to it are, to at least some extent, predictable, and thus provide potentially important information to policymakers and practitioners about whether their region is at risk. We also argue that, in the short term, state, local, and regional economic development policy has relatively little impact on recovery from shocks once they have occurred, but can have an important effect on the potential for emerging from periods of chronic economic distress and for avoiding such periods altogether.

Economic shocks are exogenous events that have a sudden and immediate impact. They can be of various kinds and can be caused by a variety of factors, including national recessions that play out differentially on regional economies; sudden declines, either nationally or regionally in an export industry critical to a specific region's economy; the closure or relocation outside of the region of a major employer; natural disasters such as earthquakes, floods, or hurricanes; or other nonnatural disasters such as terrorist attacks, chemical spills, or nuclear plant accidents. (See chapter 1 for an operational definition of shocks.)

In contrast to a decline resulting from a sudden shock, a period of *chronic economic distress* is a long period of regional economic stagnation, slow growth, or decline. Chronic distress may be initiated by one or more of the kinds of sudden shocks described above from which the region is unable to recover,[1] and which lead to economic stagnation or, through what Myrdal (1957) termed a process of cumulative causation, a long downward spiral. Negative cumulative causation is frequently described as a negative path dependency. But there may be other causes as well. These include long-term secular declines at the national level in industries that constitute an important part of a region's export base; technological or other changes that erode the region's competitive advantage in one or more of its prior export industries; the exhaustion or economic irrelevance of what was once a fundamental natural resource or location; the operations of the product cycle as industries that originate from region-based innovations ultimately expand elsewhere to take advantage of lower production costs; and/or the inability to regenerate, or reload, its traded sector's portfolio of products through entrepreneurship, small firm creation, or other means as the product cycle for its once dominant industries plays out.[2] Chronic distress may be characterized by low but stable growth (relative to the national growth rate) for long periods of time or by periods of continually declining or even, though rarely, negative economic growth. (See chapter 2 for an operational definition of chronic economic distress.)

We argue that that the *role of policy* and intentional activity can best be understood through a lens that differentiates by level of government and by time period. It is important to separate the potential role of state and local policy from that of federal policy. The federal government has the ability to change interest rates, influence the value of the dollar, and run substantial budget deficits, all of which can have important impacts on national and regional economies in a relatively short period of time. However, none of these tools are available to state and local governments. Instead, for subnational governments, given the time it takes to put policies that are available to them in place and for these policies to have an effect, most actions will have little impact in the short term. This suggests that state and local policies, unlike potential federal actions, will have little if any role in responding to economic shocks, although the effect of these shocks can be cushioned through prior planning for a strong social safety net and budgetary rainy day funds. Despite the political difficulty in doing so, state and local governments can also cushion the impact of economic shocks by maintaining public spending and, if necessary, raising tax rates during an economic downturn rather than cutting spending to match reduced tax revenues.

In the longer term a regional economy's ability to avoid or recover from chronic economic distress depends on its ability to adapt to changing circumstances and to develop or improve new products and services to replace those that have either died or were spun out through the operation of the product cycle. Here the most important actions involve investments in the formal education and workforce development systems and in infrastructure as well as efforts to diversify the region's export sector. However, it is also necessary to recognize that the strategic decisions and investments undertaken not by the public sector but by the region's existing firms play a critical role in shaping the condition of the region's economy. In the longer term, state and local economic development policymakers and practitioners have limited but important roles to play in attempting to mitigate market failures and to reduce transaction costs that limit the region's growth potential. This does not mean that we recommend that state and local leaders should sit tight and ride out an economic downturn. Instead we recommend that they take advantage of an economic crisis, when public support for change is presumably greater, to put in place public policies and investments that will improve the long-term functioning of regional economies.

Resilience

Resilience as an economic development concept has been well theorized but poorly understood in practical terms. The virtue of the term is that it builds a sense of process into ideas of economic strength and weakness—that is, a healthy economy is not uniformly strong but is one that responds well to external or internal shocks and so recovers rather than collapses. The concept of *resilience* thus provides a nuanced organic model for economic health and development. The trouble is, however, that even as planners and politicians talk about resilience they are not sure what institutions, policies, and regulatory and tax regimes foster resilience, either in the short term in response to shocks or in the long term in response to chronic distress.

What does resilience mean[3] in the context of a regional economy? For regional economic analysis, perhaps the most natural conceptual meaning of economic resilience is "bounce back," the ability of a regional economy to maintain or return to a preexisting state (typically assumed to be an equilibrium state) in the presence of a shock. Although only a few studies explicitly use the term "resilience," the economic literature that deals with the idea of resilience usually is concerned with the extent to which a regional or national economy is able to return to its previous level and/or growth rate of output, employment, or population after experiencing an external shock.[4] It does not necessarily mean that the composition of that output in terms of goods and services produced remains unchanged.

The recent economic geography literature has begun to incorporate the concept of resilience as adaptive capacity. Martin (2012, 14) defines this as "the capacity of a regional economy to reconfigure, that is to adapt its structures (firms, industries, technologies, and institutions), so as to maintain an acceptable growth path in output, employment and wealth over time. This view of resilience is thus quintessentially an evolutionary one: resilience is a dynamic process, not just a characteristic or property."[5] Glaeser's study (2005a) of the successive adaptations of Boston's economy from 1603 to 2003 is an excellent example of such an approach.

Building on this conceptual discussion, we define regional economic resilience in two different ways, depending on the kind of economic adversity a regional economy faces. With respect to sudden shocks, we define resilience as the ability of the regional economy either to resist the shock or, if adversely affected, to bounce back to its prior growth path. Thus, a shock to a regional economy may have little or no adverse effect on the economy or it may have a more serious impact. If the former, we consider the region to be *shock-resistant* (which can be thought of as the strongest form of resilience). If the latter, we consider it to be *resilient* if it bounces back to its original path within a moderate period of time. We consider the regional economy to be *nonresilient* if it does not bounce back within a moderate period of time. (See chapter 1 for our operationalization of these concepts.) A regional economy may bounce back either with little or no restructuring from its prior form or with substantial restructuring.

For chronic distress, our definition of resilience relates much more to the concept of adaptive resilience. Resilience in this context means the ability of the economy to emerge from a prolonged period of slow growth relative to the national economy and to experience sustained growth: can the economy adapt so that it emerges from its long-term path of slow growth to a higher rate of growth? We do not assume that these adaptations necessarily occur because of intentional efforts to bring them about.

Adaptations frequently take the form of economic restructuring, that is, changes in the structure of the regional economy. (See chapter 2 for an operationalization of these concepts.) Examples include changes in the composition of the region's export base (those industries that are the economic drivers of the regional economy), its industrial composition, its degree of industrial concentration or diversity, its ability to generate new firms (entrepreneurship), or the size distribution of its firms. Adaptations may also occur in the factors that affect a regional economy's overall competitive advantage, such as changes in the skill levels of its labor force (through improved performance of its education and work force training institutions or through labor force in-migration), its business culture and willingness and ability to assist business, business-related public infrastructure, and amenities that attract a more skilled labor force.

It is important to note that adaptations may take other forms not as directly related to the structure of the regional economy. Instead changes may occur in the characteristics and competencies of individual firms or clusters within the region—their production technologies; their reliance on capital relative to labor; the skills they require of their workers; their planning, marketing, research; and their development and production strategies. Another possibility is that the connectedness among firms and agencies and institutions such as universities, local industry associations, or specialized workforce providers becomes a source of competitive advantage (see Dawley, Pike, and Tomaney 2010).

In general, a region that is resilient to chronic distress is one whose economy and firms have become better poised to pursue economic growth and to attract investment in industries that are growing in the national economy. As Boschma and Lambooy (1999) argue, innovation is likely to play a particularly important role in the restructuring process, either through "path dependent innovations" that build upon the existing economic structure combining with new technologies and firms or through "pathless innovations" that reflect a completely new direction for the economy not built upon its prior foundations. They term the former "adaptive restructuring" and the latter "deep restructuring."

What Do We Know about Regional Economic Resilience?

The resilience of economic systems, the concern of this book, has until recently received only a modest amount of scholarly attention (see Chapple and

Lester 2010; Davies 2011; Dhawan and Jeske 2006; ESPON 2014; Hill, Wial, and Wolman 2008; Hill et al. 2012; Rose 2004, 2009). With respect to economic shocks, the literature has focused mainly on the strength and duration of the shock effect on the level of employment, employment growth rates, and unemployment rates as well as on the mechanisms underlying the pattern of responses to shock, such as labor migration and changes in relative wage rates (see Blanchard and Katz 1992; Deryugina et al. 2014). The available evidence shows that shocks permanently lower employment (relative to their prior path, i.e., to what they otherwise would have been) in regions that experience them. Blanchard and Katz find that at the state level, employment shocks typically result in employment declines for about four years. After that, states eventually return to their preshock employment growth rates (and are, therefore, resilient in the sense in which we use that term) but they start from a permanently lower postshock employment level (see also Barro and Sala-i-Martin 1991). There are two main reasons why unemployment rates recover relatively quickly while employment levels do not. First, unemployed workers in the United States leave regions that have experienced large job losses, while the lack of in-migration of new job-seekers helps the region's unemployment rate to recover. Second, labor force participation rates fall in the area thus reducing the unemployment rate while not increasing the number of employed workers. Employers, by contrast, do not relocate jobs to regions that have experienced large employment shocks (see Bartik and Eberts 2006; Blanchard and Katz 1992; Feyrer, Sacerdote, and Stern 2007). Changes in relative wages do not appear to play a major role.

Feyrer, Sacerdote, and Stern (2007) reach a more pessimistic conclusion about economic resilience in their study of counties that lost steel and auto manufacturing jobs between 1977 and 1982. They find that employment and population in these counties grew slightly a few years after experiencing this employment shock but that they then failed to grow during the approximately two decades that followed the shock. Several studies examining shocks to U.K. regions also find that regions bounce back to prior growth rates, but experience permanent losses in employment levels and, in the case of shocks to coal-mining regions in the early 1980s, many have yet to return to the absolute level of employment prior to the shocks (see Beatty, Fothergill, and Powell 2007; Fingleton, Garretsen, and Martin 2012; Olmerod 2010).

The literature on chronically distressed or "lagging" regions has a longer history, though it has dealt considerably more with causes than with resilience (what accounts for emergence from chronic distress). Some regions lag as a result of inadequate infrastructure, peripheral location with respect to major transportation linkages, and/or low human capital, whereas others experience prosperity and then decline as a result of changes in external demand for the products of their major export industries, or reduction in their competitive advantage relative to other regions.

Regions may also decline if their product portfolios become dominated by products that are in the later stages of their product or profit cycles (see Markusen 1985; Vernon 1966, 1979) and if the region's firms are unable to "reload" with newer products.[6] Markets are organized around products, not industries, and the traded sector of any economy consists of its portfolio of traded products, or goods and services. This is what we term a metropolitan region's product portfolio. Conceptually, each product that is exported from a region has a position in the product cycle and the traded sector's product portfolio will have a median age, a diversity (or variance) of ages, and different correlations between the growth rates of the individual products. This allows one to conceptualize the traded sector of a regional economy as a mix of infant, rapidly growing, mature, and declining products where the overall growth rate is a function of the composition of its product portfolio and the growth rates of each product in that portfolio.

Neoclassical economic theory posits that long-term differences in regional income, employment, and product caused by shocks or other processes should diminish over time as a result of labor and capital mobility. Thus, a substantial amount of research has focused on whether regional economic outcomes are converging. The cumulative results of that research indicate that while movement toward convergence does occur, it does so only after a substantial passage of time (Armstrong and Taylor 2000; Pack 2002).

However, Myrdal (1957) and others argue that equilibrating responses should not necessarily be expected and that a process of cumulative causation may accelerate decline or impede recovery, thus creating regions with chronic distress. This is negative path dependency. Product cycle theory posits that new products are most likely to be developed and refined in larger, wealthier, higher skilled areas and then, as the product becomes standardized and the product market becomes subject to more intense competition, routinized production processes will be moved to lower cost regions. The resulting deconcentration can lead either to convergence, as investment moves to lower income regions and the originating region is unable to regenerate by developing new industries, or to reinforcement of existing disparities if the originating region retains its ability to continue to innovate. Empirical research in this tradition has been primarily single-region case studies of regional economic history, particularly of regions experiencing the erosion of their previously dominant economic base or regions engaged in economic revitalization efforts (see, e.g., Glaeser 2005a; Safford 2009; Saxenian 1994; see also chapters in Bingham and Eberts 1988 and Pack 2005). More systematic evidence on regional resilience to chronic

economic distress must be inferred from the large number of econometric studies of regional economic growth.

Our Research Strategy and Methods

We employ both a quantitative analysis of a large number of regions and a set of
intensive qualitative regional case studies. Our quantitative analyses describe and
explain regional economic downturns, shock-resistance, and resilience after a
downturn and after a period of chronic distress. Metropolitan areas in the United
States constitute our unit of analysis, and we refer to them as metropolitan economies or, alternatively, as regional economies throughout this book. Our datasets
include all years from 1978 to 2014. The core analysis is from 1978 to 2007. We
perform a separate analysis for the years of the Great Recession and the slow
recovery from it, 2007 to 2014, to assess whether these years constituted a break
from previously established patterns of economic resilience.

However, our quantitative analysis does not provide information on the processes that occurred or on the nature and effects of interventions or changes
of behavior. To provide a richer understanding of economic shock and resilience we undertook intensive case studies in six metropolitan regions: Charlotte,
Cleveland, Detroit, Grand Forks, Hartford, and Seattle. We chose these regions to
reflect adversity that resulted from economic shocks and chronic distress as well
as differences in resilience outcomes. We make no claim that these six regions
are a representative slice of metropolitan regions nationally; however, they do
vary in the kinds of economic adversity that they have experienced and in their
responses.

Structure of the Book and Summary of the Chapters

We begin chapter 1 by defining economic shocks and the various ways in which
they might affect regional economies. The analytic part of the chapter is devoted
to quantitative descriptions and analyses of regional economic shocks and their
determinants, causes, and consequences from 1978 to 2007 and then, separately,
in a period coinciding with the Great Recession and its recovery, from 2007 to
2014. Some of the chapter is quite technical and for those who are not concerned
with the mechanics of our econometric analysis, we suggest that the description
of our models and the results for each (pp. 39–49) can be skipped over. The
results are summarized at the end of the chapter.

We identified nearly 1,500 employment shocks to U.S. metropolitan regions
between 1978 and 2007. Regions were resistant to nearly half (47%) of these

shocks, that is they did not experience a serious economic downturn because of them. When regions were adversely affected by the shocks, they were resilient 65% of the time—they returned to their previous growth path within a four-year period. However, consistent with the literature we review in this chapter, regions returned to their prior rates of employment and gross metropolitan product (GMP) growth more rapidly than they returned to their previous levels. They also returned to their prior rates of GMP growth more rapidly than to their prior rate of employment growth, suggesting that resilience to shock was led initially by productivity gains, with employment gains following later.

The Great Recession as a shock had a much greater initial impact on the nation's regional economies. The national economic downturn of 2008 and 2009 adversely affected more than 90% of all metropolitan area economies. However, these economies were resilient in nearly 80% of all cases, a resiliency rate similar to those for national economic downturn shocks prior to the Great Recession and above that of the 65% resilience rate for all shocks.

We also employed multivariate analysis to examine possible causes of shocks, shock-resistance, resilience, and the length of time it takes resilient regions to rebound. The story our analysis tells is more complex than the findings in previous research on regional economic growth. We find, for example, that some characteristics make regions less susceptible to shocks, but also make it more difficult for them to recover once a shock takes hold of a regional economy. The importance of human capital to long-term economic growth is a consistent finding in the regional economic growth literature. However, our findings show that when facing a shock, regions with a poorly educated population are more likely to suffer from an employment downturn but are also more likely to be resilient in recovering from such a downturn. Our findings tell a similar story with respect to industrial structure. A high percentage of employment in the manufacturing sector makes it more likely that a region will suffer from an employment downturn as a result of a shock but also more likely that it will quickly recover. We attribute these findings to the difference between shocks that are purely cyclical compared to shocks that disrupt the competitive structure of a region's economy. Cyclical shocks are more common than structural shocks and cyclical shocks allow a region's economy to rebound to its pre-shock product portfolio, while recovery from structural shock requires new products to be added to that portfolio.

Chapter 2 turns to a similar set of questions with regard to chronic economic distress. We define chronic economic distress and resilience in terms of regeneration and recovery. For the period 1978–2007, we provide quantitative descriptions and analyses of chronic regional economic distress and its determinants, causes, and consequences. As in chapter 1, some of the material is quite technical, and we suggest that readers who are not interested in following the econometrics can simply skip over pages 67–73.

We identified eighty-nine metropolitan areas (nearly 25% of our sample) that experienced one or more periods of chronic economic distress between 1978 and 2007, producing an overall total of 108 periods of chronic distress. Nearly 30% of these periods of chronic distress directly followed an economic shock to which the region was not resilient. Nearly half of these regions recovered from periods of chronic distress when employment is used as the dependent variable. Thus, for many regions chronic distress, while posing serious economic hardship, nonetheless does not last forever.

Consistent with product cycle theory, nearly all of the chronically distressed regions that were resilient (thirty-three of the thirty-seven), engaged in positive restructuring (defined as a change in the region's industrial structure so that its portfolio was better positioned for growth ten years after the onset of chronic distress than it was before that). Resilience in this sense implies economic regeneration reflecting the adaptive capacity of a region's economy and occurs when existing assets are redeployed or adapted to new sources of demand; the product portfolio of the traded sector of the economy changes substantially as a response to decline.

Nonetheless, some regions' experience was more consistent with the theory of cumulative causation. Twelve regions experienced ten or more consecutive years of chronic distress and did not emerge from that condition during the time frame of the first portion of our study: 1978 to 2007. (An additional thirteen regions experienced fewer than ten years of continuous distress and were chronically distressed in 2007, which was the end-point of the first portion of our quantitative analysis.) Most of these regions are small, although Buffalo is an exception.

Our empirical models throw light both on why regions experience chronic distress and why some of these regions are resilient. Regional chronic economic distress in terms of both employment and output is associated with low educational attainment in the region at the onset of the event. The results for educational attainment conform to previous conclusions about the importance of worker skills in the U.S. economy. Factor cost explanations also received support. Controlling for regional industrial composition, high wages per worker were associated with the onset of chronic distress. Manufacturing's share of regional employment was also important and statistically significant as a predictor of chronic economic distress, but in a way that confounds popular perceptions. Regions with a high percentage of their employment in manufacturing were less likely to enter a period of chronic GMP economic distress.

However, the determinants of emergence from chronic economic distress were not always the converse of those that predisposed regions to such a period. For regions that experienced chronic distress, those with a higher proportion of their employment in manufacturing were less likely to emerge from (be resilient to) GMP distress, but were more likely to be resilient to employment distress (i.e., return to rates of total employment growth near to, or above, the national rate). The stickiness of high wages mattered as well: the longer high wages relative to other metropolitan areas persisted, the longer it took a region to emerge from chronic distress. Income inequality appeared to predispose a region to chronic distress, but it was also positively associated with recovery—the greater the extent of income *inequality* the more likely a region was to be resilient to both employment and GMP chronic distress. And the number of major export industries, while not a factor in preventing a period of chronic distress, was positively related to resilience to GMP chronic distress.

In chapters 3 and 4 we move from quantitative analysis to our case studies. We undertook the case studies to provide a richer understanding of economic shocks, chronic economic distress, and resilience, focusing particularly on the processes that occurred, the nature of interventions made by regional actors, and on their effects. Chapter 3 profiles the three less resilient case study regions (Cleveland, Detroit, and Hartford), while chapter 4 profiles the three more resilient ones (Charlotte, Grand Forks and Seattle). In each case we describe their experiences with economic shocks and chronic distress and set forth the strategies, policies, and responses to shocks and chronic distress in which they engaged during our study period.

The six regions encompass a range of different kinds of economic problems over the nearly four decades of our study. However, we found little difference among the six regions in their activities during good times and bad. Nor were there any obvious differences between the economic development activities of those regions that avoided shocks and chronic distress and the normal practice of economic development in the other regions. Our case studies failed to find any public policies put in place during the shock period that affected whether a region recovered from a shock or how long it took to do so. This is not surprising given that most of the shocks consisted of regional cyclical fluctuations where downswings were simply followed by upswings or, from the perspective of one of our interviewees, the region's policy strategy was "to hold our breath until the economy recovered." Strategies and policies that were put in place in the case study regions were sometimes motivated by shocks but were mainly longer-term efforts that could not have been expected to prevent shocks or cushion their negative impacts. These included marketing and recruiting; the creation and restructuring of economic development organizations to encompass more of a regional development perspective and with greater participation of universities, hospitals, and foundations in the region's economy; industry targeting and cluster policy; workforce development; entrepreneurship, small firm start-up, and firm assistance programs; and amenity strategies such as downtown development.

Chapters 5 and 6 assess the likely effects of the most common activities taken to bring about regional economic resilience. We identify nine of the most common approaches. Chapter 5 considers those intended to aid specific businesses and individuals: business tax incentives; industry targeting and cluster policy; technical assistance to firms; and entrepreneurial assistance and promotion. Chapter 6 considers approaches related to the provision of public goods and to improve the operation of the region's economy: human capital, education, and workforce development; infrastructure improvement; amenity improvement and creation; restructuring of economic development organizations; and leadership.

We ask whether each of these intentional efforts to bring about recovery through public policy or civic action is likely to have made a difference. It would not have been practical to undertake an independent evaluation of the effect of the various policies, strategies, and tools that were brought to bear in each of the regions, and we did not attempt to do so. Furthermore, many of these policies are longer-term efforts and would likely not show results in the shorter time frame we are examining. Instead we focus on the likely effects of the various policies. We do so by setting forth and discussing the logic underlying the policy, that is why and under what circumstances the policy might (or might not) be expected to have an effect on regional economic resilience or development. We then summarize the existing research literature that evaluates the specific policies and over what time frames they are likely to occur.

We conclude that while none of the strategies is likely to have an identifiable effect on the successful short-term recovery from an economic shock, there are strategies that can make a difference in recovering from long-term chronic economic stress. Human capital strategies, especially improvements in the preschool, elementary and secondary, and community college formal education systems and, to a lesser extent, workforce development programs, as well as infrastructure spending, offer the best promise for economic resilience, both to help regions avoid and to recover from chronic stagnation. Well-planned and well-implemented firm technical assistance programs, programs directed toward stimulating entrepreneurship, and possibly state-level tax incentives (if not accompanied by reductions in public spending) also show modest promise in countering chronic stagnation.

Our concluding chapter focuses on the role of public policy in promoting regional economic resilience. To better understand the potential role of various types of policy actions, we develop a temporal framework that divides policy implementation and policy effects into three different time frames, with policies varying both in the time it takes to put in place and in the time frame over which effects, if the policy is effective, can be expected.

Different kinds of policy actions are likely to be most appropriate and most effective in the different time periods and in the face of different types of shocks. In the short term, the ability of a region's economy to avoid an economic shock, or to be resilient in the face of one, depends largely on what is happening to the demand for the region's traded products and services. In the face of longer lasting downturns infrastructure development and public job creation, undertaken by or with the assistance of the federal and state governments, can be very effective in employing people who have lost their jobs and in keeping money circulating in the regional economy. A robust social safety net and a rainy-day fund to maintain pre-shock spending on government services are critical to maintain the purchasing power of local residents and governments.

In the longer term, a regional economy's ability to avoid or recover from chronic stagnation depends on its ability to regenerate its portfolio of traded products and services by creating new products and services or substantially improving existing ones. Policies aimed at accomplishing this goal by diversifying the region's export sector or encouraging innovation or entrepreneurship are useful, but the available evidence from the United States suggests that their effects are likely to be modest. Here the most important decisions will be those undertaken by the region's existing firms in terms of adopting strategies relating to new products, new markets, and new technologies that position them for success in a changing economic environment and by the ability of entrepreneurs to create successful new firms.

Over an even longer time horizon, the issue of reducing a region's susceptibility to long-term economic stagnation merges with that of promoting long-term economic growth. Here, improving the quality of the region's labor force through investments in the formal educational system of the sort we suggested above, improvements in the pre-school, elementary and secondary, and community college formal education systems, and, to a lesser extent, workforce development programs, are likely to be the most effective set of public policies.

What this means for the practice of economic development largely depends on expectations. Traditional economic development activity can do little to ameliorate economic adversity in the short term. In the longer term, the most important drivers of the regional economy are the strategic and investment decisions made by individual firms. And with respect to public action and policy, decisions about the most important assets of a regional economy—education, training, infrastructure, communications, utilities, and logistics—all lie mostly outside of the domain of economic development organizations.

Instead, the practice of economic development takes place at the margin of the economy by addressing market failures and transaction costs. One critical market failure relates to information about the regional economy and available building sites, real estate, and the associated infrastructure. This also holds true for labor market information—the extent of the workforce and its skill mix. This set of information needs to be accessible at the scale of the labor market. The second major area of activity of economic development professionals is related to minimizing transactions costs and reducing investment risk. Most companies are not expert at opening up new locations or at expansion, and no matter how efficient a city's system of planning, zoning, permitting, and inspecting a business needs guidance through the labyrinth. There are genuine transactions costs that can be reduced by a good economic developer. The third role of an economic developer is to minimize risks and costs that are inherent in any complicated project. The largest risk is that the facility will not open on time and the best way to reduce cost is to provide a workforce that is trained at the time a facility opens. This requires coordinating with the region's workforce and education systems.

In summary, little can be done to offset the adverse short-term effects of shocks caused by macroeconomic fluctuations. However, there *are* important long-term public policies and investments that can change the value of a region's economic assets and help it to emerge from chronic economic stress. Economic development policymakers and practitioners have an important, albeit limited, role to play in this process.

1

SHOCKS AND REGIONAL ECONOMIC RESILIENCE

The overarching goal of our research is to better understand the resilience of metropolitan (regional) economies. In this chapter we examine this question quantitatively, focusing on short-term economic downturns. This chapter is devoted primarily to an analysis of the regional characteristics associated with shocks, the impact of these shocks on regional economies, and the regional response to them. It examines shocks to both employment and gross metropolitan product. The chapter begins by categorizing economic shocks and the regional responses to those shocks. It then describes metropolitan areas' experience with shocks from the 1970s through the 2007, the year the Great Recession began. This is followed by a separate description of 2007–2014, a period that involved the most severe economic shock since the 1930s depression, followed by a prolonged period of recovery. Finally we present an econometric analysis consisting of four models that attempt to explain why some metropolitan areas are resistant to shocks, why some are adversely affected by them, and why, once adversely affected, some are resilient and others are not. For readers who are not interested in following the econometric analysis, we suggest this section (pp. 39–49) can be skipped. The results of this analysis are summarized in the concluding section of the chapter.

Conceptualizing Economic Shocks and Resilience to Economic Shocks

We conceptualize regional economic shock resilience as the ability of a region (defined for the purpose of this book as a Metropolitan Statistical Area as delineated by the Office of Management and Budget) to recover successfully from shocks that throw it substantially off its prior growth path, resulting in an economic downturn. Shocks can be of three kinds: 1) shocks to the regional economy caused by downturns in the national economy (*national economic downturn shocks*); 2) shocks caused by downturns in particular industries that constitute an important component of the region's export base (*industry shocks* at either the *national* or the *regional* level); and 3) *other external shocks* (e.g., a natural disaster, closure of a military base, movement of an important firm out of the area).

These types of shocks are not mutually exclusive; a regional economy may experience more than one simultaneously. Some examples from the Great Recession illustrate this point. The Great Recession had its roots in the finance industry and deficient regulation of that industry. It had particularly severe effects in those regional economies where that industry was disproportionately concentrated, such as the Charlotte metropolitan area. Yet other metropolitan areas experienced severe regional recessions due to a combination of the initial national economic shock and to regionalized aftershocks in industries that were particularly dependent on consumer finance: Phoenix and Las Vegas in housing and Detroit and Cleveland due to their dependence on the automobile assembly industry. The shocks experienced in these metropolitan regions were both national and industrial.

Not all shocks throw a metropolitan economy substantially off its prior growth path and result in an economic downturn. We term those regions that are not adversely affected by a shock *shock-resistant*. If the region is adversely affected by the shock (i.e., undergoes a resulting downturn) we consider it *resilient* if it returns to at least its prior growth path within a relatively short period of time. If it does not, we consider it *nonresilient* (see figure 1.1). We operationalize these concepts below.

Being shock-resistant is the best outcome for a regional economy, followed by being resilient. Being nonresilient is the least desirable outcome. Note that economic resilience can occur because (1) the region's economy simply bounced back to its previous growth trend because of favorable shifts in the demand for its products; (2) it experienced changes in its industrial or occupational structure that reestablished the competitive position of the region's traded sector; or (3) new products were introduced into the region's portfolio of traded products. Note also that a return to its prior growth path is not necessarily a good thing, particularly if the prior growth path was low or stagnant (although it is presumably a better thing than stabilizing at an even lower level).

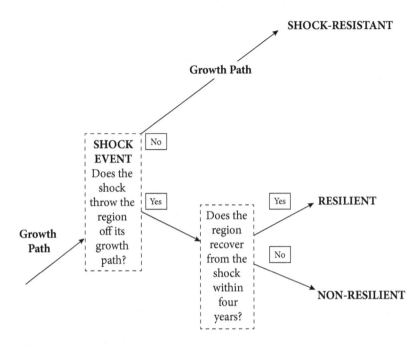

FIGURE 1.1   Resilience concepts

Operational Definitions of Shocks and Their Impacts on Regional Economies

As noted above, there are several kinds of economic shocks. A *national economic downturn shock* is a shock that results from a downturn in the national economy as a whole. We define such a shock to occur when, in any year (which we call the base year), the *national* growth rate (which is separately estimated for employment and gross metropolitan product [GMP]) declines by more than 2 percentage points from its annual growth rate over the previous eight years.[1] An *industry shock* is one that affects one or more of a region's major export industries.[2] For a given year, we define a three-digit North American Industry Classification System (NAICS) industry as a major export industry in a region if its share of regional employment is at least 1.0% *and* it is at least 80% above the same industry's share of national employment.[3]

We consider a region to suffer an industry shock when the job loss experienced by one of its major export industries in a particular year experiences a one-year annual decline of more than 0.75% of aggregate metropolitan employment. Our use of the term "shock" in this context thus refers to an inferred shock; we conclude that a shock occurred based on patterns in our data. Industry shocks can be either national (i.e., a shock to an industrial sector nationally) or a regional industrial shock (i.e., a shock that occurs to an industry in the metropolitan region but not to the industry nationally).

- A *national industry shock* occurs if the three-digit industry that contributes the *largest* share of employment loss to the region's export base when the region experiences an industry shock is also in shock at the *national* level.[4]
- A *regional industry shock* occurs if the three-digit industry that contributes the largest share of employment loss to the region's export base when the region experiences an industry shock has *not* experienced a shock at the national level.

We define shocks to GMP—regional economic output, analogous to national gross domestic product (GDP)—in the same way as employment shocks, except using GMP data.

A region's economy can also experience noneconomic shocks from natural disasters, terrorist attacks, or other noneconomic events that have the potential to adversely affect the regional economy. However, as our data do not enable us to distinguish these shocks from others, we confine our discussion of shocks within this chapter to economic shocks.

Not all shocks adversely affect regional economies. If a shock occurs and a regional economy is not adversely affected by the shock event, the regional economy is termed *shock-resistant.* A metropolitan region is determined to be adversely affected by a shock if, in the *year of the shock or the year thereafter*, its economy experiences a substantial economic downturn, defined as a decline of more than 2.0 percentage points from the annual *regional* growth rate over the previous eight years.[5] However, if the eight-year growth rate was 4.0% or higher, the region's growth rate had to decline by more than half of the previous eight-year average growth rate. (This rule was put into place to identify only major slowdowns in the growth of booming metropolitan economies.) If the region did not undergo a downturn in the year of the shock or the year thereafter, it is considered *shock-resistant*[6] to that shock.

A region that undergoes an *economic downturn* as a result of a *shock* can be either *resilient* to the shock or *nonresilient* to it. A region is *resilient* if, within four years of the onset of the downturn, its annual growth rate returns to the eight-year growth rate prior to the year the downturn occurred.[7] If it does not do so within four years, we term it *nonresilient*.[8]

Counting Shocks and Their Effects on Regions: Definitions and Descriptive Analysis

In this section we count the number of times the various types of shocks described above affected metropolitan economies from 1978 to 2007 to provide an understanding of their relative frequency. Most regional economies are resilient in the short to medium terms. However, although resilience may be the statistical norm it is far from the exclusive outcome. By our criteria, a majority of regions are either shock-resistant to shock episodes or resilient to them after they absorb their initial adverse effect. However, some shocks result in the launching point for negative cumulative causation or negative path dependency, leading to chronic economic distress. With the exception of our analysis of the Great Recession, the discussion in this chapter focuses mainly on employment shocks, although reference is made to GMP shocks when their pattern or results differ substantially from employment data.

Given our operational definition of a regional downturn, it is possible that each of the 361 metropolitan areas could experience either or both an employment and/or a GMP downturn in each of years in our data set (here we do not count as shocks those instances in which a region experiences a shock while it is already in the midst of an existing shock). Using metropolitan-level data from Moody's Analytics for 1970–2007 for 361 metropolitan statistical areas in the United States, we identify 1,476 distinct employment shocks to metropolitan regions between 1978 and 2007 and 1,393 GMP shocks for 1986–2007 (see tables 1.1 and 1.2).[9]

National economic downturn shocks accounted for 661 of the 1,476 distinct employment shocks, occurring in conjunction with the 1981, 1990, and 2000–2001 recessions.[10] Eighty-two of the national employment shocks occurred in conjunction with a *regional industry shock* and 173 occurred with a *national industry shock*.

There were 663 instances of regional industry shocks and 407 instances of national industry shocks to regions. In addition there were 292 downturns due to causes that are not linked to our data; that is, cases where a region's employment growth rate declined by 2 or more percentage points from that of the prior eight year average even in the absence of a national economic downturn or a national or regional industrial shock. Unidentifiable shocks that cause downturns in our data set include natural events such as earthquakes, hurricanes, floods, and other noneconomic occurrences that adversely affected the regional economy.

Regions were shock-resistant to almost half (47%) of the 1,476 identifiable employment shocks, meaning that they did not suffer an economic downturn as a result of the event. Regions were less likely to be resistant to national economic

TABLE 1.1 Employment shocks by type and their effects on regions

TYPE	SHOCK TYPE AND EFFECT			REGIONAL OUTCOME OF SHOCKS RESULTING IN DOWNTURNS		
	NUMBER OF SHOCKS THAT DID NOT RESULT IN DOWNTURN	NUMBER OF SHOCKS THAT RESULTED IN DOWNTURN	TOTAL NUMBER OF SHOCKS	REGION WAS RESILIENT	REGION WAS NONRESILIENT	AVERAGE TIME TO RECOVERY FOR RESILIENT REGIONS
National economic shock	221 (33%)	440 (67%)	661 (100%)	245 (56%)	195 (44%)	2.8 years
Alone	183 (45%)	223 (55%)	406 (100%)	122 (55%)	101 (45%)	2.8 years
With regional industry shock	9 (11%)	73 (89%)	82 (100%)	44 (60%)	29 (40%)	3.0 years
With national industry shock	29 (17%)	144 (83%)	173 (100%)	79 (55%)	65 (45%)	2.6 years
Regional industry shock	383 (58%)	280 (42%)	663 (100%)	204 (73%)	76 (27%)	2.9 years
Alone	374 (64%)	207 (36%)	581 (100%)	160 (77%)	47 (23%)	2.8 years
With national economic shock	9 (11%)	73 (89%)	82 (100%)	44 (60%)	29 (40%)	3.0 years
National industry shock	135 (33%)	272 (67%)	407 (100%)	181 (67%)	91 (33%)	2.9 years
Alone	106 (45%)	128 (55%)	234 (100%)	102 (80%)	26 (20%)	3.1 years
With national economic shock	29 (17%)	144 (83%)	173 (100%)	79 (55%)	65 (45%)	2.6 years
Total shocks (not double-counting)	701 (47%)	775 (53%)	1,476 (100%)	507 (65%)	268 (35%)	2.9 years

Source: Authors' analysis of Moody's Analytics data

TABLE 1.2 GMP shocks by type and their effects on regions

TYPE	SHOCK TYPE AND EFFECT			REGIONAL OUTCOME OF SHOCKS RESULTING IN DOWNTURNS		
	NUMBER OF SHOCKS THAT DID NOT RESULT IN DOWNTURN	NUMBER OF SHOCKS THAT RESULTED IN DOWNTURN	TOTAL NUMBER OF SHOCKS	REGION WAS RESILIENT	REGION WAS NONRESILIENT	AVERAGE TIME TO RECOVERY FOR RESILIENT REGIONS
National economic shock	233 (55%)	188 (45%)	421 (100%)	148 (79%)	40 (21%)	2.3 years
Alone	178 (74%)	62 (26%)	240 (100%)	45 (73%)	17(27%)	2.3 years
With regional industry shock	24 (32%)	50 (68%)	74 (100%)	42 (84%)	8 (16%)	2.0 years
With national industry shock	31 (29%)	76 (71%)	107 (100%)	61 (80%)	15 (20%)	2.5 years
Regional industry shock	414 (58%)	297 (42%)	711 (100%)	258 (87%)	39 (13%)	2.4 years
Alone	390 (61%)	247 (39%)	637 (100%)	216 (87%)	31 (13%)	2.4 years
With national economic shock	24 (32%)	50 (68%)	74 (100%)	42 (84%)	8 (16%)	2.0 years
National industry shock	184 (42%)	258 (58%)	442 (100%)	226 (88%)	32 (12%)	2.4 years
Alone	153 (46%)	182 (54%)	335 (100%)	165 (91%)	17 (9%)	2.4 years
With national economic shock	31 (29%)	76 (71%)	107 (100%)	61 (80%)	15 (20%)	2.5 years
Total shocks (not double-counting)	776 (56%)	617 (44%)	1,393 (100%)	529 (86%)	88 (14%)	2.4 years

Source: Authors' analysis of Moody's Analytics data

downturn shocks and national industry shocks than to regional industry shocks. Not surprisingly, they were also less likely to be resistant to multiple shocks, that is when two types of economic shocks occurred simultaneously. Regions suffered a substantial economic downturn in 775 (53%) of these shock incidents.

Regions suffering a downturn as a result of a shock were resilient 65% of the time, that is, they returned to at least their prior eight-year average employment growth rate within a reasonably short period of time (four years). The average length of time from the onset of the downturn to recovery for a region was 2.9 years.

As table 1.1 indicates, regions that were adversely affected by a shock were less likely to be resilient if the shock was a national economic downturn alone (to which 55% of adversely affected regions were resilient) than if it was a national industry shock alone (80% resilient) or a regional industry shock alone (77% resilient).

We examined regional resilience to shocks in a series of cross-tabulations to see whether there were descriptive variations in the results controlling for a small number of potential explanatory variables: Census region—Northeast, South, Midwest, and West—metropolitan area population size, manufacturing employment in 2000, and educational attainment, among others. The potential explanatory variables considered are listed in tables 1.3 and 1.4.

Although some of the differences reported are statistically significant they are simply bivariate descriptive relationships *not* controlling for other factors. In fact, several of these relationships are not statistically significant in the more fully specified multivariate models on which we report in the next section. There was virtually no variation by Census Region in the extent to which metropolitan areas were resistant to instances of shock. There was modest variation among regions in the degree to which once a metropolitan region was adversely affected it was resilient. When faced with employment shocks, metropolitan areas in the Northeast were resilient only 53% of the time compared to 71% of the time for southern metropolitan statistical areas (MSAs) (the national average resiliency rate was 65%). Much the same pattern held for GMP: there was virtually no variation in resistance to GMP shocks by Census Region, but of those MSAs adversely affected by a GMP shock those metropolitan areas located in the Northeast Census Region were less resilient (71% of the time) than the national average of 86%.

Population size provided a much different story. While metropolitan regions as a whole were shock-resistant to employment shocks 53% of the time, the sixty-nine largest regions (over 1,000,000 in population) were resistant to employment shocks only 23% of the time. These large metropolitan regions were also less likely to be resilient to those shocks that adversely affected them (50% compared to 65% of all regions).

TABLE 1.3 Means of shock-resistant metropolitan areas versus all other metropolitan areas

	EMPLOYMENT			GMP		
	METROPOLITAN AREAS THAT EXPERIENCED FEWER THAN THREE DOWNTURNS	METROPOLITAN AREAS THAT EXPERIENCED THREE OR MORE DOWNTURNS	DIFFERENCE	METROPOLITAN AREAS THAT EXPERIENCED FEWER THAN THREE DOWNTURNS	METROPOLITAN AREAS THAT EXPERIENCED THREE OR MORE DOWNTURNS	DIFFERENCE
Percent employment in manufacturing (2000)	11.3	14.4	−3.1***	12.5	14.7	−2.2***
Number of major export industries (2000)	4.86	5.05	−0.19	6.63	6.89	−0.27
Percent of population 25+ with a high school education or less (2000)	48.8	49.1	−0.3	48.0	50.0	−1.9**
Percent Hispanic (2000)	9.51	9.26	0.24	9.83	8.81	1.02
Average July temperature	76.3	75.9	0.4	75.7	76.2	−0.5
Right-to-work state (2000)	0.44	0.46	−0.02	0.42	0.49	−0.07
Herfindahl index	4.24	4.66	−0.41	4.35	4.76	−0.40
Number of research institutions	0.59	0.48	0.12	0.69	0.32	0.37***
Distance to large metro	2.13	1.63	0.50	1.63	1.88	0.25
Population (2000) – Medians	207,355	226,522	−19,167	288,309	181,269	107,040***

Note: * p < 0.10, ** p < 0.05, *** p < 0.01

TABLE 1.4 Means of resilient metropolitan areas versus all other metropolitan areas

	EMPLOYMENT			GMP		
	METROPOLITAN AREAS THAT WERE RESILIENT TO ALL DOWNTURNS	ALL OTHER METROPOLITAN AREAS	DIFFERENCE	METROPOLITAN AREAS THAT WERE RESILIENT TO ALL DOWNTURNS	ALL OTHER METROPOLITAN AREAS	DIFFERENCE
Percent employment in manufacturing (2000)	14.3	13.3	0.9	14.2	12.6	1.6*
Number of major export industries (2000)	5.22	4.93	0.30	7.08	6.23	0.86***
Percent of population 25+ with a high school education or less (2000)	52.8	47.7	5.1***	50.2	47.1	3.1***
Percent Hispanic (2000)	12.0	8.4	3.6**	9.78	8.58	1.20
Average July temperature	77.6	75.4	2.1***	76.3	75.4	0.92
Right-to-work state (2000)	0.52	0.43	0.08	0.48	0.41	0.07
Herfindahl index	5.23	4.32	0.91	4.72	4.28	0.44
Number of research institutions	0.21	0.60	-0.39***	0.29	0.86	0.57***
Distance to large metro	2.03	1.67	0.36	2.03	1.31	0.72***
Population (2000) – Medians	160,026	251,494	-91,468***	180,936	341,851	-160,915

* p < 0.10, ** p < 0.05, *** p < 0.01

The simple comparisons discussed immediately above show only limited evidence that metropolitan regions with common characteristics were more predisposed to suffer shock-induced economic downturns than other areas. However, the number of downturns a metropolitan region experienced has statistically significant associations with four independent variables. Regions that experienced three or more downturns were more dependent on the manufacturing sector in 2000 then were those that experienced fewer than three downturns. The downturn-prone regions had 3.1 percentage point higher shares of manufacturing employment and a 2.2 percentage point higher share of GMP from manufacturing (see table 1.3). Those regions that were susceptible to downturns in GMP had a 1.9 percentage points higher share of population with educational attainment of high school education or less, fewer research institutions, and smaller populations.

We also identified differences among regions that were resilient to *all* shock-induced downturns compared to those that were nonresilient to one or more downturns. Those regions that were resilient to all shock-induced employment downturns averaged a 5.1 percentage point higher share of their adult population with educational attainment above a high school diploma, 3.6 percentage points higher share of Hispanics in their population, a relatively small metropolitan area population, and fewer research institutions compared to those regions that were nonresilient to one or more downturns (see table 1.4). In terms of GMP downturns, resilient regions had a 1.6 percentage point *greater* manufacturing share of employment, a greater *number* of major export industries, a higher percentage of their adult population with greater than a high school education, fewer research institutions, and were more distant from the next most populous metropolitan area.

Existing research discussed in the previous chapter suggested that regions that lost either employment or GMP return to their prior *rates* of growth much more rapidly than they return to their *prior levels* of employment or GMP. We find that 75% of regions that were adversely affected by a shock actually lost employment relative to their base year (i.e., the year prior to its first year of economic downturn) during some period of one or more years following the shock, while 61% experienced a loss of GMP. Of those that did lose employment, the average amount of time it took to return to preshock employment levels was 5.6 years, with a maximum of twenty-nine years, while the mean time to return to prior GMP levels was 3.5 years.

For regions that were resilient (all of which, by our definition, returned to their prior *rate* of growth within four years), the average number of years needed to return to prior employment *levels* was 5.1 and the average number of years required to return to prior GMP levels was 3.5 years. For nonresilient regions that lost employment and/or GMP, the average amount of time needed to return to preshock employment levels was 6.7 years and to preshock GMP levels was 4 years.

Some regions took much longer. For instance, the Hartford metropolitan area experienced a downturn in 1988 to which it was nonresilient. Twenty years later, employment in the region had yet to return to its 1988 level. New Orleans suffered a downturn in 1981 in tandem with the national economic downturn and did not return to its prior level of employment until 1994.

In sum, resilient regions returned to their prior *rates* of employment and GMP growth relatively quickly (the average time was 2.9 years for employment shocks and 2.4 years for GMP shocks), but for those regions that lost employment and/or GMP, the time to return to prior *levels* was longer, and sometimes much longer. Furthermore the return to prior GMP levels was considerably more rapid than the return to prior employment levels, indicating that the recovery to a shock was led by increased productivity with additional employment following in its wake.

The Great Recession and Regional Economic Resilience

Beginning at the end of 2007 and lasting through the middle of 2009, the U.S. economy experienced the greatest economic downturn since the Great Depression. Gross domestic product declined in real terms by 2.1% in 2008 and by an additional 1.7% in 2009. It rose by 2.1% in 2010, but then increased by a paltry 0.5% in 2011 as the effects of the stimulus wore off and a regime of fiscal austerity was imposed.

Applying the definition of economic downturn that we have used for this study (i.e., a decline from the economy's previous eight year annual average), GDP fell by 4.5 percentage points from its prior eight-year annual average in 2008 and an additional 3.5 percentage points in 2009. Both of these declines exceeded 2 percentage points from the prior eight-year annual average and thus qualified as a national economic downturn and an economic shock affecting all metropolitan economies. We therefore extend our data set from 2007 to 2014 in order to examine the effect of the Great Recession period on metropolitan economies. We focus on gross metropolitan product because the first-order effects of the national economic downturn were more visible and immediate on output than on employment.[11]

Following our definition in the prior paragraph, the Great Recession was manifested in the national economic downturns of 2008 and 2009. In measuring its effect, the national downturn of 2008 could have had its impact on metropolitan area economies in 2008 or 2009, while the national economic downturn of 2009 could have had its impact in 2009 or 2010. By definition, metropolitan areas whose economies were not adversely affected (i.e., declined by more than two percentage points from their previous eight year average annual growth rate) were deemed shock-resistant. Altogether the 2008 and 2009 national economic downturns resulted in 518 cases of downturns, with some metropolitan economies being adversely affected more than once. In 2008 alone, 258 metropolitan economies were adversely affected, 71.5% of all metropolitan area economies. Together, and adjusting for double-counting, the Great Recession of 2008 and 2009 adversely affected 331 (91.7%) of all metropolitan areas (see table 1.5).

The severity of the shock that the Great Recession imposed on metropolitan economies can be gauged through comparing its impact to those of previous national economic downturns. In the entire period from 1978 to 2007, only 45% of metropolitan areas were adversely affected by national economic shock downturns, while 55% were shock-resistant. During the Great Recession period, 91.7% were adversely affected and only 8.3% were shock-resistant. Of those metropolitan economies that were shock-resistant to the national economic downturn shocks of 2008, 84% could be classified as healthy economies in that their prior eight-year average annual growth rate was positive. The remaining 16% were economies that were previously in decline; that is, their prior eight-year average annual growth rate was negative. For those 331 metropolitan economies that were adversely affected by the Great Recession from 2008 to 2010, 165 could be classified as previously healthy, while 166 were already in decline prior to the shock. Half of the nation's metropolitan areas that experienced a downturn between 2008 and 2010 experienced a precursor-shock either in 2006 or 2007, or in both years. (See table 1.6 for examples from eleven metropolitan areas.)

However, while the Great Recession did not officially[12] begin until December 2007, it was partially triggered by the decline and then collapse of the housing market that began in 2006. Housing prices, inflated by the housing bubble, began to decline in 2006 and by September 2008 had fallen 20% from their 2006 peak. Household equity in real estate began a similar decline, falling by 25.9% from the first quarter of 2006 to the fourth quarter of 2007. New housing construction began a precipitous decline from its peak in January 2006. Domestic automobile and light truck production was at 382,000 units a month in April 2006 and declined by 23% in September 2007.

As a consequence, we extend our definition of the Great Recession to include 2006 and 2007 as well as 2008 and 2009. Thus, the "2008" national economic downturn could have been manifested in metropolitan economies in 2006, 2007, 2008, 2009, or 2010. Using this definition, the 2008 and 2009 national economic

TABLE 1.5 Shocks, shock-resistance, and downturns during the Great Recession

YEAR	REGIONS THAT WERE NOT IN AN EXISTING GREAT RECESSION DOWNTURN AT BEGINNING OF YEAR (1)	REGIONS EXPERIENCING SHOCK DURING YEAR (2)	NUMBER OF TOTAL REGIONAL ECONOMIC DOWNTURNS THAT WERE NEW(3)	REGIONS THAT WERE SHOCK-RESISTANT
2008	361	258 (71.5%)	258	103 (28.5%)
2009(4)	103	176	40 (4)	63 (61.2%)
2010(5)	63	84	33 (5)	30 (47.6%)
Total	NA	518	331	30

Source: Authors' analysis of Moody's Analytics data

Notes:

1) This column assumes the Great Recession began in 2008. Regions that were in a downturn for whatever reason prior to 2008 are nonetheless not counted in this table as having experienced a Great Recession downturn. Thus it ignores regions that were in already in a downturn in 2006 or 2007.

2) This column contains all regions experiencing a downturn due to the start of the Great Recession in 2008. Thus regions experiencing more than one downturn (e.g., both in 2008 and in 2010) are double-counted.

3) For this column, 2008 begins with all regions experiencing a downturn in 2008, the first year of the recession. The figure for 2009 is for those regions that did not experience a downturn in 2008, but did in 2009. The figure for 2010 is for all regions that did not experience a downturn in 2008 or 2009 but did in 2010. All areas that experienced downturns in 2008 were considered to be not shocked in 2009, since they were already in a downturn.

4) All downturns in 2009 were considered to result from shocks in 2009 (in other words, even though the shock of 2008 could have resulted in a downturn in either 2008 or one year later, 2009, all downturns in 2009 were considered to result from the shock of 2009, not the shock of 2008.

5) In the absence of a national shock in 2010, all downturns in 2010 were considered to result from the shock of 2009.

6) All downturn is 2008, 2009, and 2010 are assumed to result from the Great Recession rather than other possible shocks, such as natural disasters, national or regional industry shocks, etc.

TABLE 1.6 Annual growth rates in gross product in the United States and eleven metropolitan areas, 2006–2011

YEAR	UNITED STATES	BRIDGEPORT	CHARLOTTE	CHICAGO	CLEVELAND	DETROIT	GRAND FORKS	HARTFORD	LAS VEGAS	PHOENIX	SAN JOSE	SEATTLE
2006	2.5%	4.4%	4.9%	2.4%	-0.2%	-4.6%	1.8%	1.8%	4.0%	5.9%	3.5%	3.8%
2007	1.6%	4.3%	-3.8%	1.5%	-0.6%	-1.4%	2.3%	4.9%	2.2%	2.5%	3.6%	6.8%
2008*	-2.1%	-7.9%	-0.7%	-4.5%	-3.2%	-8.2%	1.6%	-4.9%	-6.2%	-5.2%	-3.9%	-0.9%
2009*	-1.7%	-3.6%	-3.0%	-1.6%	-3.7%	-7.8%	2.0%	1.6%	-8.0%	-6.3%	-4.5%	-0.6%
2010	2.1%	1.8%	3.0%	0.7%	2.3%	4.4%	2.6%	0.9%	-3.3%	0.0%	7.3%	1.6%
2011	0.5%	-2.1%	1.9%	0.2%	2.1%	1.1%	1.5%	-2.1%	-2.5%	0.4%	4.9%	0.0%
CYCLE STATUS												
2010	Resilient	Resilient	Recovering	Resilient	Resilient	Resilient	Shock-resistant, growing	Recovering	Follow-on downturn	Continued decline	Resilient	Recovering
2011	Shock-resistant, growing	New downturn	Recovering	Shock-resistant, growing	Shock-resistant, growing	Shock-resistant, growing	Shock-resistant, growing	Follow-on downturn	Follow-on downturn	Recovering	Shock-resistant, growing	Follow-on downturn

* National downturn occurred in this year according to the definition used in this book. Definition of cycle status labels: Resistant, growing: Resistant to a downturn or shock with a positive 1-year annual growth rate; Resistant, declining: Resistant to a downturn or shock with a negative 1-year annual growth rate; Resilient: 8-year annual average growth rate equals the 8-year rate for the year the downturn occurred within the appropriate 4-year recovery window; Not resilient: 8-year annual average growth rate did not equal the 8-year rate for the year before the downturn occurred within the appropriate 4 year recovery window; New downturn: The year before a downturn occurs the region's cycle status is either: Resistant, Resilient, or Not Resilient; Follow-on downturn: A downturn is registered while the region is still within a recovery window from a previous downturn; Recovering: The region suffered a downturn in a previous year and is still within the appropriate 4-year recovery window and the 1-year growth rate is positive; Continued decline: The region suffered a downturn in a previous year and is still within the appropriate 4-year recovery window and the 1-year growth rate is negative.

Office of Management and Budget names for the metropolitan areas listed: Bridgeport, Norwalk-Stamford, CT; Hartford-West Hartford-East Hartford, CT; Charlotte-Gastonia-Concord, NC-SC; Las Vegas-Henderson-Paradise, NV; Chicago-Naperville-Joliet, IL-IN-WI; Phoenix-Mesa-Scottsdale, AZ; Cleveland-Elyria-Mentor, OH; San Jose-Sunnyvale-Santa Clara, CA; Detroit-Warren-Livonia, MI; Seattle-Tacoma-Bellevue, WA downturns adversely affected all but 24 (93.4%) of the 361 metropolitan areas.[13] As we did in analyzing the 1978–2007 period, we excluded from our count of a particular year's downturns those metropolitan areas that were in an existing downturn without having resolved it (through being either resilient or nonresilient over a four-year period following the initial downturn) when that area experienced a new downturn (we extended the four year period in which it could establish resiliency so that the four-year recovery window opened after the region experienced its last annual downturn).[14]

Of the 337 metropolitan areas that were not shock-resistant to the Great Recession, 70 (20.8%) were not resilient within the appropriate four-year recovery window; the remaining 267 (79.2%) were resilient to the shock. The resiliency rate from the Great Recession was virtually the same as the resiliency rate for regions adversely affected by national economic downturn shocks from 1978 to 2007 (79%). These results indicate that while the effects of the Great Recession were wide and deep and a large number of metropolitan regions had to recover from an initial downturn and follow-on downturns, metropolitan areas were ultimately as resilient to these effects as they had been in previous economic downturns. However, the length of time it took for a region to reestablish its resilience was greater than in previous downturns. The average time for a region adversely affected in 2006 to achieve resilience (i.e., return to at least its annual average eight-year growth rate prior to its downturn) was 3.5 years. The return to resilience declined for those first suffering downturns in 2007 and beyond. Overall the average number of years needed to return to resilience for metropolitan economies after experiencing a downturn in 2006, 2007, 2008, 2009, and 2010 was 2.7, compared to 2.3 years for downturns resulting from national economic shocks prior to the Great Recession.

The connection between national economic policy and metropolitan economies is clearly evident (table 1.6). In early 2009 Congress passed the American Recovery and Reinvestment Act, a fiscal package meant to stimulate the economy. Gross domestic product, which had declined by 2.1% in 2008 compared to 2007 and by 1.7% in the following year, increased by 2.1% between 2009 and 2010 as the stimulus effects filtered through the national economy. However, from 2010 to 2011, federal spending, which had increased by 11.7% from 2008 to 2009 and 3.8% from 2009 to 2010, fell by 1.4%. U.S. GDP increased by only 0.5% between 2010 and 2011 as the stimulus was curtailed. At the metropolitan level, gross metropolitan product, which had increased by 1.9% in 2010, increased by only 0.4% in 2011. As a result, 171 metropolitan areas suffered a downturn in 2011.[15] Two-thirds of these regional economies were in the midst of recovering from previous downturns and their recoveries were set back. The downturn for the other 58 was new.

TABLE 1.7 Metropolitan area shock-resistance, resilience, and nonresilience during the Great Recession

YEAR	NOT IN DOWNTURN AT START OF YEAR (1)	SHOCK-RESISTANT DURING YEAR	DOWNTURN DURING YEAR (2)	RESOLUTION				AVERAGE YEARS TO RESILIENCE
				NUMBER RESILIENT	% RESILIENT	NUMBER NOT RESILIENT	% NOT RESILIENT	
2006	361	267	94	77	81.9%	17	18.1%	3.5
2007	267	167	100	81	81.0%	19	19.0%	2.7
2008	167	56	111	87	78.4%	24	21.6%	2.3
2009	56	33	23	17	73.9%	6	26.1%	1.3
2010	33	24	9	5	55.6%	4	44.4%	1.7
Total	24		337 (93.3%)	267	79.2%	70	20.8%	2.7

Notes:

1) This column assumes that the effects of the Great Recession began to be manifested through pre-cursors in 2006 and 2007. Regions that were in a downturn for whatever reason prior to 2006 are not counted in this table as having experienced a Great Recession downturn.

2) For this column, 2006 begins with all regions experiencing a downturn in 2006, the first year of the recession's effects. The figure for 2007 is for those regions that did not experience a downturn in 2006, but did in 2007. The figure for 2010 is for all regions that did not experience a downturn in 2006 or 2007 but did in 2008, and so forth for following years . All areas that experienced downturns in a year were considered to be not shocked in later years, since they were already in a downturn.

3) All downturns listed for a year were considered to result from shocks in that year (in other words, even though the shock of 2006 could have resulted in a downturn in either 2006 or one year later, 2007, all downturns in 2007 were considered to result from the shock of 2009, not the shock of 2008).

4) In the absence of a national shock in 2010, all downturns in 2010 were considered to result from the shock of 2009.

5) All downturn are assumed to result from the Great Recession or its precursors rather than other possible shocks, such as natural disasters, national or regional industry shocks, etc.

The impact of the premature end of the stimulus is evident in the regional economies listed in table 1.6. In 2010 the national economy achieved resilience from the downturns suffered in the previous two years, as did the Bridgeport, Chicago, Cleveland, Detroit, and San Jose regions. Grand Forks benefited from North Dakota's shale boom and also was resilient. Charlotte, Hartford, and Seattle were not yet resilient, but experienced positive GMP growth from 2009 to 2010. Phoenix's GMP fell from 2009 to 2010, but the drop was not step enough to become a follow-on downturn. Las Vegas did experience a follow-on downturn from 2009 to 2010. As we noted above, the shallow broad-based, recovery that began in 2010 nearly halted in 2011. Bridgeport experienced a new downturn and the drops in GMP in Hartford, Las Vegas, and Seattle were steep enough to become follow-on downturns. The recovery continued in Charlotte and Phoenix but they were not yet resilient. The national economy, Chicago, Cleveland, Grand Forks, and San Jose were shock resistant.

Since the period we define for recoveries for those affected stretches for four years beyond 2011 to 2015 and since, at the time of the writing we did not have data beyond 2014, we were unable to calculate the resilience ratio for these metropolitan areas.

Explaining Shock-Resistance and Resilience

In this section we move from description to analysis. We consider four questions:

1. What accounts for metropolitan regional economic downturns, as we have defined them, i.e., what are the characteristics associated with areas that experience downturns of their regional economies compared to those that do not?
2. What makes regions *shock resistant*? Why are some regions adversely affected when an economic shock occurs (i.e., they experience an economic downturn as we define it), while others are not?
3. When experiencing an economic downturn, why are some areas "resilient" in that they return to their previous growth rate within a relatively short period of time while others do not?
4. What accounts for the length of time it takes a region that is experiencing an economic downturn to recover (i.e., to be "resilient" by our definition)?

We specify and estimate econometric models addressed to each of these questions, with the previous literature providing guidance about the variables that belong in these models.

INSIGHTS FROM PREVIOUS LITERATURE. The empirical findings in the regional literature point to several features of regions that may contribute to either shock-resistance or resilience.[16] Feyer, Sacerdote, and Stern (2007, 59) find that regions with higher levels of human capital were no less likely to experience shocks or to recover from them more quickly than were regions with lower levels of human capital. Regions with slower rates of growth prior to the shock were more likely to be more adversely affected and to be less resilient. With respect to industrial structure, they find that counties that experienced auto and steel job losses in the late 1970s and early 1980s had higher post-shock population growth if they had warm, sunny climates and were located near large metropolitan areas.[17]

Kolko and Neumark (2010), in a study of the impact of regional and industry employment shocks on establishment-level employment, find that employment in corporate headquarters and, to a lesser extent, in small, locally owned chains, is less likely to decline in response to these shocks. Therefore, high concentrations of these types of businesses would be expected to make regions more shock-resistant. Chapple and Lester (2007; 2010) find evidence that regions in which technology and knowledge-based work are growing rapidly exhibit greater resilience in terms of average earnings per job.

It has also been suggested that quality and age of a region's public and private infrastructure is related to cyclical volatility and to growth. Howland (1984) finds that states with new private capital stocks experience more severe recessions. She reasons that such states have a larger proportion of newer and smaller firms and that such firms are more susceptible to bankruptcy during a recession. This contradicts earlier findings by Variaya and Wiseman (1977), who argue that regions with older capital stock may experience more severe regional recessions because older (and more obsolete) capital is that most likely to be retired during a recession. However, Howland (1984) also finds that once small firms are eliminated from the sample, states with older capital stock experience more severe recessions. Age of the metropolitan area is sometimes used as a proxy for the condition of both private and public capital infrastructure. It is also used as a match between an area's urban form and modern transportation needs (with the implication that older areas are likely to have less effective and efficient infrastructure, more prone to breakdown and need for repair; see Blumenthal, Wolman, and Hill 2009). In the case of both public and private infrastructure, older areas are hypothesized to be less "resilient."

Other literature on regional economic growth, although not about shock resilience per se, suggests hypotheses that may be relevant to the analysis of resilience to shocks. As noted earlier, research suggests that human capital (the educational attainment or skills of the region's workforce) is a major driver of growth

(Glaeser and Saiz 2004; Glaeser, Scheinkman, and Shleifer 1995; Gottlieb and Fogarty 2003.). Another strand of research examines the unresolved question of whether industrial specialization or industrial diversification better promotes growth (Glaeser et al. 1992; Harrison, Kelley, and Gant 1996; Henderson 2003; Henderson, Kuncaro, and Turner 1995). A small literature explores whether local government fragmentation within a metropolitan area promotes or inhibits growth, although the findings tend to be inconclusive (Carr and Feiock 1999; Hamilton, Miller, and Paytas 2004). Some research has linked regional economic growth to a low level of income inequality within a region (Glaeser, Resseger, and Tobio 2009; Morrow 2008; Pastor and Benner 2008). All these potential determinants of regional growth are potentially determinants of regional economic resilience as well.

The literature on international economic development may also contribute some insights that are relevant to regional economic resilience. Duval, Elmeskov, and Vogel (2007), in a study of the reasons why shocks to national economies occur and persist, find that public policies that restrict firms' ability to lay off or reassign workers make shock effects less severe but also make them last longer. At the regional level, this may suggest that state and local policies that inhibit layoffs or promote unionization have similar effects. Briguglio et al. (2006) develop an index of national economic resilience based on several hypotheses about resilience, including the hypothesis that the concentration of a nation's exports in a few industries inhibits resilience. This suggests a similar hypothesis for regional export industries (as distinct from the hypotheses about overall regional economic diversification noted above). Finally, there is a growing body of international quantitative evidence that national and region-specific institutions, behavioral norms and customs, knowledge, and technology have long-lasting impacts on the economic development of countries and regions.[18] Although these concepts are difficult to apply in quantitative studies of regional economies within the United States, they are relevant to regions' ability to avoid or recover from economic shocks.

The broader literature on regional resilience, especially the literature on resilience to natural disasters, also has insights that may be relevant to regional economic resilience. For example, a common finding in that literature is that access to economic resources promotes regional or community resilience in the face of natural disasters (Norris et al. 2008; Paton and Johnston 2001; Rozario 2005). This suggests that regions with higher average incomes or wages (independently of human capital) may recover more quickly from economic shocks.

DATA AND ANALYSIS. The data for all of our models consist of total employment from 1970 through 2007 and GMP from 1978 through 2007 for the 361 metropolitan statistical areas in the United States.[19] (The post-2007 Great Recession and recovery period may be sufficiently different from prior experience that it deserves separate consideration. Unfortunately the time period is not sufficient to conduct similar econometric analysis for that period.) Because our definition of an economic downturn requires eight prior years of employment data, the years available for analysis are limited to the thirty years from 1978 through 2007 for total employment and twenty-two years from 1986 through 2007 for GMP. Each of the models includes only a subset of observations depending on the dependent variable of interest.

The literature reviewed above guides the selection of variables we test for the models, though we were unable to find data to test all of the hypotheses. We employ a series of independent variables in the regressions that attempt to capture features of the different regions' economic structure, labor force, demographic, and other characteristics that are expected be related to shock-resistance and/or resilience. Our dependent variable in each case is a dummy variable that takes on a value of 1 when the event of interest takes place in a given year and a value of 0 when it does not. The dependent variable will represent either an economic downturn or a recovery depending on the intent of the model. (See table 1.8 for data sources and summary statistics.)

To test whether regional economic resilience is related to characteristics of the region's economy, we include the percentages of regional employment that are in selected industries that either are part of an region's economic base (durable manufacturing, nondurable manufacturing, and tourism-related industries) or are rapidly growing due to structural shifts in the economy nationally (health care and social assistance).[20] Although we were unable to include data on employment in higher education (which is an export industry for some metropolitan regions), we do include a variable consisting of a count of the number of research universities in the metropolitan area involved in high and very high research activity (according to the Carnegie Foundation's classification system). The research output of these research intense universities is an export product (Hill and Lendel 2007). We also include two measures of industrial diversity—a Herfindahl index (which measures the extent to which the regional economy is concentrated in a few industries or diversified among many) and the number of major export industries in the region—to assess the frequently asserted proposition that more diverse and less concentrated regional economies are more resilient. We also included earnings per worker as a crude variable for regional wage rate, although we note that this variable could also proxy regional resource capacity. Finally, to test whether previously rapidly growing regions are more likely to experience economic downturns, be susceptible to shock, and/or be less resilient, we include a variable that captures the rate of growth prior to a downturn.

TABLE 1.8 Summary statistics

VARIABLE	SOURCE	EMPLOYMENT (1978–2007)			GMP (1986–2007)		
		MEAN	MINIMUM	MAXIMUM	MEAN	MINIMUM	MAXIMUM
Percent of population with high school education or less	Census/ DataFerrett/ GeoLytics	58	22	83	52	22	76
Lagged employment (thousands of jobs)	Moody's Analytics	271	5	8532	—	—	—
Lagged GMP (millions)	Moody's Analytics	—	—	—	23	0.5	1110
Earnings per job (thousands of 2005 dollars)	Moody's Analytics/ authors' calculations	31	18	87	32	20	87
Percent of employment in durable manufacturing (NAICS 33)	Moody's Analytics/ authors' calculations	9	0	43	8	0	41
Percent of employment in nondurable manufacturing (NAICS 31, 32)	Moody's Analytics/ authors' calculations	6	0	38	6	0	38
Percent of employment in health care and social assistance (NAICS 62)	Moody's Analytics/ authors' calculations	9	1	36	10	2	36
Percent of employment in tourism-related industries (arts, entertainment, recreation, accommodations, and food services) (NAICS 71, 72)	Moody's Analytics/ authors' calculations	9	3	41	9	3	41
Number of major export industries	Moody's Analytics/ authors' calculations	5	0	15	6	0	16
Herfindahl index	Moody's Analytics/ authors' calculations	5	2	42	5	2	38
Eight-year growth rate	Moody's Analytics/ authors' calculations	0.02	-0.06	0.15	0.03	-0.11	0.12
Number of years in secondary downturn	Moody's Analytics/ authors' calculations	0.29	0	4	0.22	0	3
National economic downturn shock	Moody's Analytics/ authors' calculations	0.06	0	1	0.05	0	1

	Source	Mean	Min	Max	Mean	Min	Max
Regional industry shock alone	Moody's Analytics/ authors' calculations	0.09	0	1	0.14	0	1
National industry shock alone	Moody's Analytics/ authors' calculations	0.03	0	1	0.06	0	1
National economic downturn shock and regional industry shock	Moody's Analytics/ authors' calculations	0.01	0	1	0.02	0	1
National economic downturn shock and national industry shock	Moody's Analytics/ authors' calculations	0.02	0	1	0.02	0	1
Northeast	Census	0.12	0	1	0.12	0	1
Midwest	Census	0.25	0	1	0.25	0	1
South	Census	0.41	0	1	0.41	0	1
West	Census	0.22	0	1	0.22	0	1
MSA age (numbers of years since principal city passed 50,000 in population in a decennial census)	Historical census data	52	0	210	52	0	210
Percent of population in principal city	Census/DataFerrett/ GeoLytics	44	10	100	43	10	100
Number of research institutions (universities classified by the Carnegie Foundation as involved in either high or very high research activity)	Carnegie Foundation	0.51	0	13	0.5	0	13
Right-to-work state	National Right to Work Legal Defense Foundation	0.43	0	1	0.44	0	1
Percent of population non-Hispanic black	Census/ DataFerrett/ GeoLytics	10	0	48	10	0	48
Percent of population Hispanic	Census/ DataFerrett/ GeoLytics	7	0	94	8	0	94
Income ratio 80–20	Census/ DataFerrett/ GeoLytics	4.17	2.94	7.95	4.18	2.98	7.95

Note: Statistics are for fully pooled data. Models will exclude certain observations.

To examine the effect of labor force and labor market institutions, we include an educational attainment variable—the percentage of the population aged twenty-five and older who possess no more than a high school diploma—to assess whether areas with a higher proportion of less educated residents are likely to be more susceptible to economic downturns and less resilient in terms of recovery. We also include the percentages of the population that are non-Hispanic black and Hispanic, respectively.[21]

As one indicator of labor market flexibility, we include a variable for whether the region is wholly or predominantly in a state that has a right-to-work law. This is a contested area; some research (Blumenthal, Wolman, and Hill 2009; Grimes and Ray 1988; Holmes 1998) has found the existence of right-to-work laws associated with state economic growth, while other studies that control for a broader set of economic and policy variables (Belman, Block, and Roberts 2009; Stevans 2009) find no relationship. We use the existence of such laws as a proxy for wage flexibility and/or firms' perceptions of a business-friendly climate that might make regions both more resilient and less shock-resistant.

We also include background characteristics of metropolitan areas that might affect shock-resistance and/or resilience. To determine whether the size of a region's economy matters to its performance (and also to standardize other variables for size differences), we include a lagged employment variable (lagged GMP in the case of the GMP models). Because some literature suggests that resilience is related to resource capacity, we include earnings per job as a proxy indicator for regional personal income (though as we noted earlier this could also be a proxy for regional wage rates). The age of the metropolitan area (as expressed by the number of years since the principal city attained a population of 50,000) is included as an indicator of infrastructure age.

The proportion of the metropolitan population residing in principal cities in the region is used as a rough proxy for regional decision making, since the larger the proportion the more a single jurisdiction (i.e., the principal city) can make decisions on its own that are nearly regional in their scope. It is also likely that local governments in regions with a less fragmented governmental structure can make capital investments that are more likely to be supportive of the entire regional economy. Because some of the literature reviewed above argues that income inequality makes flexible regional responses more difficult we include the ratio of the income of each region's high-income households (defined as those at the 80th percentile of the metropolitan area's income distribution) to that of its low-income households (defined as those at the 20th percentile).

We also include variables capturing the three different kinds of shocks (national economic downturn shock, national industry shock, and regional industry shock as previously defined) in tandem with each other or alone to test whether shock-resistance and/or resilience are related to shock type.[22] Finally, to capture the effect of omitted variables that might vary by Census region, we include dummy variables for each of the four regions of the country (Northeast, Midwest, West, and South); the West is the baseline region to which the other regions are compared.[23]

MODEL 1: EXPLAINING THE OCCURRENCE OF REGIONAL ECONOMIC DOWN-TURNS. Our first model examines the characteristics that lead regions to suffer a downturn for any reason, whether as a result of exogenous economic shock, natural disaster or other perturbations. We employ a hazard model, a model in which the dependent variable measures the duration of time that an entity spends in a steady state before experiencing a particular event. Specifically, we use the Cox proportional hazard model. The Cox model is different from parametric models in that it leaves the hazard rate unparameterized; that is, it makes no a priori assumptions about the shape of the hazard. The hazard rate represents the risk of experiencing an event, given that the entity in question hasn't experienced it yet. Box-Steffensmeier and Jones (2004) have argued that in most settings the Cox model is preferable to parametric alternatives due to its less strict assumptions about the data-generating process.[24]

A hazard model estimates when the event is likely to occur, and the independent variables in the model measure the effect of each on the probability that it will occur in a given year. The event of interest in this case is a regional economic downturn, defined as a decline of at least two percentage points in the prior eight-year average annual growth rate. Model 1 thus estimates how much time occurs until a metropolitan area experiences a downturn. This is equivalent to asking what conditions contribute to an area suffering a downturn in a given year.

The unit of analysis is a regional economy year (i.e., each of the 361 metropolitan areas in each of the thirty years is a separate observation). Since the model seeks to examine what determines how much time occurs until a metropolitan area experiences a downturn, we used only those observations when a metropolitan area was not already in a downturn and thus was capable of suffering from a new one.

The results of this model are presented in table 1.9. The resulting coefficients here are discussed in terms of hazard ratios, which allow for easier substantive interpretation. A hazard ratio of 1 suggest that a one-unit increase in a variable does not change the risk of experiencing the event in question, given that it has not already occurred. A hazard ratio of 2 suggests that a one unit increase in a variable doubles the risk of experiencing the event, given that it has not already occurred. Variables that are expressed as a percentage have been standardized so that their values fall between 0 and 100 (rather than 0 and 1.0), allowing for more meaningful interpretation of the hazard ratios.

TABLE 1.9 Likelihood of a metropolitan area experiencing a downturn in a given year (Model 1)

VARIABLE	COX MODEL: HAZARD RATIO (STANDARD ERROR)	
	EXPERIENCED AN EMPLOYMENT DOWNTURN	EXPERIENCED A GMP DOWNTURN
Percent of population with high school education or less	1.049 (0.008)***	1.056 (0.010)***
Lagged employment	1.000 (0.000)	—
Lagged GMP	—	1.000 (0.000)
Earnings per job	1.002 (0.012)	1.022 (0.012)
Percent of employment in durable manufacturing	1.028 (0.008)***	1.024 (0.010)***
Percent of employment in nondurable manufacturing	1.013 (0.013)	0.999 (0.014)
Percent of employment in health care and social assistance	0.921 (0.025)***	0.961 (0.022)*
Percent of employment in tourism-related industries	0.985 (0.013)	0.996 (0.012)
Number of major export industries	0.927 (0.022)***	0.920 (0.020)***
Herfindahl index	1.028 (0.015)*	1.010 (0.019)
Eight-year growth rate	1.235 (0.041)***	1.205 (0.037)***
National economic downturn shock	2.791 (0.219)***	1.073 (0.13)
Regional industry shock alone	3.410 (0.363)***	2.167 (0.202)***
National industry shock alone	4.655 (0.631)***	2.906 (0.302)***
National economic downturn shock and regional industry shock	3.386 (0.462)***	2.334 (0.362)***
National economic downturn shock and national industry shock	4.509 (0.411)***	2.618 (0.330)***
Northeast	0.453 (0.096)***	0.923 (0.229)
Midwest	0.913 (0.154)	0.976 (0.190)
South	0.420 (0.068)***	0.873 (0.170)
MSA age	1.003 (0.001)**	0.999 (0.001)
Percent of population in principal city	0.998 (0.003)	1.007 (0.003)**
Number of research universities	1.002 (0.079)	1.144 (0.095)
Right-to-work law	1.159 (0.147)	0.765 (0.101)**
Percent of population non-Hispanic black	1.000 (0.006)	1.012 (0.008)
Percent of population Hispanic	0.989 (0.004)***	0.981 (0.006)***
Income ratio 80–20	1.315 (0.146)**	0.942 (0.098)
N	6,518	5,025

* $p < 0.10$, ** $p < 0.05$, *** $p < 0.01$

The main results from this model are the following:

- A region's industry structure affects the probability that the region will experience a downturn. Higher employment in durable goods manufacturing as a percentage of total employment makes a region *more* susceptible to downturns in both employment and GMP, while higher employment in health care and social assistance makes it *less* so. A 1-percentage point increase in a region's employment in durable manufacturing increases a region's risk of seeing an employment downturn in a given year by 2.8 percentage points, and increases its risk of GMP downturn by 2.4 percentage points, all else equal.
- Having a large number of major export industries makes a region *less* likely to experience a downturn in both employment and in GMP (by approximately 8 percentage points for each additional export industry, as we have defined it). This suggests that the less concentrated the export sector (i.e., the larger the number of industries that are major exporters), the more protected the region is from economic shocks.
- Regions in which a large share of the population has low levels of formal schooling (no more than a high school diploma) are *more* susceptible to downturns. An increase of 1 percentage point in population with a high school education or less was associated with an increase of 4.9 percentage points in the risk of experiencing a downturn in employment and 5.6 percentage points in the risk of experiencing a downturn in GMP.
- Regions experiencing a national industry shock are *more* likely to have a downturn in employment and in GMP than regions facing other types of shocks, while regions are least likely to experience a downturn from a national economic shock.
- Metropolitan areas in the Northeast and South are *less* susceptible to downturns in employment than those in the West, but there is no statistically significant difference among the regions with respect to downturns in GMP.
- A region in a state with a right-to-work law is 23.5 percentage points *less* likely to experience a downturn in GMP compared to one without such a law, all else equal. However, there is *no relationship* between right-to-work laws and employment downturns.
- Regions with large income gaps between high- and low-income households are *more* susceptible to downturns in employment (but *not* GMP) than those with lower levels of income inequality; a one-unit increase in the 80–20 income ratio is associated with a 32-percentage point increase in the risk of an employment downturn.

Most of these results make sense in light of the cyclical nature of employment and output patterns. Durable goods manufacturers will produce more and hire more workers when demand for these goods rises and lay them off when demand falls (thus, a cyclical effect). Export industries, many of which are in manufacturing, may have output and employment patterns that are more cyclical than other industries, but, except in general national economic downturns, they are unlikely to follow similar cycles. Therefore, the more major export industries a region has, the less likely that all or a large number of these industries will suffer industry shocks simultaneously; the lack of concentration in a small number of major export industries protects them against industry shocks substantial enough to trigger a regional economic downturn (a portfolio diversification effect). The findings on our education/human capital measure are also expected. In response to a decline in the demand for their products or services, employers of all types are more likely to lay off nonprofessional and nonmanagerial workers, who typically have lower levels of formal education than professionals and managers.

Endogeneity may be a concern insofar as the model does not account for migration. Working age adults, especially those with higher levels of formal education (who are somewhat more likely to make long-distance moves; see Bartik 2009) may flee from regions that are hard-hit in favor of regions that are doing well. To account for this, we also ran a specification that included a variable for lagged net migration as a percentage of the population. Migration data are only available since 1991, which severely limits the number of observations. When the model was run, all the variables discussed above retained their signs except for the number of major export industries, which was no longer statistically significant.

MODEL 2: EXPLAINING SHOCK RESISTANCE. Our second model examines what makes regions "shock-resistant" (i.e., they do not suffer an economic downturn) once they have experienced a shock as we define it. In contrast to the first model, this model only includes instances in which a region has experienced some sort of identifiable shock. Consequently, we abandon the hazard model and utilize instead a simple logistic regression to examine the probability of a downturn occurring.

As with the previous model, we exclude those observations where a region was already in a downturn and thus could not be adversely affected by further shocks. We include variables for type of shock, but exclude national economic downturn shocks from the model. Thus, the results for the other types of shocks should be interpreted as the probability of a type of shock causing a downturn *relative to* the probability of a national economic shock causing a downturn.

To make for easier substantive interpretation of the findings in table 1.10, we calculate marginal effects for each variable, which can be interpreted as the increase in the probability of a downturn occurring produced by a one-unit increase in the independent variable (from half a unit below its mean value to

TABLE 1.10   Did shock result in downturn? (Model 2)

	LOGIT REGRESSION: MARGINAL EFFECT (STANDARD ERROR)	
VARIABLE	DOWNTURN RESULTS FROM EMPLOYMENT SHOCK	DOWNTURN RESULTS FROMGMP SHOCK
Percent of population with high school education or less	0.009 (0.002)***	0.009 (0.003)***
Lagged employment	0.000 (0.000)	—
Lagged GMP	—	0.000 (0.000)
Earnings per job	0.018 (0.005)***	0.027 (0.005)
Percent of employment in durable manufacturing	0.009 (0.003)***	0.004 (0.004)***
Percent of employment in nondurable manufacturing	0.008 (0.004)**	−0.004 (0.005)
Percent of employment in health care and social assistance	0.001 (0.006)	0.000 (0.006)
Percent of employment in tourism-related industries	−0.007 (0.006)	−0.008 (0.005)
Number of major export industries	−0.022 (0.008)***	−0.011 (0.008)
Herfindahl index	0.008 (0.004)*	0.005 (0.007)
Eight-year growth rate	0.190 (0.019)***	0.107 (0.013)***
Regional industry shock alone	−0.091 (0.042)**	0.192 (0.047)***
National industry shock alone	−0.010 (0.051)	0.328 (0.045)***
National economic downturn shock and regional industry shock	0.398 (0.036)	0.470 (0.042)***
National economic downturn shock and national industry shock	0.321 (0.039)***	0.414 (0.045)***
Northeast	0.040 (0.086)***	0.012 (0.076)
Midwest	0.098 (0.062)	0.075 (0.065)
South	−0.087 (0.071)	0.050 (0.062)
MSA age	0.001 (0.001)*	0.000 (0.001)
Percent of population in principal city	−0.002 (0.001)*	0.002 (0.001)**
Number of research universities	0.014 (0.039)	−0.003 (0.044)
Right-to-work law	−0.053 (0.044)	−0.051 (0.043)
Percent of population non-Hispanic black	0.007 (0.002)***	0.000 (0.002)
Percent of population Hispanic	0.001 (0.001)	−0.002 (0.002)
Income ratio 80–20	0.003 (0.004)	0.064 (0.032)**
N	1,476	1,393

* p < 0.10, ** p < 0.05, *** p < 0.01

half a unit above), holding all other variables at their mean values. If the variable in question is a dummy variable, then the marginal effect represents the effect of the dummy changing from 0 to 1, holding all other variables at their mean values. Standard errors are robust and clustered by metro area.

The principal results of this model are as follows:

- Regions with a high proportion of employment in durable goods manufacturing and a *less* educated population are less likely to be resistant to (i.e., they are more likely to be adversely affected by) both employment and GMP shocks. By contrast, regions with a large number of major export industries are *more* likely to be resistant to an employment shock but not a GMP one. Thus, for example, a one-point increase in the percentage of an area's population that did not have more than a high school degree increased the probability of the area being adversely affected by either an employment or a GMP shock by 0.9 percentage points. Regions whose export base is more diverse are more likely to be resistant to employment shocks. Each additional export base industry was associated with an increase of 2.2 percentage points in the probability that the region would be shock-resistant.
- Regions experiencing national economic downturn shocks in tandem with local or national industry shocks are *more* likely to experience economic downturns.
- Regions with higher average earnings per job are *more* likely to experience both employment and GMP downturns, all else equal. A one-unit increase in average earnings per job ($1,000) made a region 1.8 percentage points less likely to be resistant to an employment shock and 2.7 percentage points less likely to be resistant to a GMP shock. This is consistent with the hypothesis that high wage rates, controlling for industry composition, make regions more likely to be adversely affected by shock. It also suggests that this variable is proxying relative wage rates rather than resource capacity.
- Regions whose prior eight-year annual growth rate was higher were *less* likely to be resistant to either an employment or GMP shock, all else equal. An extra 1 percentage point of average annual eight-year growth prior to a shock was associated with a 19.0-percentage point increase in the probability of being adversely affected by an employment shock and a 10.7-percentage point increase of being adversely affected by a GMP shock. This could be, in part, a regression to the mean effect, but it also suggests that high-flying economies are particularly susceptible to shocks.

MODEL 3: EXPLAINING RESILIENCE TO SHOCKS. Our third model is a logistic regression that examines the regional characteristics that influence whether a metropolitan area economy that experienced an economic downturn was resilient, i.e., it rebounded to its annual average eight-year growth rate prior to the downturn. This model treats each of the downturns that metropolitan areas experience as separate observations and looks at the factors that contribute to whether or not a metropolitan area is resilient to a particular downturn. As with the previous model, standard errors are robust and clustered by metro area.

Results are presented in table 1.11. For employment they are broadly similar to those of model 1, the model accounting for regional economic downturns. Contrary to expectations, having a large percentage of the population with a high school education or less and a large percentage of employment in durable manufacturing make metropolitan areas *more* resilient to employment downturns caused by shocks. A 1-percentage point increase in the percentage of residents with a high school education or less increased the probability of resilience

TABLE 1.11   Was metropolitan area resilient to downturn? (Model 3)

	LOGIT REGRESSION: MARGINAL EFFECT (STANDARD ERROR)	
VARIABLE	RESILIENCE TO DOWNTURN FROM EMPLOYMENT SHOCK	RESILIENCE TO DOWNTURN FROM GMP SHOCK
Percent of population with high school education or less	0.016 (0.002)***	−0.001 (0.001)
Lagged employment	0.000 (0.000)	—
Lagged GMP	—	0.000 (0.000)
Earnings per job	−0.005 (0.004)	0.003 (0.002)
Percent of employment in durable manufacturing	0.008 (0.003)**	0.001 (0.002)
Percent of employment in nondurable manufacturing	−0.008 (0.004)*	−0.002 (0.002)
Percent of employment in health care and social assistance	−0.016 (0.009)*	−0.009 (0.004)**
Percent of employment in tourism-related industries	0.006 (0.004)	0.002 (0.002)
Number of major export industries	−0.004 (0.009)	0.001 (0.003)
Herfindahl index	0.012 (0.010)	0.000 (0.003)
Pre-downturn growth rate	−0.075 (0.011)***	−0.054 (0.006)***
Number of years in downturn	−0.059 (0.020)***	−0.031 (0.012)**
National economic downturn shock	−0.010 (0.047)	−0.060 (0.042)
Regional industry shock alone	−0.001 (0.051)	−0.028 (0.027)
National industry shock alone	0.006 (0.059)	−0.009 (0.029)
National economic downturn shock and regional industry shock	−0.183 (0.083)**	−0.075 (0.065)

(Continued)

TABLE 1.11   (Continued)

| | LOGIT REGRESSION: MARGINAL EFFECT (STANDARD ERROR) | |
VARIABLE	RESILIENCE TO DOWNTURN FROM EMPLOYMENT SHOCK	RESILIENCE TO DOWNTURN FROM GMP SHOCK
Northeast	−0.290 (0.092)***	−0.076 (0.057)
Midwest	−0.203 (0.068)***	0.031 (0.030)
South	−0.206 (0.067)***	0.008 (0.032)
MSA age	0.000 (0.000)	−0.001 (0.000)***
Percent of population in principal city	0.001 (0.001)	0.000 (0.001)
Number of research universities	0.010 (0.030)	−0.021 (0.017)
Right-to-work law	0.161 (0.044)***	0.046 (0.024)*
Percent of population non-Hispanic black	0.001 (0.003)	−0.003 (0.001)**
Percent of population Hispanic	0.002 (0.001)	0.001 (0.001)
Income ratio 80–20	−0.006 (0.003)**	0.037 (0.019)**
N	1,076	952

* $p < 0.10$, ** $p < 0.05$, *** $p < 0.01$

to a manufacturing shock by 1.6 percentage points, while a 1-percentage point increase in durable goods manufacturing employment increased the probability of resilience by 0.8 percentage points. The explanation, we believe, is just as cyclical demand for durable goods makes employment in that sector susceptible to downturns, so too does the eventual uptick in demand allow it to be resilient. These variables may simply express the cyclical nature of durable goods manufacturing and of the low-skilled labor market.

However, the results for GMP are quite different. There is no relationship between durable goods employment and GMP resilience, nor is there a relationship between educational attainment and GMP resilience. Taken together with the employment results, this suggests that regions with lower levels of education (and substantial employment in durable goods) were resilient as a result of employment rebounds (presumably during cyclical upswings during which employment in durable goods rebounded) but without major change in productivity.

Other important findings from the model are:

- Wage flexibility and/or a "business-friendly" environment (as perceived by firms), proxied by right-to-work laws, appear to have a *positive* effect on resilience with respect to both employment and GMP downturns. Regions with one or both of these characteristics may be more likely to recover employment after it has been temporarily lost. The probability of a region being resilient to employment downturns is 16.1 percentage points greater and to a GMP downturn 4.6 percentage points greater if it is located in a state with a right-to-work law than if it is located in a state without such a law (holding all other variables at their mean).

- Regional income inequality *reduces* employment resilience (i.e., the greater the extent of income inequality, the less likely the region is to be resilient) but *increases* GMP resilience (the greater the income inequality, the more likely the region is to be resilient). One possible interpretation is that causation actually runs the other way, and that regions that are GMP resilient rather than employment resilient actually increase income inequality as productivity gains accrue disproportionately to higher income groups.
- Having a large percentage of employment in health care and social assistance makes a region *less* resilient to both employment and GMP downturns. Because employment in these industries is not especially cyclical, health care and social assistance employment makes a region less susceptible to downturns but makes it more difficult for the region to recover from downturns once they occur.
- Metropolitan areas with lower preshock average annual growth rates were *less* likely to be resilient in the face of both employment and GMP downturns and the greater the number of years that they experienced the downturn, the less likely they were to be resilient. Thus, while faster growing regional economies were more susceptible to shocks (see discussion of model 2, above), they were also more likely to be resilient in recovering from shock effects.

MODEL 4: EXPLAINING LENGTH OF TIME TO RESILIENCE. In our final model the concern is not what determines *whether* a region is resilient, but what determines *how long* it takes after a downturn occurs for a region to become resilient. The model is a hazard model in the form of model 1. The data are limited to those observations when metropolitan areas are already in a downturn and excludes years when a metropolitan area is in a growth period. We censor those observations in which a metro area is deemed nonresilient to a downturn; that is, the full amount of time it takes for these regions to recover from the downturn, if they do recover, is considered to be unobserved in the data. By exploiting the full time-series/cross-sectional nature of the data, the hazard model includes more observations than does the logit model used for model 3.

Results are presented in table 1.12. Some of the results of this model are the same as those of model 3. A high percentage of the population with no more than a high school education, a high percentage of employment in durable manufacturing, a low percentage of employment in health care and social assistance, the presence of right-to-work laws, and low levels of income inequality all reduce the amount of time it takes the region to become resilient following a regional employment downturn. Thus, for example, a 1-percentage point increase in the percentage of a region's residents with a high school degree or less increased the probability of the region being resilient to an employment shock in a given year by 3.2 percentage points. For GMP downturns, as in the previous model, low health care and social assistance employment, right-to-work laws, and high inequality reduce the amount of time to become resilient. In addition:

TABLE 1.12   Did metropolitan area recover from a downturn in a given year? (Model 4)

VARIABLE	COX MODEL: HAZARD RATIO (STANDARD ERROR)	
	RECOVERED FROM EMPLOYMENT DOWNTURN	RECOVERED FROM GMP DOWNTURN
Percent of population with high school education or less	1.032 (0.010)***	1.008 (0.011)
Lagged employment	1.000 (0.000)*	—
Lagged GMP	—	1.000 (0.000)
Earnings per job	0.939 (0.016)***	0.972 (0.019)
Percent of employment in durable manufacturing	1.028 (0.010)***	1.000 (0.011)
Percent of employment in nondurable manufacturing	0.997 (0.012)	0.977 (0.016)
Percent of employment in health care and social assistance	0.912 (0.025)***	0.922 (0.025)***
Percent of employment in tourism-related industries	1.044 (0.012)***	0.986 (0.021)
Number of major export industries	0.987 (0.025)	1.005 (0.024)
Herfindahl index	0.997 (0.024)	0.994 (0.026)
Pre-downturn growth rate	0.665 (0.027)***	0.684 (0.022)***
Number of years in downturn	0.460 (0.035)***	0.237 (0.024)***
National economic downturn shock	1.419 (0.236)**	1.304 (0.290)
Regional industry shock alone	1.341 (0.227)*	0.933 (0.159)
National industry shock alone	1.176 (0.218)	1.052 (0.181)
National economic downturn shock and regional industry shock	1.418 (0.272)*	1.018 (0.197)
National economic downturn shock and national industry shock	1.590 (0.267)***	1.238 (0.216)
Northeast	0.489 (0.118)***	0.540 (0.139)**
Midwest	0.472 (0.095)***	1.011 (0.203)
South	0.671 (0.141)*	0.793 (0.180)
MSA age	1.002 (0.001)	1.000 (0.001)
Percent of population in principal city	1.001 (0.004)	1.006 (0.003)
Number of research universities	1.226 (0.115)**	0.999 (0.116)
Right-to-work law	1.339 (0.177)**	1.521 (0.240)***
Percent of population non-Hispanic black	1.005 (0.008)	0.978 (0.007)***
Percent of population Hispanic	1.007 (0.006)	0.998 (0.005)
Income ratio 80–20	0.724 (0.087)***	1.528 (0.158)***
N	5,018	3,508

* $p < 0.10$, ** $p < 0.05$, *** $p < 0.01$

- For both employment and GMP downturns, the higher a region's predownturn growth rate, the longer it will take for the region's economy to become resilient.
- Neither the degree of concentration of a region's economy (as measured by its Herfindahl index) nor the diversity of its export sector is significantly related to resilience to either employment or GMP downturns.
- The presence of a large number of research universities appears to enable a region's economy to recover more quickly from employment, but not GMP, downturns.

As with model 1, we reestimated model 4 adding a variable for lagged net migration as a percent of the population. This enabled us to address potential sources of simultaneity, though the decreased number of observations made it more difficult to achieve statistically significant results. All the variables discussed achieved the same sign in the re-estimated model, with the exception of the 80–20 income ratio.

Summary and Conclusion

Regions that experienced shocks over the course of the 1978–2007 period were shock-resistant nearly half of the time. Of those that were adversely affected by a shock (i.e., not resistant to it), they were resilient 65% of the time. Consistent with findings from previous literature, regions returned to their prior *rates* of employment and GMP growth more rapidly than they returned to their previous *levels*; indeed, in some cases returns to prior *levels* took a prolonged period of time. They also returned to their prior rates of GMP growth more rapidly than to their prior rate of employment growth, suggesting that resilience to shock was led initially by productivity gains, with employment gains following later.

The Great Recession was the most severe national economic downturn since the Depression. More than 93% of the nations' metropolitan area economies were adversely affected by the shock, while fewer than 7% were shock resistant. However, of those that were adversely affected, 79% were resilient within our defined four year time period after adjusting the recovery window for the last downturn the region experienced (i.e., returned to at least their annual average growth rate for the eight years prior to the Great Recession), a resilience rate similar to that of regions adversely affected by prior national economic downturns.

Through regression analysis, we have been able to test some of the hypotheses suggested by the literature we cited and reviewed in the first part of the chapter. Our analysis shows that there are no specific characteristics that both insulate regions from the harmful impacts of economic downturns and help them recover quickly from downturns. No regional characteristics produce shock resistance or, in the case of nonresistance, resilience with respect to both employment and GMP.

TABLE 1.13 Summary of quantitative results on regional resistance and resilience

	LIKELIHOOD OF EXPERIENCING DOWNTURN (HAZARD MODEL)		DID SHOCK RESULT IN DOWNTURN (LOGIT MODEL)		WAS REGION RESILIENT TO DOWNTURN (LOGIT MODEL)		SHORTNESS OF TIME TO RESILIENCE (HAZARD MODEL)	
	EMPLOYMENT	GMP	EMPLOYMENT	GMP	EMPLOYMENT	GMP	EMPLOYMENT	GMP
Low educational attainment	+	+	+	+	+	0	+	0
Earnings per job	0	0	+	0	0	0	–	0
Percent employed in durable manufacturing	+	+	+	0	+	0	+	0
Percent employed in nondurable manufacturing	0	0	+	0	–	0	0	0
Percent of employment in health care and social assistance	–	–	0	0	–	–	–	–
Percent employed in tourism-related industries	0	0	0	0	0	0	+	0
Economic diversity	–	–	–	0	0	0	0	0
Economic concentration	+	0	+	0	0	0	0	0
Prior eight year growth rate	+	+	+	+	–	–	–	–
Number of research universities	0	0	0	0	0	0	+	0
Right-to-work	0	–	+	0	+	+	+	+
Percent black	0	0	+	0	0	–	0	–
Percent Hispanic	–	–	0	0	0	0	0	0
High income inequality	+	0	0	+	–	+	–	+

Note: Plus sign (+) indicates a positive impact that is substantively significant (with at least a 1 percentage point change) and statistically significant (at the 10% level or better); minus sign (–) indicates a negative impact that is substantively significant and statistically significant; zero (0) indicates an impact that is not statistically significant or, if statistically significant, not substantively important.

Table 1.13 summarizes our major findings about the impacts of regional characteristics and public policies on regions' vulnerability and resilience to downturns. The story it tells is more complex than the findings in some of the previous research. It shows, for example, that some characteristics make regions less susceptible to downturns resulting from shocks but also make it more difficult for them to recover. Although the importance of human capital to long-term economic growth is a consistent finding in the regional economic growth literature, our findings show that when facing a shock, regions with a poorly educated population are more likely to suffer from an employment downturn but are also more likely to be resilient in recovering from such a downturn. Our findings tell a similar story with respect to industrial structure. A high percentage of employment in the manufacturing sector makes it more likely that a region will suffer from an employment downturn as a result of a shock but more likely that it will quickly recover. We believe both of these findings reflect the inherent short-term cyclical effects of most shocks. These shocks expose lower skilled workers and the manufacturing sector disproportionately to downturns, but the cyclical nature of the downturns also makes them more likely to rebound as the economy recovers.

As suggested by Briguglio et al. (2006), we found that export industry diversity made a region less likely to experience a shock and more likely to be resistant to a shock when it occurred, at least with respect to employment. We also found that right-to-work laws, which we use as a crude proxy for wage flexibility and/or a perceived "business-friendly" environment, were positively related to regional resilience to both employment and GMP shocks. Income inequality presented particularly complex results. High income inequality made a region *less* likely to have its GMP adversely affected by a shock, and *more* likely to be resilient and to return to its prior growth rate more rapidly. At the same time it made regions *less* likely to be resilient in terms of employment.

Table 1.13 also shows that some regional characteristics that have desirable impacts on employment have negligible or even undesirable impacts on GMP, and vice versa. For example, low educational attainment promotes employment resilience to shocks but has no effect on GMP resilience, while a high degree of income inequality promotes GMP resilience but actually undermines employment resilience. Finally, every regional characteristic shown in table 1.13 affects some outcomes but has no meaningful impact on others.

CHRONIC DISTRESS AND REGIONAL ECONOMIC RESILIENCE

Unlike the previous chapter, which dealt with regional economic adversity resulting from shocks, this chapter's focus is on regions that experience adversity in the form of chronic economic stress. As in the previous chapter, we suggest readers not concerned with the mechanics of our econometric analysis, might want to skip over this section (pages 67–73).

Chronically distressed regions are regions that experience prolonged periods of slow growth or decline relative to the national economy. These may be "lagging" regions that suffer from inadequate infrastructure or low human capital. Or they may be regions that were once prosperous, but have declined as a result of changes in external demand, shifts in their competitive and comparative advantage, or the maturation of the product cycle of its main export(s). Some of these once prosperous regions are able to "reload" the product portfolios of their traded sectors and regain prosperity after a period of slow growth, while others experience a more severe and prolonged period of relative decline.

Chronic regional economic stagnation or distress has received less attention in the research literature than the ability of regions to "bounce back" from shocks. Regional economic resilience, conceived of as bounce back and regaining historic growth trajectories, is the subject of a specialized research tradition that we discussed in the introduction and chapter 1. The literature on resilience in the face of long-term economic stagnation is less well developed, and much of it is descriptive in nature.

Textbook neoclassical economic theory[1] suggests that regional disparities in economic outcomes should not persist and that regions should not face long-term chronic distress. Instead, the mobility of labor and capital should result in equilibrating processes that produce convergence as factor out-migration reduces supplies of capital and labor in regions experiencing distress, which over time, brings about increases in wages and returns to capital in these regions as factor supplies come more in line with demand. If this theory is correct, then resilience should not be dissimilar to bounce back, albeit over a longer time period and perhaps with a greater amount of economic restructuring. Indeed, Armstrong and Taylor (2000, 85) review the research literature on convergence and observe, "The general conclusion . . . is that convergence in per capita incomes between regions has certainly occurred, but at a very slow rate. This is true even in the US where factor flows between states are substantial."

Myrdal (1957) and others offer an alternative theory to account for chronic distress, whether caused by a specific shock from which the region does not bounce back or by longer-term processes related to the product cycle or sectoral changes at the national level. Instead of equilibrating processes, Myrdal sees a process of cumulative causation that accelerates trends of either growth or decline. Once a region suffering from negative path dependence has reached a lower level, recovery to some previous higher level becomes extremely difficult.

There are a variety of reasons that have been suggested to explain these occurrences. Endogenous growth theory suggests the critical role of human capital and focuses on the importance of knowledge developed and interchanged among a region's residents and businesses as a critical factor in innovation and economic renewal (see, for example, Romer 1986). However, migration in response to economic distress is likely to be selective, with the best-educated individuals, those for whom migration often offers the highest rate of return, leaving for jobs elsewhere, thus depriving the region of an important stock of human capital. Krugman (1993) also argues that the factor adjustment process is dominated by migration rather than by relative wage decline and thus the region remains unattractive to new economic activity.

Product and profit cycle theories provide a more encompassing framework that elaborates the dynamics undergirding cumulative causation, but also makes cumulative causation (as opposed to convergence) contingent. The life cycle of a product is viewed as consisting of four stages: introduction or development, growth, maturation, and decline.[2] As James and Moeller (2013: 5) note, "Each stage has a unique cost and profit structure, which cause the profitable production locations to change as products cycle through the stages." Markusen et al. (1986) note that early product cycle theories focused on individual products and estimated a short cycle of six to eight years, but later elaborations extended the theory to entire industries or related industries rather than solely to individual products and posited a much longer cycle.

Vernon (1966, 1979) and Markusen (1985) theorize that the locale where new products are developed is likely to also be where those products are initially produced as the product continues to be refined, the company retains a monopoly, and/or demand for the new product is not highly price elastic. However, as the product becomes more standardized, competition appears, demand becomes more price elastic, cost minimization becomes a major concern, and production facilities move to areas where the cost of production is lower.

Although this process could lead to convergence, as income rises in lower cost regions that are recipients of the new production facilities, it could also be self-reinforcing rather than leading to convergence. Vernon and others (see Malizia and Feser 1999, 183) argue that product innovation is not random with respect to location, but is likely to occur disproportionately in high-income and high-skill places, while production of standardized goods will occur disproportionately in low-income, low-skill regions. If the high-income, high-skill regions continue to be the centers of new product innovation, then the product cycle process will reinforce spatial disparities and work against convergence.

It is also possible, however, that leading regions will lose their ability to engage in product innovation as their products reach the maturity stage and cycles slow and dispersion sets in, thus leading to episodes of longer term economic decline and resulting in convergence trends. Ryan and Moeller (2013) in their empirical study of income convergence, product cycles, and space, find evidence of both of these processes.

A growing body of literature also emphasizes the importance of path dependence and institutional lock-in as an impediment to economic resilience and to convergence. Boschma and Lambooy (1999, 396) contend:

> The danger exists—and can be observed in reality—that regions develop path-dependency, developing more of the same, sustained by monopolies and cartels, even when the market needs entirely new technologies, organizational approaches and products. This "lock-in" of old production structures exists in technologies, products, organization, but also in the environment of firms: institutions, markets and physical structures. Old mature regions display the combination of the negative attributes of the three elements. Its institutions are sclerotic, its market structure is closed and its physical structure in unattractive.

Boschma and Lambooy (1999) also note that the restructuring required to break the lock-in and revitalize may be of two different kinds. It can be based on "path-dependent innovations" that build on the region's prior industries and skill sets, but adapting them to new circumstances (e.g., Detroit's automobile industry emerging from its history as a producer of machine steam engines, including the internal combustion engine first developed for boats, and related machine engine suppliers and metal fabricators). Alternatively, it may occur through "deep restructuring" through "pathless innovations" that are related only minimally, if at all, to previous history.

If, as Myrdal (1957) and others argue, equilibrating responses do not necessarily occur automatically, what is known about factors that do bring about resilience in the face of chronic distress? Literature in this area consists of theory (or sometimes merely assertions masquerading as theory), intensive case studies of one or a small number of regions, and econometric work on long-term regional economic performance from which characteristics that promote recovery from long-term chronic distress can be inferred.

Economic geographers and public policy advocates who specialize in regional economic development have focused on institutional and cultural impediments to economic revitalization and have advocated "collective learning" and "learning regions" as policies for economic revitalization of chronically distressed regions (see, e.g., Gregersen and Johnson 1997; Hudson 1999; Morgan 1997). Their focus is often on building learning networks and enhancing clusters and fostering agglomeration economies. The large body of empirical case study research has suggested a variety of diverse factors related to resilience in the face of chronic distress including effective social networks (Glaeser 2005a; Morgan 1997; Safford 2009; Saxenian 1994;), cluster development (Bachellor 2000; Rosenfeld 2000; Saxenian 1994), leadership (Katz and Bradley 2013), and myriad other factors.

Inferences from regional economic theory and econometric studies of economic growth suggest a myriad of plausible factors to pursue in determining why some metropolitan areas have experienced prolonged episodes of decline and why some regions that have experienced such decline are able to nonetheless recover (see also Blumenthal, Wolman, and Hill 2008; Glaeser and Saiz 2004; Shapiro 2005). One proximate factor for the onset of periods of chronic distress that has been suggested (Myrdal 1957) is specific shocks from which the economy does not bounce back.

The product and profit cycle theories discussed above suggest another proximate cause of chronic distress. One implication of product cycle theory is that the region where a major product or industry originally develops is likely after a period of time to experience a decline in production and employment in that industry that could, if the industry is not regenerated or replaced, result in a prolonged period of economic distress. In some cases, these regions are simply able to absorb the declines resulting from product cycles or to adapt and recover from them. Others are not. Why is this the case? Why are some regions able to easily recover from shocks or from changes brought about by product cycles, while others are not? Explanations for the inability to recover from chronic distress include:

- *Human capital.* Consistent with endogenous growth theory, Edward Glaeser and coauthors, among others, point to low levels of human capital as an important reason for slow regional growth (Glaeser 2005a, 2009; Glaeser and Saiz 2004; Glaeser, Scheinkman, and Shleifer 1995; Gottlieb and Fogarty 2003; Lin 2012;).
- *Relative wage costs.* Regions whose wages are high relative to other regions for similarly productive labor may become less attractive places for locating or expanding business activity. Thus high wages have sometimes been found to be associated with poor economic performance (Flynn 1984; Harrison 1984). Under textbook neoclassical assumptions, wages that are much higher than necessary to clear the local labor market would lead to a bidding down of wages until the region regained its labor cost competitiveness.[3] However, if wages are "sticky" and do not decline when there is a substantial excess supply of labor, a much longer period of employment decline might result.
- *Industrial structure.* In view of the relative decline of manufacturing in the national economy since the 1980s in terms of both share of gross domestic product and share of employment, some studies have found that regions more dependent on manufacturing are likely to grow more slowly (Desmet and Rossi-Hansberg 2009; Glaeser et al. 1995; Lin 2012; Norton and Rees 1979).[4] Other research (Markusen 1985) has found that regions whose major industry is characterized by an oligopolistic structure are less likely to quickly recover from decline of that industry than are those with a competitive structure. Chinitz (1961) suggests that this may be because oligopolistic industries deter entrepreneurial behavior.
- *Economic diversity.* Although it is frequently asserted that regions with greater economic diversity have higher rates of growth, the question whether industrial specialization or industrial diversification better promotes growth remains unresolved (Blumenthal, Hill, and Wolman 2009; Glaeser 2005a; Glaeser et al. 1992; Harrison, Kelley, and Gant 1996; Henderson 2003; Henderson, Kuncaro, and Turner 1995). A related hypothesis is that the domination of regional labor markets, suppliers, research and development pipelines, or channels of informal business association and communication by a few large, vertically integrated firms may inhibit the growth of other firms (Chinitz 1961; Christopherson and Clark 2007; Lin 2012; Markusen 1985; Safford 2009).

- *Agglomeration economies.* Agglomeration economies are external benefits that accrue to firms (e.g., cost-savings from lower search costs for skilled labor or from lower input costs as a result of suppliers close by) as a result of large numbers of other firms (and people) locating in the same area. Empirically, increases in metropolitan population size, a proxy for agglomeration, have been related to increased productivity and higher average wages (Beeson 1992; Glaeser, Kolko, and Saiz 2001).[5]
- *Proximity to large metropolitan areas.* The distance to a large metropolitan area reflects the strength of industrial linkages and access to capital. According to the urban hierarchy literature, the markets for certain goods will tend to cluster in larger central places in order to take advantage of economies of agglomeration, while those that are smaller and more isolated will contain fewer services and fewer types of firms (Heilbrun 1987).
- *Demographic composition.* The percentage of blacks in the population is associated with poor regional economic performance (Blumenthal, Wolman, and Hill 2009; Glaeser and Shapiro 2001), even after controlling for educational attainment. (This finding undoubtedly reflects the poor quality of schools that the average black student attends relative to that of the average white student.)
- *Crime and amenities.* Economic growth has been found to be associated with low crime rates and other place-based amenities (Gabriel, Mattey, and Wascher 1999; Glaeser and Shapiro 2001).
- *Innovation, technology, and the presence of research universities.* The presence of one or more research universities in a region promotes economic growth as a result of the labor force impacts of the institutions, the federal research funds attracted, and the commercial spin-offs of new and innovative products (Felsenstein 1996; Glaeser and Saiz 2004; Hill and Lendel 2007; Pack 2002). Norton and Rees (1979) argue that locations that are sources of product innovation are fundamentally those that are path dependent on a dominant production technology (e.g., machine tools in the manufacturing belt in the northeast and Midwest). When this technology is displaced by newer ones ("high tech" and electronics), regions dependent on the old technology are likely to go into a period of decline.
- *Business environment.* Controlling for other factors, some studies find that state right-to-work laws (possibly serving as a proxy for firms' perceptions of the business environment) are positively correlated with economic growth (Blumenthal, Wolman, and Hill 2009; Holmes 1998; see also Grimes and Ray 1988; Tannenwald 1997). However, studies that

control more carefully for other "business climate" indicators have found that these laws have no impact on growth (Belman, Block, and Roberts 2009; Stevans 2009).

- *Income inequality.* Some researchers have found lower degrees of income inequality related to higher rates of regional economic growth (Glaeser, Resseger, and Tobio 2009; Morrow 2008; Pastor and Benner 2008). The rationale is that higher degrees of inequality may contribute to the deterioration of the social and political fabric of a region and thus impede cooperative activity and growth.
- *Government fragmentation.* It has been argued that greater fragmentation of local governments within a region hinders regional economic development planning and cooperation and thus reduces regional economic performance. However, research findings have been inconclusive (Carr and Feiock 1999; Hamilton, Miller, and Paytas 2004).

In terms of policies that can promote recovery from chronic economic distress, current economic development theory and empirical research provide little guidance to those regions that are worst off. General agreement exists that regional economic restructuring, resulting in a shift in the region's industrial portfolio toward faster growing economic activities, is a prerequisite, but this is supported by little research evidence on how to bring that about.[6] Boschma and Lambooy (1999, 398) observe that, "When discussing the policy options, the literature tends not to offer much." Glasmeier (2000, 568) writes, "Very few [economic development policies] are designed to confront structural problems of enduring importance. Although reducing poverty and uneven development and providing jobs for disadvantaged citizens are often invoked as the rationale behind development policies, in fact these policies are not designed to reconcile problems of deep poverty and economic abandonment. . . . Conventional policy has yet to find the key that unlocks the fate of truly troubled locales."

Regions and Chronic Economic Distress: Definitions and Descriptive Statistics

We conceptualize a chronically distressed region as one whose rate of growth is slow relative to the national economy over a long period of time. We define a chronically distressed region as follows: In a given year, a region is growing slowly if its growth rate over the previous eight years (defined in chapter 1 as the slope of the regression line of the natural logarithm of employment or GMP [gross metropolitan product] on a time trend) is less than 50% of the national eight-year growth rate and at least 1 percentage point less than the national growth rate.

A region is chronically distressed if it meets this criterion for seven consecutive years; that is, its eight-year growth rate is less than 50% of the national eight-year growth rate and at least 1 percentage point less than the national growth rate for seven consecutive years.

Appendix 1 table A1 provides a list of regions that, during the 1978–2007 period, met this definition of chronically distressed based on their employment growth. It includes 89 metropolitan areas that together experienced 108 periods of chronic distress (since some metropolitan areas experienced more than one such period). The 89 metropolitan areas represent 25% of the 361 metropolitan areas in our universe of metropolitan regions. Appendix 1 table A2 lists regions that satisfy this definition based on GMP growth. It includes 102 periods of GMP slow growth, representing 90 unique metropolitan areas or 25% of our universe.

Tables A1 and A2 include some entries that are predictable and others that are perhaps more surprising. For instance, the Boston area remains a hub of universities, hospitals, and technology. Yet the MSA suffered from seven consecutive years of slow job growth in the late 1980s and early 1990s. However, the slow growth in total employment is due to broader industrial shifts that helped cause the area to shed low-wage nondurable manufacturing jobs and gain higher wage jobs in information technology and health care (Bluestone and Stevenson 2010). Indeed, Boston does not show up on the comparable GMP list. In fact, many of the highly populated regions from table A1, including Boston, Los Angeles, and New York, are absent from table A2. Conversely, both tables A1 and A2 include smaller industrial regions such as Youngstown, which has been chronicled by Safford (2009) as an example of post-industrial decline, with high unemployment and low wages into the 2000s.

Of the 108 instances of chronic regional economic distress in employment, 20 of the instances occurred within four years of a shock to which the region was not shock-resistant and to which it was also not resilient within the four-year period. In other words, in these cases, a shock occurred directly prior to the onset of a period of chronic distress and quite likely led to it. In an additional eleven cases, the onset of chronic economic distress occurred during the fifth year after the onset of a shock to which the region was not resilient.

How many of these chronically distressed metropolitan areas were able to recover from chronic low-growth during the period we examined? We define recovery in this context as occurring when a formerly chronically distressed region's eight-year annual growth rate reaches 75% or within 0.5 percentage points of the nation's eight-year annual growth rate and remains at that level for a period of seven consecutive years. Appendix 1 tables A3 and A4 provide lists of chronically distressed regions that show recovery with respect to employment and GMP respectively. Forty-two (47%) of the eighty-nine metropolitan areas that were chronically distressed with respect to employment growth saw a period of recovery within the timeframe of our dataset. It is important to note that regions that experience slow growth near the tail end of our dataset will be unable to see recovery within the time frame of study.[7] Of the ninety regions that were chronically distressed with respect to GMP, however, only eleven demonstrated recovery within the time frame of study. This may be attributed in part to the fact that our GMP data are more limited, consisting of only twenty-two years (1986–2007) in which a region could show decline and recovery. (Unless otherwise noted, descriptive statistics from this point on are for employment.)

Appendix 1 tables A5 and A6 provide lists of chronically distressed regions that did not show recovery. Once again, the lists only tell part of the story. The Boston metropolitan area is included in table A5 as a region that did not recover from chronic slow growth. However, the region did show six consecutive years of recovery before experiencing a slight downturn in the 2000s, thereby preventing it from meeting the criteria for recovery. The Youngstown MSA, by contrast, experienced another period of slow growth almost immediately after its first episode and therefore is not included on either of the lists because it was still experiencing slow growth. (Tables A5 and A6 do not include regions still experiencing chronic slow growth as of 2001.)

Table 2.1 highlights the fact that there are considerable regional differences in terms of the number of chronically distressed regions as well as the percentage of chronically distressed regions that showed recovery. Unlike Pack (2000), who finds that the majority of chronically distressed metropolitan areas were in the South at the time of her writing, our criteria suggest that a large number are in the Northeast and Midwest. In fact, over half of the metropolitan regions in the Northeast meet the criteria for being chronically distressed with respect to employment growth (38% meet the GMP criteria). This is substantially higher than any other region, with the Midwest being the second most affected at 37%. The Midwest has the largest number of chronically distressed regions in terms of employment (33), while the South has the largest number of chronically distressed regions in terms of GMP (37).

We next provide descriptive statistics that highlight some of the differences in averages for specific variables between both chronically distressed metropolitan areas and all other metropolitan areas in table 2.2 and differences between chronically distressed metropolitan areas that showed recovery and chronically distressed regions that did not show recovery in table 2.3.

The most striking takeaway from table 2.2 is that there appear to be considerable differences between chronically distressed regions and healthy regions

TABLE 2.1 Regional differences

			EMPLOYMENT		
REGION	NUMBER OF METROPOLITAN AREAS IN EACH REGION	NUMBER OF CHRONICALLY DISTRESSED METROPOLITAN AREAS	PERCENT OF METROPOLITAN AREAS CHRONICALLY DISTRESSED	NUMBER OF CHRONICALLY DISTRESSED METROPOLITAN AREAS THAT RECOVERED	PERCENTAGE OF CHRONICALLY DISTRESSED METROPOLITAN AREAS THAT RECOVERED
Northeast	45	27	60%	8	30%
Midwest	90	33	37%	19	58%
South	147	22	15%	10	45%
West	79	7	9%	5	71%
U.S. total	361	89	25%	42	47%
			GMP		
Northeast	45	17	38%	0	0
Midwest	90	25	28%	0	0
South	147	37	25%	8	22%
West	79	11	14%	3	27%
U.S. total	361	90	25%	11	12%

in a number of key categories. Chronically distressed regions appear to be less well educated (53.9% of the adult population with a high school education or less vs. 47.4%) and less populous (with a median population of 163,000 versus 238,000). Chronically distressed regions also had a higher percentage of their employment in manufacturing, lower average populations (implying fewer opportunities to develop agglomeration economies), and greater industrial diversity. They were also less likely to be in right-to-work states. Although each of these differences in mean values discussed above is statistically significant, they do not control for the influence of other variables as we do in a later section of this chapter.

In contrast to table 2.2, table 2.3 finds fewer differences between chronically distressed regions that recovered and those that did not, though more differences reveal themselves in the GMP data. For example, as the percent of the population employed in manufacturing in chronically distressed regions increased, the regions were less likely to recover, while as the average July temperature, an amenity feature, increased and if the state had a right-to-work law, chronically distressed regions were more likely to recover. Meanwhile, the only variable that attains statistical significance in the employment data is the percent of the population that was Hispanic in 2000. Chronically distressed regions that recovered had a Hispanic population (10.1% of the total) that was much larger

TABLE 2.2 Chronically distressed metropolitan area means vs. all other metropolitan area means

	EMPLOYMENT			GMP		
	CHRONICALLY DISTRESSED METROPOLITAN AREAS	ALL OTHER METROPOLITAN AREAS	DIFFERENCE	CHRONICALLY DISTRESSED METROPOLITAN AREAS	ALL OTHER METROPOLITAN AREAS	DIFFERENCE
Percent employment in manufacturing (2000)	16.2	12.7	3.4***	14.3	13.3	0.98
Number of export industries (2000)	5.49	4.84	0.66**	7.77	6.42	1.3***
Percent of population 25+ with a high school education or less (2000)	53.9	47.4	6.5***	53.2	47.6	5.6***
Percent Hispanic (2000)	6.86	10.1	-3.3*	6.04	10.4	-4.4**
Average July temperature	74.8	76.3	-1.5**	75.4	76.2	-0.78
Right-to-work state (2000)	0.24	0.53	-0.29***	0.37	0.48	-0.10*
Herfindahl index	4.71	4.06	0.65**	4.29	4.64	-0.35
Number of research institutions	0.61	0.47	0.13	0.19	0.61	-0.42***
Distance to large metropolitan area	189	185	5	283	153	130***
Population (2000)—Median	163,706	238,314	-74,608**	146,438	273,170	-126,732***

* $p < 0.10$, ** $p < 0.05$, *** $p < 0.01$

TABLE 2.3 Chronically distressed region means that showed recovery vs. chronically distressed region means that did not recover

	EMPLOYMENT			GMP		
	CHRONICALLY DISTRESSED METROPOLITAN AREAS THAT DID RECOVER	CHRONICALLY DISTRESSED METROPOLITAN AREAS THAT DID NOT RECOVER	DIFFERENCE	CHRONICALLY DISTRESSED METROPOLITAN AREAS THAT DID RECOVER	CHRONICALLY DISTRESSED METROPOLITAN AREAS THAT DID NOT RECOVER	DIFFERENCE
Percent employment in manufacturing (2000)	15.0	17.2	-2.14	8.89	15.1	-6.2***
Number of export industries (2000)	5.40	5.57	-0.17	6.90	7.89	-0.98
Percent of population 25+ with a high school education or less (2000)	53.3	54.4	-1.11	52.5	53.3	-0.82
Percent Hispanic (2000)	10.07	3.99	6.09**	4.80	6.22	-1.4
Average July temperature	75.24	74.43	0.81	79.5	74.8	4.8***
Right-to-work state (2000)	0.29	0.19	0.09	0.73	0.33	0.40**
Herfindahl index	4.16	3.98	0.18	4.19	4.30	0.11
Number of research institutions	0.69	0.53	0.16	0.36	0.16	0.20
Distance to large metropolitan area	181	197	-16	247	289	-41.
Population (2000)—Medians	164,624	162,453	2,171	194,042	142,950	51,092*

* p < 0.10, ** p < 0.05, *** p < 0.01

as a percentage than regions that did not recover (4.0%). As with many of the variables, it is difficult to infer the direction of causality, but we theorize that it is likely that growing regions attract a greater number of immigrants.

Of the instances of chronic distress, there were 63 cases (out of a total of 108) in which a region actually lost employment during the first year that it entered the category of chronically distressed. The average time it took to return to the prior level of employment was 9.1 years, but for some regions a return to prior levels took much longer; in a few cases, it has not yet occurred. Both Anderson, IN and Danville, IL suffered declines in employment throughout almost the entire period of study, losing 25% and 22% of jobs, respectively, from 1978 to 2007.

To what extent did chronically distressed regions recover through restructuring, that is, through a change in the region's traded sector industrial portfolio so that it was more oriented toward growth? To explore this question we calculated a restructuring score based on the potential job growth rate for each chronically distressed region at the onset of its period of chronic distress.

The restructuring score is based loosely on the concept of the industry-mix effect in a shift-share analysis. We first calculated a potential growth rate for each region on the assumption that each of the region's three-digit NAICS industries would grow at the same rate as that industry grew nationally over the next ten years from the time of the onset of the region's chronic distress. The resulting potential growth rate is a measure of the extent to which a region was poised for growth. We then performed a similar calculation ten years after the onset of chronic distress for each region. The difference between the region's potential growth rate ten years after the onset of distress and its potential growth rate at the onset is the "restructuring score." A positive restructuring score means that the region was better positioned to take advantage of nationwide industry growth trends ten years after the onset of chronic distress than it was when chronic distress began. A negative score means that the region was less well positioned to do so after ten years.

Of the thirty-seven chronically distressed regions that emerged from chronic distress and for which we had a full data set, thirty-three had positive restructuring scores, that is, they were better poised for growth ten years after the onset of chronic distress than they were when they entered chronic distress. However, of the twenty-six chronically distressed regions that were not resilient, twenty-three also had positive restructuring scores. The median resilient region had a slightly higher amount of positive restructuring than did the median region that did not emerge from chronic distress, but the mean restructuring score was slightly higher for the unsuccessful regions. There was a negative (and statistically significant) correlation of 0.45 between a region's potential growth score at the onset of its chronic distress and the number of years of consecutive slow growth once in that condition.

The major difference between regions that recovered and regions that did not was their starting points. Chronically distressed regions that recovered (i.e., emerged from chronic distress) were not as poorly poised for growth at the onset of chronic distress as were those that did not. Both groups underwent positive restructuring, but those that did not emerge from chronic distress simply had farther to go to meet our resilience standards. Indeed, of the seven regions with the highest degree of restructuring as measured by our restructuring scores, four— Weirton-Steubenville, Johnstown, Youngstown, and Abilene—were among the nonresilient regions. These descriptive findings suggest that even chronically distressed regions engage in economic restructuring that improves their position and that, to some extent, convergence processes are able to overcome path dependence and stasis over time.

Explaining Chronic Distress and Resilience to It

In this section, we move beyond descriptive statistics and employ regression analysis to better understand those factors that are associated with regions falling victim to chronic distress and the ability to recover from such a state.[8] Our analysis is confined to the 1978–2007 period. We concern ourselves with the following questions:

- What accounts for chronic distress as we have defined it, that is, what factors contribute to a region becoming chronically distressed?
- What characteristics distinguish those regions that are able to recover from chronic distress (i.e., are resilient) from those that are not able to do so?
- For those regions that do recover from chronic distress, what accounts for the length of time it takes a region to do so?

To answer these questions, we employ a series of cross-sectional and longitudinal models. To the extent possible we employ independent variables that test the various hypotheses discussed earlier in this chapter, guided by the findings contained in chapter 1. Because we examine a much smaller subset of regions here than we did in chapter 1, and thus have less data to draw on, we employ more parsimonious models. Table 2.4 presents summary statistics for the economic and demographic variables included in the models.

TABLE 2.4 Summary statistics

VARIABLE	SOURCE	EMPLOYMENT (1978–2007)			GMP (1986–2007)		
		MEAN	MINIMUM	MAXIMUM	MEAN	MINIMUM	MAXIMUM
Percent of population with high school education or less (population age over 25)	Census/ DataFerrett/ GeoLytics	58	22	83	52	22	76
Lagged employment (thousands of jobs)	Economy.com	271	5	8532	—	—	—
Lagged GMP (millions of 2005$)	Economy.com	—	—	—	23	0.5	1110
Earnings per job (thousands of 2005$)	Economy.com/ authors' calculations	31	18	87	32	20	87
Percent of employment in manufacturing (NAICS 31, 32, 33)	Economy.com/ authors' calculations	15	1	55	14	1	51
Percent of employment in health care and social assistance (NAICS 62)	Economy.com/ authors' calculations	9	1	36	10	2	36
Percent of employment in tourism-related industries (arts, entertainment, recreation, accommodation, and food-services) (NAICS 71, 72)	Economy.com/ authors' calculations	9	3	41	9	3	41
Number of major export industries	Economy.com/ authors' calculations	5	0	15	6	0	16
Herfindahl index	Economy.com/ authors' calculations	5	2	42	5	2	38
Northeast	Census	0.12	0	1	0.12	0	1
Midwest	Census	0.25	0	1	0.25	0	1
South	Census	0.41	0	1	0.41	0	1
West	Census	0.22	0	1	0.22	0	1
Number of research institutions (universities classified by the Carnegie Foundation as involved in either high or very high research activity)	Carnegie Foundation	0.51	0	13	0.51	0	13
Right-to-work state	National Right to Work Legal Defense Foundation	0.43	0	1	0.44	0	1
Percent of population non-Hispanic black	Census/ DataFerrett/ GeoLytics	10	0	48	10	0	48
Percent of population Hispanic	Census/ DataFerrett/ GeoLytics	7	0	94	8	0	94
Income Ratio 80–20 (Times 10)	Census/ DataFerrett/ GeoLytics	42	30	79	42	29	80
Distance in hundreds of miles to large metropolitan area (with a population of 1 million or more)	Census/ GIS	1.8	0	24	1.8	0	24

Results from Empirical Models

MODEL 1: EXPLAINING THE OCCURRENCE OF CHRONIC DISTRESS CROSS-SECTIONALLY. To address this question, we first employ a cross-sectional logit model where the dependent variable equals 1 in those cases when a region is chronically distressed at any point in our time frame of study (1978–2007) and is 0 otherwise. The independent variables used in the model are from 2000. Table 2.5 presents the results of model 1. Two variables are statistically significant at the 1% level: the percentage of the adult (ages 25 and over) population with a high school diploma or less and the 80–20 income ratio. In the former case, a 1-percentage point increase in the percent of the adult population with a high school degree or less (from half a percentage point below the mean to half

TABLE 2.5 Explaining the occurrence of chronic distress cross-sectionally (Model 1)

VARIABLE	CROSS-SECTIONAL LOGIT REGRESSION: MARGINAL EFFECT (STANDARD ERROR)	
	REGION IS CHRONICALLY DISTRESSED IN EMPLOYMENT	REGION IS CHRONICALLY DISTRESSED IN GMP
Percent population with high school education or less	0.019 (0.004)***	0.010 (0.004)**
Lagged employment	0.000 (0.000)	—
Lagged GMP	—	0.000 (0.000)*
Earnings per job	0.006 (0.005)	0.008 (0.005)*
Percent of employment in manufacturing	0.001 (0.004)	−0.002 (0.003)
Percent of employment in health care and social assistance	0.014 (0.008)*	0.010 (0.007)
Percent of employment in tourism-related industries	−0.004 (0.006)	0.004 (0.005)
Number of export industries	−0.003 (0.010)	0.006 (0.007)
Herfindahl index	−0.001 (0.012)	0.003 (0.009)
Northeast	0.303 (0.162)*	0.166 (0.127)
Midwest	0.218 (0.124)*	0.154 (0.104)
Southern	−0.100 (0.093)	0.077 (0.083)
Number of research universities	−0.011 (0.034)	−0.029 (0.047)
Right-to-work law	−0.027 (0.064)	−0.076 (0.054)
Percent of population non-Hispanic black	−0.001 (0.003)	−0.001 (0.002)
Percent of population Hispanic	−0.003 (0.002)	−0.003 (0.002)**
Income ratio 80–20	0.016 (0.005)***	0.013 (0.005)**
Distance to large metropolitan area	0.019 (0.010)*	0.050 (0.021)**
N	360	360

* p < 0.10, ** p < 0.05, *** p < 0.01

a point above) increases the probability that a region will experience chronic distress by 1.9 percentage points, given that all other covariates are at their mean. In the latter case, a one-unit increase in the 80–20 income ratio (in this case, one unit equals one-tenth of a percentage point in the ratio, i.e., increasing a ratio of 4.0:1.0 to 4.1:1.0) increases the probability of a region experiencing chronic distress by 1.6 percentage points, given that all other covariates are at their mean. The coefficients on the distance to a large metropolitan area and on the percent of employment in health care and social assistance are also statistically significant at the 10% level, such that regions that are more isolated from other large metropolitan areas and with a higher degree of employment in health care may be more likely to experience chronic low growth. These findings are largely supported by the GMP data. Education level, income ratio, and distance to a large metropolitan have coefficients that are of a similar magnitude as the employment results.

The finding on the education variable is not surprising, as much of the growth literature has stressed the importance of human capital. Similarly, the relationship between chronic low growth and distance from another large metropolitan area is consistent with Glasmeier's (2000) argument that industrial linkages are necessary in order for economic activity to accumulate. The finding for income inequality is perhaps more surprising, particularly in the GMP data. This result has also been documented by other researchers (Glaeser, Resseger, and Tobio 2009; Morrow 2008; Pastor and Benner 2008), who contend that inequality has its own economic costs, including social unrest and political fragmentation. As we noted in the previous chapter there is a question about the direction of causation and simultaneous determination: is chronic distress caused by income inequality or does chronic distress cause income inequality? The answer is not clear due to the fact that the income inequality measure is from 2000. The model that follows examines chronic distress longitudinally and provides further insights.

MODEL 2: EXPLAINING THE OCCURRENCE OF CHRONIC DISTRESS LONGITUDINALLY. This model asks a question similar to model 1 except that it makes use of the full longitudinal nature of our data. The dependent variable in this model equals 1 in the first year that a region begins to undergo chronic low growth. As a result, the model only includes observations up to that point in time. Again, we employ a Cox proportional hazard model that examines the factors that contribute to a region becoming chronically distressed (if at all), with the results shown in table 2.6. The coefficients are hazard ratios, the ratio between the predicted risk for a unit difference in the explanatory variable.

TABLE 2.6 Explaining the occurrence of chronic distress longitudinally (Model 2)

	COX MODEL: HAZARD RATIO (STANDARD ERROR)	
VARIABLE	REGION IS CHRONICALLY DISTRESSED IN EMPLOYMENT	REGION IS CHRONICALLY DISTRESSED IN GMP
Percent population with high school education or less	1.322 (0.033)***	1.205 (0.032)***
Lagged employment	1.000 (0.001)	—
Lagged GMP	—	1.000 (0.000)*
Earnings per job	1.182 (0.031)***	1.129 (0.042)***
Percent of employment in manufacturing	0.981 (0.017)	0.933 (0.027)**
Percent of employment in health care and social assistance	0.979 (0.075)	0.872 (0.058)**
Percent of employment in tourism-related industries	0.917 (0.038)**	1.002 (0.031)
Number of export industries	0.970 (0.082)	0.908 (0.057)
Herfindahl index	1.016 (0.047)	0.886 (0.096)
Northeast	3.007 (2.577)	0.906 (0.763)
Midwest	1.808 (1.388)	1.819 (1.342)
Southern	0.447 (0.378)	1.441 (1.210)
Number of research universities	1.353 (0.455)	0.721 (0.317)
Right-to-work law	0.386 (0.243)	0.178 (0.112)***
Percent of population non-Hispanic black	0.992 (0.019)	0.978 (0.016)
Percent of population Hispanic	0.978 (0.012)*	0.952 (0.012)***
Income ratio 80–20	1.082 (0.037)**	1.139 (0.028)***
Distance to large metropolitan area	1.107 (0.058)*	1.256 (0.051)***
N	7,187	4,806

* $p < 0.10$, ** $p < 0.05$, *** $p < 0.01$

In this case, the hazard or event of interest is the onset of chronic distress. A hazard ratio of one indicates that the explanatory variable has no effect on the probability of the region becoming chronically distressed in a given year. A hazard ratio of two indicates that a one-unit increase in the explanatory variable doubles the risk of the region becoming chronically distressed.

As in model 1, low educational attainment and income inequality are positively related to chronic distress. A one-unit increase (1 percentage point) in the percentage of adults with a high school degree or less is associated with an increase in the probability of chronic distress of 32.2 percentage points. For income inequality, a one-unit increase increases the probability of chronic distress by 8.2 percentage points.

In addition to educational attainment and income inequality, two new variables attain statistical significance in our second model: earnings per job and the percent of the population employed in tourism-related industries. Controlling for the industrial composition of regional employment, a one-unit ($1,000) increase in earnings per job increases the risk of experiencing chronic distress by 18 percentage points. A one-unit increase (1 percentage point) in the percent of employment that is in tourism-related industries reduces the risk of chronic distress by approximately 8 percentage points.

Table 2.6 also presents the GMP results. There are several statistically significant hazard ratios that show a negative relationship (hazard ratios less than 1.0), which indicates risk reduction. The risk of a metropolitan regional economy experiencing chronic distress is reduced by the following: the percent of employment in health care (regions with a higher percentage of employment in health care are less likely to experience chronic distress; note that this was positive in the employment regression in the previous model); regions with a higher percentage of Hispanic population are less likely to be chronically distressed; and a region in a right-to-work state is less likely to experience chronic distress.

We interpret these findings for both educational attainment and income inequality in the same fashion as for model 1. The finding that a higher wage (controlling for industrial composition) is associated with lower employment than would otherwise occur confirms the expectation from standard economic theory. Since tourism is a labor-intensive export industry, it appears that the more a region's economy is tourist-driven, the less likely it is to experience employment-related chronic distress than are other regions holding other factors constant. A region with an above average share of its GMP being generated in the health care sector is likely to be an exporter of health care services (i.e., they are serving patients from out of the region) and thus is less likely to experience chronic distress. Finally, we interpret the right-to-work variable as a proxy for either perception of business climate or wage flexibility or both; hence, this finding need not be read as providing support for a specific policy.

MODEL 3: WHAT DISTINGUISHES THOSE REGIONS THAT ARE ABLE TO RECOVER FROM CHRONIC DISTRESS (I.E., ARE RESILIENT) FROM THOSE THAT DID NOT? Once again we employ a cross-sectional logit model using data from 2000. In this case, we seek to distinguish regions that recovered from chronic low-growth from those that did not. Hence, we limit our sample to those regions that experienced chronic low-growth, substantially reducing our number of observations. The dependent variable in this case is a 1 in the case that a region recovered and 0 otherwise.

TABLE 2.7 If region recovers from chronic distress (Model 3)

VARIABLE	CROSS-SECTIONAL LOGIT REGRESSION: MARGINAL EFFECT (STANDARD ERROR)	
	REGION IS CHRONICALLY DISTRESSED IN EMPLOYMENT	REGION IS CHRONICALLY DISTRESSED IN GMP
Percent population with high school education or less	−0.007 (0.013)	0.000 (0.002)
Lagged employment	0.000 (0.000)*	—
Lagged GMP	—	0.000 (0.000)
Earnings per job	−0.015 (0.017)	−0.004 (0.004)
Percent of employment in manufacturing	−0.005 (0.014)	−0.005 (0.004)
Percent of employment in nondurable manufacturing	0.003 (0.030)	—
Percent of employment in health care and social assistance	−0.045 (0.039)	−0.006 (0.006)
Percent of employment in tourism-related industries	0.063 (0.043)	−0.007 (0.007)
Number of export industries	0.005 (0.033)	−0.001 (0.003)
Herfindahl index	−0.039 (0.067)	−0.007 (0.009)
Number of research universities	−0.173 (0.139)	−0.010 (0.024)
Right-to-work law	0.130 (0.222)	0.018 (0.036)
Percent of population non-Hispanic black	−0.024 (0.012)**	−0.001 (0.001)
Percent of population Hispanic	0.011 (0.011)	−0.001 (0.002)
Income ratio 80–20	−0.006 (0.022)	0.003 (0.003)
Distance to large metropolitan area	0.042 (0.082)	−0.001 (0.003)
N	89	89

* $p < 0.10$, ** $p < 0.05$, *** $p < 0.01$

Table 2.7 presents the employment results for model 3. Because we examine here only those regions that are undergoing chronic distress, we use a more parsimonious model to focus on those factors that specifically relate to recovery. Only one variable attains statistical significance at the 5% level: the percent of the population that is non-Hispanic black. Metropolitan areas with a 1-percentage point increase in the percent of their population that is non-Hispanic black are 2.9 percentage points less likely to recover from chronic distress. We believe that this finding should be interpreted as a human capital finding that is not captured by the educational attainment variable we use as a measure of human capital. It suggests that the quality of education afforded to the average black person at any specific level of educational attainment is actually lower than that afforded whites and other non-blacks, a factor which, if our expectation is correct, would not be controlled for through educational attainment, but instead would be picked up through percentage of blacks in a region's population. Table 2.7 finds no statistically significant results in the GMP data.

MODEL 4: FOR THOSE REGIONS THAT DID RECOVER, WHAT ACCOUNTS FOR THE DURATION OF THEIR RECOVERY? To further probe the factors that contribute to a region's recovery from chronic low-growth, we employ a hazard model similar to model 2 that attempts to explain how long it takes for a region to recover. The dependent variable is a 1 in the first year of a region's recovery, and 0 otherwise.

The coefficients in model 4, as with those of model 2, are presented as hazard ratios. Three variables are associated with *increases* in a region's probability of recovering from chronic employment distress in the first year: the 80–20 income ratio, manufacturing's share of employment, and number of research universities located in the region. A one-unit increase in the income ratio, meaning increased income disparity, is associated with a 26-percentage point increase in the probability of recovering (see table 2.8). This is significant at the 1% level. The variables that follow are at the 5% level of statistical significance. A one-unit increase in the share of manufacturing employment increases the probability of recovery by 10 percentage points. And, the presence of an additional research university in a metropolitan region effectively doubles the probability of recovering in a given year.

The other variables with closest statistical association with the dependent variable all are associated with decreases in the odds of recovery. At the 1% level of statistical significance they are: earnings per job, percent of employment in health care and social assistance, the degree of industrial concentration as measured by the Herfindahl index, and the portion of the population that is non-Hispanic black.

Controlling for industrial composition, an increase of one unit ($1,000) in earnings per job is associated with a decrease in the probability that a chronically distressed region will recover in the first year (or, if it does not in the first year, in the next year, etc.) by 28%. A one-unit increase in the proportion of the population employed in the health care and social services sector decreases the probability of recovery, as does a one-unit increase in the level of industrial concentration; each by about 37 percentage points. A one-unit increase in the percent of the region's population that is non-Hispanic black is also associated with a 14% lower probability of recovery from chronic distress. As we noted earlier, we interpret this as an indication of consistent lower quality of education received by the African American population.

The GMP results show that two variables are *positively* associated with recovery: the number of export industries and the 80–20 income ratio. In the case

TABLE 2.8   Likelihood that region recovers from chronic distress (Model 4)

| | COX MODEL: HAZARD RATIO (STANDARD ERROR) | |
VARIABLE	REGION IS CHRONICALLY DISTRESSED IN EMPLOYMENT	REGION IS CHRONICALLY DISTRESSED IN GMP
Percent population with high school education or less	1.011 (0.032)	0.546 (0.245)
Lagged employment	1.000 (0.000)	—
Lagged GMP	–	1.000 (0.000)*
Earnings per job	0.719 (0.088)***	0.254 (0.175)**
Percent of employment in manufacturing	1.100 (0.050)**	0.581 (0.117)***
Percent of employment in health care and social assistance	0.616 (0.060)***	0.114 (0.093)***
Percent of employment in tourism-related industries	1.190 (0.278)	0.108 (0.084)***
Number of export industries	0.878 (0.087)	3.013 (1.077)***
Herfindahl index	0.629 (0.103)***	0.003 (0.007)**
Number of research universities	2.002 (0.687)**	0.055 (0.095)*
Right-to-work law	1.545 (1.203)	52.030 (242.900)
Percent of population non-Hispanic black	0.861 (0.041)***	0.794 (0.159)
Percent of population Hispanic	1.004 (0.020)	0.968 (0.063)
Income ratio 80–20	1.260 (0.075)***	3.453 (1.947)**
Distance to large metropolitan area	1.025 (0.181)	0.769 (0.714)
N	445	268

* $p < 0.10$, ** $p < 0.05$, *** $p < 0.01$

of the income ratio, the effect appears even larger for GMP than for employment. The ratio for export industries suggests that increasing the number of large industries that are significant to the regional economy may contribute to a recovery of GMP but not necessarily in overall employment. Decreases in the odds of GMP recovery are statistically associated with increased shares of employment in each of the sectors included in the model: manufacturing, health care and social service employment, and tourism employment.

Summary and Conclusion

Textbook neoclassical theory suggests that periods of chronic distress are temporary and that chronically distressed regions will bounce back to their previous growth rates after a reasonably short adjustment period. Cumulative causation theory, as postulated by Myrdahl (1957), suggests that chronic distress will be prolonged and recovery will result only from substantial restructuring. Our empirical models are not capable of testing either theory rigorously. However, our findings indicate some support for both theories' implications about the prospects for economic recovery in chronically distressed regions.

Many regions recovered from chronic distress. Nearly half of the regions that were chronically distressed in employment (i.e., regions that experienced at least eight consecutive years of job growth at a rate less than half of the national average) emerged from chronic distress. (The period of chronic distress was followed by at least eight consecutive years of job growth at a rate that was at least 75% of the national growth rate.) The mean time a region took from the onset of chronic distress to its emergence from that condition an event we characterize as resilience to chronic distress, was 9.1 years.

There were some regions, however, that did not recover from chronic distress within our study period. Twelve regions experienced ten or more consecutive years of chronic distress and did not emerge from that condition during the time frame of our study. (An additional thirteen regions had experienced fewer than ten years of continuous distress but were still experiencing chronic distress at the cut-off point for our data.) Most of these regions were small, although Buffalo was an exception.

In general we find that convergence in job growth rates (i.e., negative outlier regions moving closer to the national average) is the typical response to chronic distress. Nearly all of the chronically distressed regions (fifty-six of sixty-three), regardless of whether they were resilient or not, engaged in positive restructuring. The difference was that those that did not emerge simply were more distressed at the beginning of the period than were those that did emerge.

Nearly all of the regions (thirty-three of thirty-seven) that were resilient to chronic distress underwent economic restructuring as they emerged from that condition; their portfolios were comprised of industries that were better poised for national economic growth ten years after the onset of chronic distress than was the case at the onset of their distressed state. However, the ten-year time period that we used from the onset of chronic distress to measure restructuring is a considerably shorter period than is suggested by cumulative causation theory.

Our empirical models throw light both on why regions experience chronic distress and why some of these regions are resilient, that is, they are able to emerge from that condition. Table 2.9 summarizes our regression findings for the key variables. Several are consistent for both employment and GMP resilience.[9] Chronic distress is associated with low educational attainment in a region at the onset for both employment and GMP output. The results for educational

TABLE 2.9 Summary of quantitative results on chronically distressed regions

	REGION IS CHRONICALLY DISTRESSED (CROSS-SECTIONAL LOGIT MODEL)		REGION IS CHRONICALLY DISTRESSED (HAZARD MODEL)		REGION RECOVERS FROM CHRONIC DISTRESS (CROSS-SECTIONAL LOGIT MODEL)		REGION RECOVERS FROM CHRONIC DISTRESS (HAZARD MODEL)	
	EMPLOYMENT	GMP	EMPLOYMENT	GMP	EMPLOYMENT	GMP	EMPLOYMENT	GMP
Low educational attainment	+	+	+	+	0	0	0	0
Earnings per job	0	+	+	+	0	0	−	−
Percent employed in manufacturing	0	0	0	−	0	0	+	−
Percent of employment in health care and social assistance	+	0	0	−	0	0	−	−
Percent employed in tourism-related industries	0	0	−	0	0	0	0	−
Economic diversity	0	0	0	0	0	0	0	+
Economic concentration	0	0	0	0	0	0	−	−
Number of research universities	0	0	0	0	0	0	+	−
Right-to-work	0	0	0	−	0	0	0	0
Percent black	0	0	0	0	−	0	−	0
Percent Hispanic	0	−	−	−	0	0	0	0
High income inequality	+	+	+	+	0	0	+	+

Note: Plus sign (+) indicates a positive impact that is substantively significant (with at least a 1 percentage point change) and statistically significant (at the 10% level or better); minus sign (−) indicates a negative impact that is substantively significant and statistically significant; zero (0) indicates an impact that is not statistically significant or, if statistically significant, not substantively important.

attainment conform to previous conclusions about the importance of worker skills in the U.S. economy. Factor cost explanations also received support. High earnings per job (controlling for industry structure) are associated with the onset of chronic-distress. Moreover, the longer high wages relative to other areas persisted, the longer it took a region to emerge from chronic distress.

Manufacturing's share of regional employment was important and statistically significant in several of the models. Regions with a high percentage of their employment in manufacturing were less likely to enter a period of chronic GMP economic distress. For regions that experienced chronic distress, those with a higher proportion of their employment in manufacturing were less likely to emerge (i.e., be resilient) from GMP distress, but were more likely to return to rates of total employment growth near or above the national rate. This may reflect the late product cycle stages or low productivity that may have characterized the kinds of manufacturing firms found in chronically distressed regions in the late twentieth and early twenty-first centuries rather than any adverse economic impact of manufacturing per se.

Our measures of economic diversity (number of major export industries and the Herfindahl index) were unrelated to whether a region experienced chronic distress. However, for those regions that were chronically distressed, the number of major export industries was positively related to resilience from that condition, while the degree of industrial concentration in regional economies was negatively related to the amount of time it took to exit chronic distress.

There was also some support for the importance of agglomeration economies. Regions with larger GMP (a reasonable proxy for agglomeration) were less likely to enter a period of chronic GMP distress than those with smaller GMPs. For regions that experienced chronic distress, the greater total employment, the more likely the region was to be employment resilient to chronic distress. Our descriptive results with respect to population size also supported a role for agglomeration economies. Regions entering distress had higher mean population size than those that did not experience distress, and chronically distressed regions that were able to emerge from that condition had average population sizes greater than those that were not resilient. Finally, regions with populations smaller than 1,000,000 and regions that are far away from a metropolitan area of that size are more likely to experience chronic distress. This finding suggests that more isolated metropolitan areas with less than a million in population may not be able to meaningful agglomeration economies.

Demographic composition also played a role in a metropolitan area regional economy's resilience to chronic distress, after controlling for other factors. The higher the percentage of Hispanic population in a region, the less likely it was to experience a period of chronic distress (of course, this might simply reflect the tendency for Hispanic immigrants to cluster in regions in which they expect employment opportunities as a result of economic growth). For chronically distressed regions, the higher the non-Hispanic black population, the less likely the region was to emerge from a period of employment chronic-distress. Our strong sense is that this finding reflects low levels of human capital that are not picked up in the educational attainment variable, given that the quality of schools attended by the average black are lower than those attended by the average white.

Income inequality, in the form of a large gap between workers at the 80th percentile and workers at the 20th percentile of the earnings distribution is positively associated with the onset of chronic distress. However, it also appears to be positively associated with recovery.

The findings for educational attainment and income inequality largely parallel the results of chapter 1. That chapter finds that regions with low levels of education are more likely to experience downturns; and suggests that such regions are also more likely to experience periods of sustained low growth. Both chapters indicate that high-income inequality is associated with downturns, and both also find that such inequality may hasten recovery. Conversely, the findings here regarding earnings per job and distance from a large metropolitan area are novel and suggest that these variables may have long-term effects on growth that are not easily captured by studies that focus on the short term.

REGIONS THAT LACKED RESILIENCE

While the previous two chapters provide descriptive data and quantitative analysis on economic shock downturns and chronic economic distress, they do not provide information on the processes that occurred, on the nature of interventions or changes of behavior, or on their effects. In short, the quantitative analysis cannot provide depth and context. Therefore, to enable a richer understanding of economic shock, chronic distress, and resilience, we undertook intensive case studies in six regions: Charlotte, Cleveland, Detroit, Grand Forks, Hartford, and Seattle.[1] We chose regions to reflect (a) different kinds of shocks (national economic downturn (cyclical) shocks for Cleveland, Detroit, and Grand Forks; national or regional industry shocks for Charlotte, Cleveland, Detroit, Hartford, and Seattle; and a major natural disaster shock and military base downsizing for Grand Forks), (b) experience with chronic distress (Cleveland, Detroit, Grand Forks, and Hartford), and (c) different degrees of resilience in response to these events (from high resilience in Charlotte and Seattle to a lack of resilience in the 1980s in Hartford and in the 1990s in Grand Forks, and, since 2000, in Cleveland and Detroit). Although we make no claim that these six regions are a representative slice of metropolitan area economies nationally, they do vary in the kinds of shocks that they experienced the degree and length of chronic distress, and in their responses. (See appendix 2 figures 3.1–3.4 for summaries of how each of the six regions as well as the nation as a whole performed in terms of employment and gross metropolitan product [GMP] and when they experienced shocks.)

We made at least two trips to each of the regions with the exception of Grand Forks, which we visited once. During the trips, we conducted semistructured interviews with individuals who were either major participants in economic development activities (in the public, private, or nonprofit sector), were owners or managers of firms in the region's major export industries, or were well-regarded observers or analysts of the regional economy. We conducted telephone interviews with selected additional individuals whom we were unable to interview during our site visits. In most regions we interviewed individuals from organizations concerned with the region's economic future, including public and private economic development organizations, local and regional government, trade association or cluster association organizations, workforce development programs, universities (both researchers, as observers and analysts, and officials as participants), foundations, leading private sector firms in the export sector, federal statistical offices, business and economic editors, and reporters of local newspapers and economic journals.

For each region, we followed a similar process to locate the individuals who would populate these interview categories. We had initial contacts in each region who provided suggestions which we cross-compared. Instances of multiple-mentions of the same individual usually led to interviewing the individual, whom we also asked for additional contacts to fill voids in our categories. We also selected some individuals because they were prominent or likely to be highly knowledgeable about economic development in the region.

In each of the case studies, we describe the region's economic background, the extent to which the region experienced and was adversely affected by economic shocks or long-term stagnation, whether it was resilient (including those regions that were shock-resistant) or not, why the region was resilient or not, and the explicit responses undertaken by regional actors.

In this chapter we focus on three regions that had relatively little resilience: Cleveland, Detroit, and Hartford. In chapter 4 we discuss the three regions that were more successful: Charlotte, Seattle, and Grand Forks, the latter of which was an interesting mixed case.

Cleveland

ECONOMIC HISTORY. Situated on Lake Erie and the Cuyahoga River, the Cleveland region was a manufacturing powerhouse from the 1880s through the 1960s.[2] As of 1970 the region's main export industries, each accounting for more than 4% of total employment, were transportation equipment manufacturing (predominately automotive assembly), fabricated metal product manufacturing, machinery manufacturing, and primary metal manufacturing.

The eighteen companies in the Cleveland metropolitan region that were on *Fortune* magazine's list of top 500 companies in 1968 provide a sense of the diversity of the region's industrial structure. They represented automotive parts (five companies), chemicals (two companies), appliances (three companies), steel, mining, oil production, addressing and duplicating machines, printing presses, sprinklers, industrial motors, and machine tools and lathes. Cleveland was a manufacturing-dominated region.

But as the manufacturing industries dominating the Cleveland regional economy reached the late stages of their product life cycles and were not able to "reload" with new products, the regional economy became characterized by slow-growing, technically sophisticated, capital intensive, old products.

The cost of production is especially important for companies with mature products and this drives decisions on where to locate investment in plant and equipment. A former leader of a multinational manufacturing company with several divisions in the city of Cleveland explained the connection between the business cycle, capital investment, and these types of investment decisions: "When business turns down we close our highest cost operations first and when it picks up our lowest cost plants come back first. It is just following marginal costs."

Another challenge for companies with products in the late stages of their product life cycles as has been the case in the Cleveland metropolitan economy is that significant product innovations are infrequent and their ability to nurture innovation is limited. Christenssen (1997) coined the term "the innovators dilemma" to describe how market pressures to satisfy customers' immediate needs, drive down costs, and meet quality standards can result in the death of the company. Focusing intently on the immediate needs of customers can result in missing the disruptive innovation that will eventually kill the company or its customer.

The founder of a major venture capital firms recounted to us how in the early 1980s his CEO-peers chided him for not investing in Cleveland technology. In response he was guided through the region's corporate laboratories and shown the science that was underway at Sohio/BP, the paint and chemical companies, and in the metals companies. His response was that there was good work going on but it was much more development than research. As a venture capitalist he was not going to invest in following the customer product development; he was interested in innovation that was going to create new product classes and new markets.

It is no surprise that a former Cleveland area business executive observed, "People here don't think in terms of entrepreneurship. Their mentality has been [one of] big business." The result is that Northeast Ohio, which includes the Cleveland region, had become what another interviewee called "the Mount Rushmore of dead manufacturing companies," such as Firestone, Royal Appliance,

Republic Steel, Standard Oil, White Motors, and Warner & Swasey; all companies that were once leaders in product innovation but no longer exist. Leaders
in the region recognized the need to engage in economic development planning and organizing to diversify and grow the local economy as early as 1980,
hiring both the Rand Corporation and McKinsey & Company to conduct
studies on the economy and to propose strategies. The region's philanthropic
foundations, regional chamber of commerce, and others have funded numerous studies since that time to assess the economy and recommend actions to
make both the Cleveland metropolitan region, its central cities, and the larger
Northeast Ohio region more competitive. However, the region has suffered
repeated and sustained challenges. The eight-year average employment growth
rate for Cleveland between 1979 and 2010 ranged from –0.85% to 1.85%,[3] experiencing negative employment growth in every year but one from 2000 and
2010. From 1970 to 2010, regional employment grew by only 8%, real GMP
per worker grew by 38%, but average wages per worker increased by only 4%,
clearly reflecting the shift from high-paying manufacturing jobs to jobs in lower
wage industries.

SHOCKS, DOWNTURNS, AND RESILIENCE. Cleveland is susceptible to
regional economic downturns when national downturns occur because of its
specialization on cyclically sensitive durable goods manufacturing, with a deep
dependence on the Detroit headquartered assemblers. Thus, the Cleveland
region experienced nine shocks from 1979 to 2010, and was resistant to none.
These shocks caused five separate downturns (in two cases shocks were simultaneous) including downturns resulting from the national industry shock around
1979 (after which the region lost 98,500 jobs prior to the 1982 recession) and the
national economic shocks of 1990, 2000, and 2008. The region ultimately was
resilient to all economic shocks except the national economic shock in 2000 and
it did not experience any regional industry shocks.

Although it took ten years for the region to regain its 1979 level of employment, by 1983 it had regained its prior growth rate and employment was increasing at a 3.7% annual rate. The 1991 downturn was smaller, with the region losing
24,450 jobs between 1990 and 1992. The recovery from the 1990 downturn
occurred even more quickly. However, the downturn that began as a result of the
2000 shock was different. From 2000 to 2010, the Cleveland region experienced
annual loss in employment for every year but one, losing 146,000 jobs by the end
of the decade. The region also experienced two periods of chronic distress, from
1981 to 1988 (from which it never recovered, according to our criteria laid out
in the previous chapter) and from 2003 until at least 2010. The first decade of
the twenty-first century was one of economic decline and stagnation. The region

never recovered from the 2000 recession and entered the Great Recession in 2006, earlier than the nation as a whole.

In mid-2011 the private sector, under the leadership of the Greater Cleveland Partnership and the metropolitan area chambers of commerce in Akron, Canton, and Youngstown, joined with the Fund for Our Economic Future (Fund), an umbrella organization of the region's foundation community. These organizations started the Regional Economic Competitiveness Strategy (RECS). The RECS was a review of the economic performance of the sixteen counties in Northeast Ohio and of the economic development infrastructure.[4] As part of the review a shift-share analysis on the performance of the sixteen-county region was performed, looking at the change in employment and gross regional product between 2000 and 2010 (Hill 2012). During this decade the region lost 284,000 jobs in total; 72% of the job loss, or 205,000 positions, was attributed to a decline in local competitive conditions and an additional 16%, or 45,000, was attributed to the mix of industries in the region. The fall in gross product was not as severe, but was still a stunning $31.3 billion. One-third of the loss was due to the mix of industries in the region, and two-thirds was attributed to deteriorating regional competitive conditions. Fourteen industries were responsible for 41% of the loss, with the leading two being automotive parts and automotive assembly.

The RECS leadership concluded, "The specific mix of industries which drive NEO's [Northeast Ohio's] economy have lost many jobs nationally, accounting for much of NEO's economic decline. But NEO's driver industries perform even worse than the US average of similar industries" (Fulford 2013). This is an echo of a finding of a 2006 report conducted by the Upjohn Institute for the Fund, which found that region's "subpar industrial performance is due to two factors: . . . most of its traditional core industries face shrinking national and international markets . . . [and] the competitiveness of industries in the region is mediocre" (Eberts, Erickcek, and Kleinhenz 2006, 1.[5]

STRATEGIES, POLICIES, AND RESPONSES. The region's foundations funded numerous studies since those of the Rand Corporation (Kingsley 1982) and McKinsey & Company to assess the economy and recommend actions to make Cleveland more competitive. Policymakers in the region perceived that an economic transition was occurring and that they needed to respond. Nonetheless, the decline in manufacturing was a wrenching experience for the Cleveland region. A businessman we interviewed saw the trajectory of these changes as one of "mourning the loss of manufacturing to accepting the economic transition." Another participant viewed the transition brought on by the decline of the manufacturing sector as involving three phases: in the 1980s it was "save the patient," the 1990s involved helping industries with more of a future, and in the 2000s regional leaders recognized the need to invest in a tapestry of development initiatives.

Policymakers and regional leaders undertook a range of responses, including the creation and reorganization of economic development institutions and changing the focus of economic development first from the city to the Cleveland metropolitan area, and then, later, to the broader region that includes Akron and Youngstown. Foundations, corporations, and governments have spent significant sums during the last twenty-five years to address the region's challenges. Despite their efforts, Cleveland and its broader labor market have continued to struggle.

In the local public sector, the city's government focused on tax abatements as the major component of an implicit amenities strategy to develop downtown, initially supporting professional sports and other attractions and then, from 2000 forward, branching into downtown residential development and residential amenities. Throughout the 1990s, as part of a downtown revitalization strategy, the city provided property tax abatements for construction projects. This included the Gateway project and Tower City Center, although it has been suggested that this strategy mostly transferred business activity from one area of the city to another (Miller and Wheeler 1997, 195). The Gateway project, completed in 1994, focused on developing a new baseball field for the Cleveland Indians and an arena for the Cleveland Cavaliers professional basketball team. Although the Cleveland football team moved to Baltimore in 1995, the city was able to obtain an expansion team (now the Cleveland Browns), for which it completed a new stadium in 1999. One of the main reasons given for these investments is that, to be a "big league" city, Cleveland needed major league sports. At the same time, the Rock and Roll Hall of Fame was being built as part of a tourism strategy (Miller and Wheeler 1997, 194). None of these projects appear to have significantly altered the development path of the city or region, but have helped create noticeable changes in the function of the city's downtown. What was a nearly exclusive office and retail destination in the 1970s, transforming into a struggling office market in the 1980s, emerged after 2010 as a mixed-use work-live neighborhood. Downtown Cleveland was heralded as an overnight success; albeit one that was thirty years in the making.

The 1990 Census of Population counted 7,261 people in the tracts that are a close approximation to the Downtown core. The Downtown Cleveland Alliance in its 3rd Quarter 2014 Market Update estimated that there were 13,728 downtown residents and that the housing projects that either were under construction or had committed financing would result in a population approaching 18,000 in 2017 and 23,000 in 2020 (Downtown Cleveland Alliance 2014, 5).

There were a series of initiatives in the Cleveland region that can be considered at the forefront of economic development strategy and thinking. The history of regional responses was one of continual organizational creation and restructuring resulting in a network of specialized organizations with responsibility for the Cleveland, Akron, Canton, and Youngstown metropolitan areas by partnering with each metropolitan region's chamber of commerce and local governmental entities. These are specialized economic intermediaries targeting specific industries or companies in different stages of their life cycles so that, as one interviewee noted, "now we focus on the whole continuum of development." The first phase, in the wake of the 1979 recession, saw a range of efforts to reinvigorate the regional economy after the city's bankruptcy declaration and the election of George Voinovich as mayor. Voinovich had a productive relationship with the local business community that enabled significant progress on a number of initiatives. These initiatives included the formation of Cleveland Tomorrow in 1981 by the CEOs of the fifty largest Cleveland businesses, the funding of the Rand and McKinsey studies on the Cleveland economy, and projects resulting from these activities.

Cleveland Tomorrow became one of the biggest drivers of policies to restructure the local economy. It supported the Work in Northeast Ohio Council, an independent labor-management organization that promoted productivity programs and quality of work life programs in manufacturing industries; the Cleveland Advanced Manufacturing Program, a partnership among the state government, Cleveland Tomorrow, local universities, and the community college to expand research and services to promote advanced manufacturing; a Center for Venture Development, to assist entrepreneurs with business plans, build their boards, identify professional services and find funding; and Primus Ventures, seeded with $30 million raised by Cleveland Tomorrow's Board with the initial purpose of providing venture capital.

Partly as a response to the sustained downturn after 2000, Cleveland Tomorrow, the Greater Cleveland Growth Association, and the Greater Cleveland Roundtable merged in 2004 to form the Greater Cleveland Partnership (GCP). One of the board members explained, "The goal of the merger was to use savings from removing duplication to expand economic development activities." Compared to Cleveland Tomorrow, whose membership consisted of primarily larger firms, GCP's sixty board members represented firms of all sizes and a diverse set of industries, including professional services, higher education, and others in recognition of the growing role of nonprofit institutions as well as banks and law firms in the city and regional economy.

Foundations similarly tried to adopt a more coordinated regional effort after many years of struggling to make a difference in economic development in the region, often supporting bricks and mortar projects as well as various business-led initiatives. The Cleveland and George Gund foundations, together with the

GAR Foundation of Akron, were instrumental in bringing together seventy private and corporate foundations in sixteen Northeastern Ohio counties to create the Fund for Our Economic Future in 2004. The new organization adopted a larger regional focus, incorporating all of Northeast Ohio rather than solely the Cleveland metropolitan region. Its goal was to frame a regional economic development agenda "that can lead to long-term economic transformation," track overall regional progress, and support highly promising initiatives. The Fund followed a strategy similar to that used by Cleveland Tomorrow by employing its resources to fund intermediary organizations. Two of the organizations it funded are entities that grew out of Cleveland Tomorrow's initial programs and three came out of the 1999–2000 review of the region's economic development efforts. One benefit, as explained by a foundation director, is that philanthropy tends to be viewed as neutral: "we don't have the baggage that the political or business community has, so people don't automatically turn off."

Both the Greater Cleveland Partnership and the Fund for Our Economic Future supported five specialized regional organizations, with a determined regional approach. TeamNEO was formed in 2003 to market the greater Northeast Ohio region (consisting of eighteen counties) and attract firms.[6] Its goals were to increase regional collaboration and better use available economic development funding (including significant funds from the state's development organization JobsOhio) in order to attract new businesses to the region. According to its Web site (ClevelandPlusBusiness.com 2013), it generated a return on investment of $20 in regional payroll for every $1 invested. TeamNEO also housed Cleveland+, a regional marketing campaign with a strong press and media relations focus.

The other regional organizations focused on assistance to firms and entrepreneurs in specific sectors:

- NorTech is the successor organization to the Technology Leadership Council. It promoted initiatives in biotech, polymers, electronics, advanced materials, and other emerging industries; its focus is to substantially increase entrepreneurial support and outcomes within and, especially, at the intersections of Northeast Ohio's technological strengths in biosciences and healthcare, polymers, advanced materials, and manufacturing, electronics, information and communication technology, and advanced energy. NorTech was merged into TeamNEO in late 2014.
- BioEnterprise, a joint initiative of the Cleveland Clinic, University Hospitals Health System, Case Western Reserve University, and Summa Health System, provides management counsel, clinical access, business development, and capital access services to new bioscience companies, with the aim of accelerating their growth.

- MAGNET (the Manufacturing Advocacy and Growth Network) is the new version of the Cleveland Advanced Manufacturing Program and assisted manufacturing-dependent industries by providing assistance on quality and innovation. It also brokered commercial and university intellectual property in selected manufacturing areas and delivers federal and state manufacturing Small Business Assistance programs. Cleveland's MAGNET is part of the National Institute of Standards and Technology's Manufacturing Extension Partnership program.
- JumpStart, Inc., was formed to stimulate early stage business development and investment by providing capital and technical and management support to new and promising enterprises. It has three primary tasks: to connect entrepreneurs with successful stakeholders, provide technical assistance, and assist with venture development.

It is impossible to determine how effective these activities were: "there is no victory to declare yet, no trend shifting; this is something we'll measure ten years from now," according to an economic development professional. The region remains one of the country's significant manufacturing centers, and despite the sector's downturn, the region retains a high concentration of manufacturing jobs.

Yet dissatisfaction with the region's performance on the part of the business and philanthropic communities and state government was palpable. The region's philanthropies and chambers became concerned over the cost and performance of the post-2000 economic development ecosystem and launched the RECS process in mid-2011. As of this writing the results of the latest review and restructuring are emerging.

In 2012 the region spent $67.6 million to support the ecosystem and the region's metropolitan chambers of commerce. This spending does not include public sector spending on state, county and municipality economic development functions. The members of the ecosystem generated nearly $20 million from their own direct fundraising (primarily earned income for services rendered by the chambers), businesses contributed $17.5 million through a combination of dues and specialized fundraising campaigns, and philanthropy was responsible for $13.9 million (Fulford 2013, 11). The second phase of the RECS concluded that less should be spent and the system had to become more focused and more effective. The review concluded that over time parts of the ecosystem began to overlap in terms of service provision and that organizational funding models were unsustainable with too much reliance on philanthropy.

SUMMARY. The Cleveland region, once home to a diverse and thriving manufacturing-based economy, saw that economy erode as the various industries

TABLE 3.1 Cleveland-Elyria-Mentor MSA

VARIABLE	1970	2010	% CHANGE
Population	2,419,274	2,077,240	−14%
Employment	927,416	1,004,457	8%
National employment			73%
Avg. wage per worker ($2005)	39,400	40,959	4%
U.S. avg. wage per worker	34,818	42,295	22%
GMP (millions of $2005)*	68.8	95.0	38%
GMP per worker*	68.6	94.6	38%
National GDP per worker			135%
Manufacturing employment	296,702	116,305	−61%
Employment in primary metal manufacturing (NAICS 331)	37,623	8,089	−78%
Employment in fabricated metal product manufacturing (NAICS 332)	48,540	25,576	−47%

MAJOR SHOCKS	SHOCK-RESISTANT (Y/N)	DOWNTURNS	RESILIENT (Y/N)	TYPE OF SHOCK
National industry (transportation equipment manufacturing) shock (1979)	N	1979	Y	Employment
National economic shock (1989)	N	1990	Y	GMP
National economic shock (1990)	N	1990	Y	Employment
Unidentified shock	N	1999	Y	GMP
National economic shock (2000)	N	2000	N	Employment
National economic shock (2008) and national industry (primary metal manufacturing) shock (2008)	N	2008	Y	GMP
National economic shock (2008) and national industry (fabricated metal product manufacturing) shock (2008)	N	2008	Unknown as of 2010	Employment

CHRONIC DISTRESS (Y/N)	NUMBER OF CONSECUTIVE YEARS OF SLOW GROWTH	FIRST YEAR OF CONSECUTIVE SLOW GROWTH	RECOVERY (Y/N)	TYPE OF CHRONIC DISTRESS
Y	8	1981	N	Employment
Y	8	2003	Unknown as of 2010**	Employment

* GMP data is for 1978–2010; GMP per worker 1970 uses 1978 employment and GMP data. ** Due to the data available prior to publication, we are unable to determine whether the Cleveland region recovered from this recent bout of chronic distress.

passed through the stages of the product cycle. In 1990 Hill published a book chapter on Cleveland's metropolitan economy titled "Cleveland, Ohio: Manufacturing Matters, Services Strengthen, But Earnings Erode." The title still holds true. The regional economy was unable to "reload" by generating sufficiently robust new industries and products. Employment in the Cleveland region grew by only 8% between 1970 and 2010, far below the nation's growth rate and of the growth rate of the other five regions in our study. (The next lowest, Detroit, had an employment growth rate of 15%.) GMP per worker grew by 38%, again, far below the national rate, and average wages increased by only 4%, compared to 22% nationally. Although the economy was resilient to most of the shocks it has faced, it experienced two long episodes of chronic economic distress, one of which it was still mired in at the end of our study period. It was not resilient, by our criteria, to either of these episodes.

Although the region's leaders put in place an organizational structure and set of programs and activities that are widely seen as at the cutting edge of economic development practice, the region's economy nonetheless continued to stagnate. Of course, it may be that without the activities undertaken by community leaders the regional economy would have been much worse or it may be that these activities are laying the groundwork for future growth. It is also possible that even the best current thinking on regional economic development was inadequate to cope with the problems of a region that was undergoing the kind of externally forced economic transformation that Cleveland faced in the first decade of this century.

Detroit

ECONOMIC HISTORY. The Detroit region was dominated for nearly 100 years by the Big Three automakers (now Ford Motor Company, General Motors Company, and FCA US LLC—the company that is the product of the merger between Chrysler and Fiat) and their suppliers.[7] As such, it faced periodic economic downturns (occasionally caused by factors other than a shock to the regional economy) as a result of national economic shocks. These shocks affected the sales and, thus, production of motor vehicles and other durable goods. When the national economy suffered, the automobile industry and thus the region suffered, and when the economy expanded, the auto industry and region grew. After downturns shrank regional employment both generally and in the automotive industry, the region would ultimately bounce back as the national economy recovered.

However, over time transportation equipment manufacturing, while continuing to maintain its dominance in the Detroit region's economy, declined in importance. In 2010 transportation equipment manufacturing constituted only 4.3% of the region's total employment compared to 10.3% in 1970. Total regional employment in that industry also fell by more than 50% from 1970 to 2010. The decline in employment in Detroit's major export industry was a result of 1) productivity increases in the sector, which is one reason why employment levels in the industry did not recover to the same levels as did output after recessionary shocks, 2) lost market share to foreign headquartered assemblers who established major operations outside of Detroit,[8] and 3) the decentralization of Detroit-headquartered portion of the automobile industry to other regions as automotive production increasingly moved to states in the southern United States (and Mexico) to take advantage of lower costs.[9] Thus, employment in the transportation equipment industry was increasing nationally even while it was declining in the Detroit region.

It is not surprising then that the decline in automobile industry employment severely affected the regional economy. Between 1970 and 2010, total employment in the Detroit region increased by 15% (about 230,000 jobs), while employment nationally rose by 72.5%. Gross metropolitan product for the region increased by 22.6% in real terms, compared to 134.5% nationally. Average real wages increased by only 1% (the lowest increase in any of our six case study regions), compared to 22% nationally.

In addition to the 51% decline in employment in transportation equipment manufacturing between 1970 and 2010, the region also experienced decreasing employment in many related industries, including machinery manufacturing (decrease of 64%), primary metal manufacturing (decrease of 79%), and fabricated metal product manufacturing (decrease of 47%), among others. In fact, of all manufacturing industries, only one (plastics and rubber products manufacturing) gained jobs from 1970 to 2010 and all but one of the others (apparel manufacturing) had a double-digit decrease in employment.

SHOCKS, DOWNTURNS, AND RESILIENCE. The Detroit region experienced eleven shocks between 1979 and 2010. It was resistant to a national industry shock in 1986 and resilient to all three of the shocks that caused downturns prior to 1999. The explanation for its seemingly surprising resilience to the national industry shock in 1979 and the national economic downturn in late 1980s is simple: the national economy simply recovered. After these shocks, the region's total employment even rebounded past its previous peak before the next shock. There was virtually unanimous agreement among those whom we interviewed that the recovery had nothing to do with policy or strategic interventions but rather the national economic turnaround. In effect, the region simply "held its breath" until things got better. Moreover, this is not a new facet of the regional economy. As Galster (2012) notes, the region experienced booms and busts related to national economic conditions at least back to the 1920s.

With ever-increasing competition from abroad and from lower cost production sites within the United States, the Detroit region faced more difficulty in
exhibiting resilience in the early twenty-first century. The effects of the downturn
that began in 2000 proved prolonged, with the loss of regional employment re-
enforced by the additional shock which occurred with the national recession in
the late 2000s. Interviewed during the depths of the post-2007 and 2008 shocks,
policymakers characterized the region's economic response to the post-2000
shock as "different," "too long and too deep," "the culmination of a two-generation
decline," or "not . . . experienced before in this magnitude." The region's economy
was nonresilient to the shock in 2000 and possibly was only resilient to the shocks
in 2007 and 2008 due to substantial federal cash infusions as two of the Big Three
had to undergo restructuring in order to maintain their operations. One result
was that the region was in a period of chronic distress from 2003 to at least 2010.
Prior to 2000, the region averaged an eight-year annual employment growth
rate of 1.9%. Between 2000 and 2001 employment fell by 3% and continued
to decline every year after that through 2010. Over that ten-year period, total
employment in the region declined by 21.3%.

As one of our interviewees said, "The region was hit by a truck, and no one is
resilient when hit by a truck." Another likened the auto industry to the "cavalry"
and said it was not coming this time to save the regional economy. In large part,
this is due to structural changes in the automotive industry that disproportionately affected the Detroit region; as a 2009 report by the Upjohn Institute notes:
"Michigan's auto industry has restructured in two distinct ways. The auto assembly sector reduced the number of workers in their facilities, without reducing the
number of facilities in the state. Parts producers, on the other hand, cut workers
and shut down plants. . . . in Michigan the average staffing levels of these facilities were cut in half during that period [from 2001 to 2008], while for the rest
of the nation the levels were reduced by 27 percent" (Eberts and Erickcek 2009,
2–3). In the first decade of the twenty-first century, business and civic leaders
publicly stated that although the automobile industry will still play a major role
in the regional economy, it is not going to be the job engine for the region that
it was in the past, at least with respect to providing substantial employment for
relatively low-skilled workers. Many political leaders were thought to believe in
the same sentiment though they did not say so publicly. Furthermore, a report
by Michigan Future, Inc., noted that "the engine that still drives the Michigan
economy is the troubled domestic auto industry. So for the foreseeable future,
until the Detroit Three automakers stabilize, Michigan's economy will continue
to lag the nation" (Glazer and Grimes 2008, i). Many of those that we interviewed
predicted (or hoped) that the region would remain the international center of
automotive research, development and engineering and that those parts of the

industry would continue to be the major drivers of the regional economy. No one that we interviewed thought that employment in motor vehicle production, particularly in automobile assembly work, was likely ever to return anywhere close to pre-2000 levels.

STRATEGIES, POLICIES, AND RESPONSES. Among many in the region, the response to the region's economic difficulties brought about by the decline of the automobile industry was one of hopelessness and despair. Others professed optimism in the region's ability to create a more vibrant economy, one that is more diversified and less focused on the automobile industry. Both of these responses were dramatically different from the denial of long-evident trends that seemed to characterize the response to earlier shocks even as some observers predicted these changes due to technology and globalization would ultimately have a severe long-term effect on the region's economy. Despite a reluctant acceptance that the region can no longer expect the auto industry to be the economic driver that it was in the past, most people we interviewed recognized that the automobile industry remains critical to the economy. They also believed that, particularly in the short and medium terms, the most important activities related to the region's economic future are being undertaken by the motor vehicle cluster—the individual Big Three auto firms and their suppliers.

The future of the auto suppliers is particularly important as their orders from their main purchasers decline. Many of those we interviewed said that the prolonged domination of the Big Three created a culture of dependence and entitlement, not only for area residents who looked forward to lifetime employment within the industry, but also for the industry's suppliers. Several of our interviewees said that suppliers to the auto industry were characterized by a "procurement culture" in which the suppliers could prosper and be "set" once they obtained a contract with one of the Big Three. As a result, suppliers did not try seriously to find other markets, and entrepreneurship, risk taking, and small business creation not tied to the automobile industry in the region were all stifled. Although some suppliers made inroads in diversifying to meet the needs of related industries (such as defense), those efforts were limited, especially because of the past rebounds in the auto industry, which drew suppliers' attention away from needed changes.

Building on a history of technological proficiency and adaptability going back to the earliest days of the car companies, more recent efforts focused on taking the human and physical capital acquired in the auto industry and transitioning it to other industries. Most diversification thus occurred within companies closely related to the auto industry, in fields such as green technologies (e.g., solar and wind power, next generation batteries), the defense industry (building on a regional role in the industry since automobile companies shifted to producing military hardware such as tanks during World War II), and aerospace.

The public and nonprofit sectors helped in these efforts. Both public and non-profit funding went toward helping suppliers learn how to reorient their production, market themselves to other manufacturers, and even deal with multiple buyers (rather than just one auto company, as in the past) through such initiatives as the Manufacturing Extension Partnership, a federal public/private partnership that operates in every state. Diversifying the region's economy was one of the key objectives of the New Economy Initiative, which was initially funded with $100 million from ten foundations in 2008 and provided grants for revitalization issues including workforce development, residential conversions in downtown Detroit, and entrepreneurialism. The state also played a role in the effort to encourage diversification. In the mid-2000s, the governor created state tax initiatives to support green industries. In addition, state funds were made available to companies manufacturing next generation batteries and alternative energy sources, for example, in an effort to both retain these capabilities as well as grow these new industries as a potential cluster to replace or augment the automobile industry.

Another aspect of this diversification was attempts to strengthen the health care industry in the region. These efforts took two paths. One focus—led by Detroit's nonprofit hospitals and medical school—was to position the region as a health service provider (akin to the Cleveland Clinic) to medical tourists in both the United States and across the border into Canada. These attraction efforts were largely building on a strong health system already in place in the region as a legacy of substantial benefits provided by the auto industry to its workers. The other focus—primarily by businesses but supported by nonprofits, including university technology transfer offices, and the public sector—was innovation in medical devices (again taking advantage of the engineering and other talent of the auto industry).

During our interviews, we heard repeatedly about strategies supported by various public, private, or nonprofit actors—usually working together—to take advantage of the region's location with the nearby Canadian border,[10] the presence of major highways forming a NAFTA corridor, and two airports, one with direct flights to China and other developing economies. The culmination of these desires may have reached its height in an initiative led by Wayne County to develop the airports into a new aerotropolis as a regional logistics hub. Shortly before we conducted our interviews, the effort had been dealt a serious blow, partly due to conflicts among the local jurisdictions, although, as of 2013, Wayne County was still trying to launch the aerotropolis. However, at the time of our interviews, virtually all of these proposals discussed above were either at the beginning of the implementation stage or were still being developed. Every one of the plans will require long-term commitment and development if it is to yield visible economic results.

Public and nonprofit actors are also offering or funding programs focused on generating more entrepreneurship and small firm start-up and survival in the region. Perhaps the premier example of this is TechTown, a research and technology park located in midtown Detroit that is supported by a number of regional and national foundations. Its primary function is to act as a business incubator and offer programs to support budding local entrepreneurs and new companies, but it also provides some services to companies looking to locate in the Detroit region. Michigan State University, the University of Michigan, and Wayne State University also started working together through the new University Research Corridor to support more commercialization of start-ups. Other organizations (including the region's universities and economic development organizations) also created entrepreneur development and support programs (including Bizdom, Ann Arbor Spark, and the Lowe Foundation).

The relatively low average level of human capital in the region was seen by interviewees as another critical problem. They noted that area residents long believed that they and their children would be able to find well-paid employment in the auto industry with relatively little education and with only the need to "punch a clock." They observed that one of the principal challenges is making the local population understand that the low skilled high paying jobs that existed in the past largely disappeared and are not going to return and that high paying jobs are now likely to require some familiarity with computers or technology, as are jobs in other growing sectors (such as green technologies or health care). Many of the region's nonprofit organizations (including local economic development agencies and private foundations) funded efforts to improve the region's education and workforce training programs, with the New Economy Initiative, for example, providing funding for workforce development programs at several local community colleges. Interviewees expressed concerns about the availability of and access to public training programs, but many also cited the strengths and programs of the universities and community colleges as an asset, while also calling for more collaboration among the different educational tiers to better serve residents.

The belief that the automobile industry would be unlikely to bounce back to its prior strength as it did in the past produced a variety of other long-range policy proposals, some serious and some more fanciful, for regional development alternatives. Many of these focus on building up and promoting the region's preexisting amenities, such as the Detroit Institute of the Arts, the Detroit Symphony Orchestra, and others are legacies of the wealth and philanthropy of individuals in the automotive industry. Newer developments are being advanced to attract younger, highly educated professionals. Working with the city government, several foundations funded a greenways project, building trails along the riverfront and connecting major city attractions and neighborhoods. The foundations and private actors, such as First National Bank, were funding large-scale redevelopment of the city's waterfront as well as, with other nonprofits and businesses, downtown revitalization efforts, including residential conversion supported by tax credits and the popular Campus Martius Park. Public and private actors also attempted to increase retail traffic around the city's two major league stadiums, located across the street from one another. Private developers, such as Dan Gilbert, the president of Quicken Loans, have purchased and redeveloped a substantial number of buildings in downtown Detroit, and some downtown areas, long derelict, have experienced residential growth. We also heard about various efforts to capitalize on the natural wealth of the nearby Great Lakes, and their importance for recreation, tourism, and as a water source. One interviewee referred to the Lakes as a "third coast" and noted the potential for increasing tourism from other regions to support the local economy.

Indeed, many proposals that were discussed were designed to deal with the problems of the city of Detroit, which everyone that we interviewed agreed is in desperate shape, both economically and financially.[11] Kresge's Re-Imagining Detroit, for example, focused almost exclusively on the city. Although the city suffers from population loss, poverty, crime, and extreme fiscal distress, the concern most often expressed by those we interviewed was regarding the dysfunctional school system. As an attempt to correct conditions in the notoriously poor system, in 2009 the state appointed an emergency manager who had the power to make significant changes to the school system's structure and finances.

At the rhetorical level most people that we interviewed emphasized that although the economic problem is a regional one, it cannot be solved without successfully addressing the severe social, economic, and fiscal problems of the city of Detroit. Some argued that negative perceptions of Detroit are a severe deterrent in efforts to lure new residents and businesses to the region as a whole and that there is "no respect" for Detroit although the "perception is worse than the reality." Others, though, reasoned that it is unclear whether improving the condition of the city is indeed a precondition for regional economic revival since, as one interviewee observed, until recently the region was doing very well thanks to the automobile industry while the city had been declining for decades. It is unknown whether the new focus on the importance of the city to the region is a late recognition of the city's role or a matter of "political correctness" and political necessity that provides actors with the political legitimacy to participate in regional interactions—which, nonetheless, may not bring the city many benefits.

Actors within the region historically had a difficult time coming together to discuss and develop collaborative responses to the region's problems, including its economic ones. The difficulty is, in part, a reflection of a legacy of adversarial and confrontational relationships or "culture of distrust." That history includes not only union-management conflict but also tension between policymakers in the city of Detroit and its suburbs, (there are also intersuburb conflicts), as well as between actors of various races and ethnicities, especially whites and African Americans (Galster 2012). As a consequence, positive social capital was in short supply and there is little history of cooperation at the regional level or across jurisdictional or racial lines.

Elected leaders were often said to be consumed by regional competition and historical animosities, rather than developing collaborative enterprises, although we did hear positive rumblings about new efforts by both the city and suburban executive leadership. Many interviewees agreed that the severity of the economic downturn resulted in greater recognition of the need for cooperation and that some collaborative efforts are now taking place.

The region did not lack organizations that made such attempts, and during the years of our study, both existing and new or restructured organizations attempted to devise strategies and responses to the region's economic challenges. The Detroit Regional Chamber of Commerce runs several traditional business attraction and promotion programs. City and county economic development organizations (such as the Detroit Economic Growth Corporation in the city and similar county-level organizations) continue to perform their traditional functions of promoting and attracting economic development in their own jurisdictions. Some of these once-local economic development organizations expanded into more regional agencies, such as the growth in services provided by Ann Arbor Spark outside the boundaries of its principal funder, Washtenaw County. One pioneering organization was Detroit Renaissance, a CEO-led organization that emerged after the Detroit riot in 1967. For most of its history, Detroit Renaissance focused primarily on the city of Detroit; however, in 2009 it changed its name to Business Leaders for Michigan and directed its concerns to the state level, with a focus on reducing business costs (particularly taxes) in the state.

Foundations played an increasingly important role in the region, with the large, national Ford and Kresge foundations—which were funded by regional fortunes—directing more of their giving to the region after focusing primarily elsewhere. These two organizations were two of the initial funders of the New Economy Initiative. In 2008, the Kresge Foundation also launched Re-Imagining Detroit 2020, an effort to coordinate the foundation's activities and those of other organizations focused on development in the city to limit program duplication and overlap.

As of 2010 there were few, if any, tangible effects of the above actions on Detroit's regional economy. Most of those interviewed acknowledged that the current economic situation was the result of the region's long-term dependence on the automobile industry, which had brought unparalleled (though somewhat cyclical) prosperity but was now ending. Most interviewees did not regret that dependence and the benefits it brought, although many did regret regional leaders' inability to accept some time ago that the region's motor vehicle industry would decline and to prepare for that future. Even the most optimistic felt that the effects of any policy changes will take years to show substantial results.

SUMMARY. Detroit's experience is perhaps an extreme example of the advantages and disadvantages of a regional economy hitching its star to a single dominating industry and its related cluster. The dependence on the motor vehicle industry resulted in a high-wage, high-employment economy, albeit with cyclical ups and downs, for many decades. The regional economy was resilient in the face of all of these shocks until the end of the twentieth century. However, as foreign-owned competition arose, and as the industry proceeded through the product cycle placing a greater premium on low-cost production, the regional economy suffered the consequences. Employment in transportation equipment fell by more than 80,000 jobs (51%) between 1970 and 2010 and total employment increased by only 15%, far below the national average. GMP per worker rose by only 26%, far below the national rate of 134.5%, and average wages per worker increased by less than 1%, an indication that the region's high-paying motor vehicle jobs were being replaced with lower paying jobs in other sectors. The region was not resilient to two shocks at the end of the century and entered a period of chronic economic distress from which it had not emerged (i.e., was not resilient) by the end of our study period.

Motor vehicle suppliers were not able to replace their reliance on the industry with contracts with other industries, and, despite both substantial organizational restructuring of its economic development operations and a variety of schemes, some of them fanciful, for targeting specific industries or sectors for growth and development, the region was not able to generate new industries. Despite substantial efforts, the region's businesses and policymakers were unable, at least during the period of our study, to translate Detroit's expertise and experience with the motor vehicle industry into related or new enterprises. It is widely acknowledged that better education is a critical long-range component required for sustained

TABLE 3.2 Detroit-Warren-Livonia MSA

VARIABLE	1970	2010	% CHANGE
Population	4,431,390	4,296,250	–3%
Employment	1,520,387	1,748,891	15%
National employment			73%
Avg. wage per worker ($2005)	44,093	44,420	1%
U.S. avg. wage per worker	34, 818	42,295	22%
GMP (millions of $2005)*	146.0	179.0	23%
GMP per worker*	80.9	102.4	26%
National GDP per worker			135%
Manufacturing employment	415,197	187,822	–55%
Employment in transportation equipment manufacturing (NAICS 336)	156,082	75,733	–51%
Employment in machinery manufacturing (NAICS 333)	68,844	24,727	–64%

MAJOR SHOCKS	SHOCK-RESISTANT (Y/N)	DOWNTURNS	RESILIENT (Y/N)	TYPE OF SHOCK
National industry (transportation equipment manufacturing) shock (1979)	N	1979	Y	Employment
National industry (transportation equipment manufacturing) shock (1986)	Y	—	—	GMP
Unidentified shock	N	1988	Y	GMP
Unidentified shock	N	1989	Y	Employment
National economic shock (1999)	N	1999	N	GMP
National economic shock (2000) and national industry (transportation equipment manufacturing) shock (2000)	N	2000	N	Employment
National industry (transportation equipment manufacturing) shock (2007) and national economic shock (2008)	N	2007	Y	Employment
National economic shock (2008) and national industry (management of companies and enterprises) shock (2008)	N	2008	Unknown as of 2010	GMP

CHRONIC DISTRESS (Y/N)	NUMBER OF CONSECUTIVE YEARS OF SLOW GROWTH	FIRST YEAR OF CONSECUTIVE SLOW GROWTH	RECOVERY (Y/N)	TYPE OF CHRONIC DISTRESS
Y	8	2003	Unknown as of 2010	Employment

* GMP data is for 1978–2010; GMP per worker 1970 uses 1978 employment and GMP data.

regional economic growth, but it is no clearer here than it is elsewhere how to bring this about for children coming to school with a legacy of poverty.

Hartford

ECONOMIC HISTORY. Hartford's regional economy has long been driven by its three major export industries—insurance, aerospace manufacturing, and, as the state capital, state government.[12] Known as "the insurance capital of the world," Hartford is home to the headquarters of many large insurance companies, including the Hartford Financial Services Group, Aetna, The Phoenix Companies, Inc., and major operations of Travelers Insurance Company, CIGNA, and MetLife. The region's aerospace manufacturing industry is anchored by the family of companies owned by the United Technologies Corporation, including aircraft engines manufacturer Pratt & Whitney, aerospace system manufacturer Hamilton Sundstrand (now called UTC Aerospace Systems), and helicopter manufacturer Sikorsky Aircraft.[13] These firms support a large network of aerospace component manufacturers throughout the region that form the region's aerospace supply chain.

Employment in transportation equipment manufacturing, including aerospace manufacturing, is generally cyclical, although the general trend in transportation equipment manufacturing was starkly downward during the late twentieth and early twenty-first centuries. The region lost large numbers of jobs in these industries during the late 1970s, early 1980s, and early 1990s, and none of the recoveries that followed those downturns was sufficient to regain what had been lost. From 1970 to 2010, total employment in transportation equipment manufacturing declined by almost 35,000 jobs (61%), and its share of total employment decreased from 10.1% in 1970 to 4.9% in 2010. Between 2010 and 2011, the number of transportation equipment manufacturing jobs in the region decreased by 1.1% while the employment of transportation equipment manufacturing nationwide increased by 4.1%.

Although the insurance industry's share of total regional employment remained constant at about 7%, employment in the industry increased by 26% from 1970 to 2010. However, this gain masks a substantial change in the industry's employment over time. There were consistent job gains during much of the 1970s and 1980s, followed by large-scale job losses in the 1990s. The job loss was caused partly by structural changes in the industry, which led to the movement of many jobs to lower cost regions, such as Scranton and metropolitan areas in the Great Plains.

Over the entire 1970–2010 period, the Hartford region had relatively slow overall job growth (37% from 1970–2010, compared to 75% nationally) but extremely high GMP growth (169%, slightly higher than the national rate) and average wage growth (29% compared to only 22% nationally). These data reflect the region's concentration of jobs in industries and firms producing high-value added but mature products that did not generate rapid job growth.

SHOCKS, DOWNTURNS, AND RESILIENCE. During our study period the region experienced nine shocks and downturns, with both usually attributable to national economic conditions. It was resilient to downturns in 1980, 2000, and 2001, but was nonresilient to the 1988 downturn, an event that severely altered its growth path for many years. The 1988 downturn was also the most severe in terms of job loss and triggered a period of chronic slow growth that persisted from 1992 to 2002.

The timing and magnitude of losses in insurance and aerospace contributed to an aggregate economic downturn in the region that occurred earlier and lasted longer than the nationwide recession that began in 1990 and precipitated a period of chronic employment distress beginning in 1992. Aerospace manufacturing was especially hurt by decreased demand for spare parts due to the nationwide recession as well as cuts in defense spending (Hicks 1991). Hartford's insurance companies, which had invested heavily in commercial real estate during the 1980s, were hurt by the bursting of the commercial real estate bubble of the late 1980s and early 1990s. One employee in insurance industry said, "The real estate bubble hit us hard. At that time, assets lost value every day, and it destroyed profitability." From 1988 to 1993, Hartford lost 68,000 jobs (a decline of 10.2%), and it continued to lose jobs slowly for another two years. Although the region subsequently gained jobs from 1995 to 2000 and recovered from its period of chronic distress, it failed to reach its 1988 level of employment before the 2001 downturn halted its recovery.[14] Despite this, Hartford was resistant to the regional industry shock in the transportation equipment industry in 1998 (i.e., although the region lost substantial employment in this industry, the shock did not throw the regional economy as a whole into a downturn). It also was resistant to national economic shocks immediately prior to the Great Recession.

STRATEGIES, POLICIES, AND RESPONSES. Hartford is notable among our case study regions for the relative *lack* of large-scale local and regional responses to shocks and chronic distress. One possible reason is that, although the region had periods of low employment growth (including a long period of chronic slow growth), it nonetheless had very high median per capita income and productivity growth, possibly reflecting the out-migration of low-wage, low-skill jobs and the retention and growth of higher paid ones. These measures of economic success may have made policymakers less likely to perceive a need to take action, particularly since the problem manifested itself more as a slow but steady decline rather than a sudden drop. One of the interviewees commented,

"In the recession of the 1970s, the reaction was immediate because the losses were so dramatic. But the recession of the 1990s was less dramatic—a slower bleed."

Structural and historical reasons may also have contributed. Local government in Connecticut is weak, and the local government system is fragmented. Cooperation on a regional level is particularly difficult. A faculty member observed, "The state has a long and rich history of fragmentation—it is made up of 169 municipalities. There is a lot of fragmentation, lack of cooperation, and a lot of duplication." Given this fragmentation as well as the small geographic size of the state, major economic development efforts affecting the state's regions—including Hartford—have been more likely to be undertaken by the state than by local or regional entities. The state was the first to establish Enterprise Zones (EZ) in 1982, with Hartford as one of the six initial communities designated as an EZ, and there were still seventeen EZs in the state as of 2013.

The state also undertook a major state cluster initiative on the heels of the wrenching 1990s downturn. Governor John G. Rowland's administration (1995–2004) identified six broad industry groupings for the initiative to target—financial services, telecommunications and information, health care services, manufacturing, high technology, and tourism—and convened industry cluster advisory boards for each. After a year of deliberation, the advisory boards concluded that the broad industry groupings should be formalized as industry clusters and that additional clusters should be encouraged. The policy consisted of making state funding available to firms in clusters that the state government predefined on a statewide basis; it was not a "bottom-up," regionally based policy.

The statewide cluster initiative was relevant for the Hartford region because the initiative targeted the region's two key export industries, with an aerospace cluster that was established in 1999 and an insurance and financial services (IFS) cluster that was created in 2003.[15] Hartford's aerospace cluster, by far the most active of the state's cluster organizations, was led by Aerospace Components Manufacturers (ACM), a network of mainly small- to medium-sized aerospace companies in the state. Member firms put together a workforce development curriculum, including basic skills, for the shared training, with costs shared by the firms. It arranged customized training courses for its members, provided consolidated purchasing agreements, and organized a roundtable forum to discuss business development. One interviewee argued that the aerospace cluster was self-sustainable because of this cost-sharing (which was necessary since the cluster did not do training itself but worked with the region's Manufacturing Extension Partnership affiliate, CONNSTEP, and outside consultants). Another told us, "The greatest advantage of [the] ACM [cluster] is peer-to-peer support."

The insurance and financial services cluster was formally established in response to industry concerns that there were few specific policies directed at one of the state's leading industries (most of which is located in the Hartford region) and was designed to benefit from the region's highly educated workforce and high per capita income. One interviewee involved in the cluster recalled, "It felt like there was no one in state government who really understood insurance." The cluster's leaders created one of the first associate's degrees for the IFS industry and established the IFS Center for Educational Excellence, funded by the Department of Labor. We were told that the IFS cluster—along with the biosciences cluster—was successful at supporting the needs of its member companies, particularly providing educational support and lobbying for legislation in support of the cluster. The IFS cluster functions as an important mechanism for the Hartford region by tracking job posting of major IFS firms and monitoring worker skills so that needed aspects of training are met.

Some of the comments of our interviewees in the Hartford region are instructive in terms of suggesting difficulties in designing and implementing a clusters policy. First, the mission of the clusters was not well defined (e.g., it was unclear how the clusters were supposed to interface with and become "full partners" with government, higher education, and other economic development organizations, as initially envisioned), and most simply devolved into trade organizations shortly after they were formed. One interviewee observed, "The clusters are not economic clusters; they're groups to give the industries a public voice." In addition, a former state economic development official we interviewed argued that another difficulty with the cluster policy was operationalizing the cluster agenda, and it was not until 2006 that it finally got rolling. Moreover, after the initiating governor resigned from office in 2004, his successor's administration continued the program, but interviewees suggested that it suffered as a result of the discontinuity in leadership. All in all, our interviewees suggested that the ACM cluster was the most successful in the support system it provides to its members.

The Rowland administration also focused on amenity-based strategies, particularly on downtown redevelopment and revitalization. The Six Pillars initiative, announced in 1998, envisioned the state spending $350 million in the hope that accompanying federal and private investments would reach $1 billion (State of Connecticut 1998). The initiative included waterfront redevelopment, rejuvenating the civic center, and building a new sports and convention center, the location of an institution of higher education, converting vacant properties into housing, and increased parking (ibid.). It is not clear how Governor Rowland viewed the initiative in terms of region-wide economic impact, but the "suburbs also strongly supported the plans to redevelop Hartford," believing that the city's "dismal national reputation" was an impediment to attracting people to the region (Burns 2002).

Although the major economic development efforts in the region were primarily the responsibility of the state government, organizations concerned with the economy of the Hartford region do exist at the local and regional level. The region is notable for its many small- to medium-size economic development organizations, the size and number of which mirror the political fragmentation in the region. At the regional level, there was a substantial amount of organizational creation and restructuring in these organizations. The MetroHartford Alliance grew out of the 2001 merger of the Hartford Chamber of Commerce and the economic development-focused MetroHartford Economic Growth Council in response to the region's downturns in the late 1980s and early 1990s. The Alliance functions as a vehicle for traditional economic development activities. In addition, the Hartford-Springfield Economic Partnership was formally launched in 2000 as an interstate collaboration of regional economic development, planning, business, tourism, and educational institutions designed to establish the Hartford-Springfield area as a major corridor connecting Connecticut and Massachusetts. One interviewee stated, "The Hartford-Springfield Partnership is interesting because it has been done *despite* government."

The Hartford region also is home to multiple organizations that tried to increase the technological sophistication of the state's industries. The Connecticut Center for Advanced Technology is a nonprofit corporation that was founded to assist aerospace suppliers. A second organization, the Connecticut Technology Council, is a statewide association of technology-oriented companies and institutions that was founded in early 1990s. It became the first point of contact for new IT companies in the state and lobbies the state on behalf of the IT companies, providing leadership in areas of policy advocacy. The third organization, the BEACON Alliance, is an association of companies, universities, and health care institutions in central and southern Connecticut and neighboring western Massachusetts. It was founded in 2000 to promote collaboration, technology commercialization, industry development, and education in medical device manufacturing and other applications of biomedical engineering.

Economic development activity at the regional level was hampered by the lack of a unified business leadership substantially engaged in the region's economic and political arenas. Until the early 1980s, an informal group of insurance executives referred to as "the Bishops" did fill that role, but their influence waned as firms from outside the region acquired locally owned insurance companies and as politicians and corporate leaders left their posts. More recently, the region struggled for consistent leadership. One interviewee described a disconnect between the corporate and city infrastructure in the Hartford region such that, as residents moved further out of the central city in order to avoid urban problems, middle management in the city's major companies (especially insurance companies) was not capable of stepping up in an entrepreneurial role. One interviewee from a state-level business association noted, "The end result of this was a dual structure where the city of Hartford rejected the corporate leadership and the [corporate] leadership only came into the city during the day." Hartford did demonstrate a regional focus in its workforce development programs. These programs shifted to a "regional focus" before national policy changes, when Regional Workforce Development Boards were launched in 1992 to administer employment and training activities at the local level in five state regions in partnership with local elected officials.

As in the other regions, various organizations offer entrepreneurship and firm assistance programs. The University of Hartford promotes entrepreneurship in the region through the Entrepreneurial Center, which provides hands-on training and guidance for qualifying small businesses located in Hartford through the Hartford Small Business Technical Assistance Program. The Center not only provides one-on-one business counseling, but also offers various educational programs (some free of charge) and conferences. MetroHartford Alliance provides business-related assistance to firms in the Hartford region. It offers financing and consulting services for export-minded small businesses, through working cooperatively with all parts of the region on issues related to their common economic health. Another organization, Connecticut Innovations, Inc., provides information on start-up capital needs, relocation, financing, and investment. Connecticut Innovations also helps emerging companies to research, develop, and market new products and services. CONNSTEP provides MEP services to small and medium-sized manufacturers throughout Connecticut. The BEACON Alliance (medical device manufacturing) and Aerospace Components Manufacturers are industry-specific organizations that provide technical assistance to their members.

There was little effort by public or private organizations in terms of undertaking or planning any policy or strategy to restructure the regional economy in response to the Great Recession. Some of our interviewees thought that restructuring of the regional economy was necessary, but none thought it possible within the region's existing structure of governments and private organizations. One businessman in the technology industry said, "It is hard for Hartford to accept the true global position of New Haven and Stamford for its position [*sic*] as a destination for new capital.

SUMMARY. Hartford was resilient in terms of responding to all but one of the shocks it experienced and to its one period of chronic distress. However, its overall performance from 1970 to 2010 reflects an economic restructuring that resulted in slow job growth, but high productivity growth with increases in average earnings, suggesting a shedding of low-wage jobs. Of its two main export industries in 1970, the region had lost 35,000 jobs in transportation equipment (a decline of 61%) by 2010. The other, insurance, grew by 9,000 jobs (26%).

TABLE 3.3 Hartford-West Hartford-East Hartford MSA

VARIABLE	1970	2010	% CHANGE
Population	1,035,195	1,212,381	17%
Employment	465,975	636,704	37%
National employment			72%
Avg. wage per worker ($2005)	38,867	49,953	29%
U.S. avg. wage per worker	34,818	42,295	22%
GMP (millions of $2005)*	30.1	81.0	169%
GMP per worker*	57.9	127.2	120%
National GDP per worker			135%
Manufacturing employment	143,269	66,749	−53%
Employment in insurance carriers and related activities (NAICS 524)	35,676	44,802	26%
Employment in transportation equipment manufacturing (NAICS 336)	56,083	21,616	−61%

MAJOR SHOCKS	SHOCK-RESISTANT (Y/N)	DOWNTURNS	RESILIENT (Y/N)	TYPE OF SHOCK
Unidentified shock	—	1980	Y	Employment
Unidentified shock	—	1988	N	Employment and GMP
Local (transportation equipment manufacturing) industry shock (1998)	Y	—	—	GMP
National economic shock (2000) and national industry (insurance carriers and related activities) shock (2000)	N	2000	Y	GMP
National economic shock (2000)	N	2001	Y	Employment
National industry transportation equipment manufacturing shock (2007)	Y	—	—	GMP
National economic shock (2008)	Y	—	—	GMP
National economic shock (2008)	Y	—	—	Employment

CHRONIC DISTRESS (Y/N)	NUMBER OF CONSECUTIVE YEARS OF SLOW GROWTH	FIRST YEAR OF CONSECUTIVE SLOW GROWTH	RECOVERY (Y/N)	TYPE OF CHRONIC DISTRESS
Y	10	1992	Y	Employment

Unlike the other regions that we examined, the state government, rather than regional organizations or local governments, played the major role in attempting to bring about growth in the region. It identified six clusters, two of which were the major export industries of the Hartford region, and attempted to put in place policies to promote growth in them. It also provided financial assistance to Hartford for an amenity-based downtown development and revitalization effort. Economic development at the regional level was hampered by a lack of formal and informal regional leadership. There were a large number of economic development organizations within the region that engaged in the usual variety of local economic development programs.

Conclusion

All three of the regions we examined in this chapter have experienced both economic shocks and long-term chronic economic distress. All three have responded with a variety of efforts to regain their footing and become resilient. None, at the time of this writing, have yet to succeed in doing so. The conclusion to chapter 4 provides material that integrates the findings for both regions that were not resilient (considered in this chapter) and those that were (considered in the next chapter)

RESILIENT REGIONS

In the previous chapter we focused on the three of our case study regions that had relatively little resilience in the face of economic shocks and/or chronic economic distress. In this chapter we turn to the three case study regions that proved to be more resilient—Charlotte, Grand Forks, and Seattle. Charlotte and Seattle are both examples of regions that have been able to successfully "reload"; they were able to move from reliance on a prior major export base to new ones. Grand Forks is a more mixed success. It has been less successful in replacing the decline in its previous export base. By our statistical criteria, it has had a mixed record of resilience and nonresilience to shocks and chronic distress but it has nonetheless diversified in a way that its residents consider successful.

Charlotte

ECONOMIC HISTORY. The economic face of the Charlotte region during much of the twentieth century was manufacturing, which accounted for about one-third of the region's jobs in 1980.[1] Textile mills, textile product manufacturing, and apparel manufacturing accounted for more than half of manufacturing jobs and just under one-sixth of all jobs in 1980. Global competition eroded the profitability of those three subsectors between 1980 and 2010, when they collectively shed 54,144 jobs, declining 89%, even as the region as a whole had a net gain of more than 404,000 jobs over the period.

As employment in the manufacturing sector weakened, Charlotte's banking sector grew, and in the wake of federal banking deregulation Charlotte became the nation's second-largest financial center (measured by assets). By 2000 the banking and related service sectors constituted the region's largest export industry. The groundwork for this expansion was laid decades earlier in the form of favorable banking laws in North Carolina. Historically, branch banking had not been allowed in most U.S. states; indeed, the fear of monopoly by the large Northeastern banks led most states to prohibit branching (Roussakis 1997, 43). Early on North Carolina's bank leaders when provided with the legal authority by their state legislature to branch statewide soon learned how to effectively and efficiently acquire other banks, merge their operations, and run the merged bank as a branch facility. North Carolina's banks exhibited expansion-minded behavior as early as the 1950s. Extensive experience with handling multiple branches statewide and the opportune protection provided by implementation of the Southeastern Regional Banking Compact in January 1985 gave North Carolina bank CEOs an advantageous boost into interstate merger opportunities nationwide when the U.S. Supreme Court declared interstate banking constitutional in June 1985 (Frieder 1988).

Bank mergers and acquisitions allowed the region to prosper even as employment in the region's textile and apparel industries declined at a precipitous rate. By 2010, manufacturing had dropped to 8.0% of regional employment (from over 30% in 1980) and finance and insurance had doubled (from 3.7% to 7.4%). Jobs in credit intermediation and related activities (commercial banking and related industries, such as mortgages and credit cards) increased by 286% during 1980–2010, growing from 9,102 to 35,165. Overall, employment in the Charlotte region increased by 164% between 1970 and 2010 and from 1980 to 2010 average earnings per worker increased by 44% compared to 22% nationally.

However, the economic downturn beginning at the end of 2007 resulted in the collapse of large financial corporations across the nation. Banks in the metropolitan Charlotte region were major factors in the region's quick turnarounds from prior downturns, and the dependence of the Charlotte region's economy on those now-ailing financial institutions made it especially vulnerable to the Great Recession. Between 2008 and 2010, the Charlotte region lost 60,000 jobs (6.9% of its 2008 total). Business and community leaders observed that this recession was "the worst" that they had ever seen and that the jobs that were lost "will not be coming back" to the Charlotte region. Finance and insurance lost 3,800 jobs (3.8%) over the two-year period.

In December 2008, San Francisco-based Wells Fargo took over Charlotte-based Wachovia. Bank of America, the other major Charlotte-based bank, acquired Merrill Lynch (which is based in New York City) in the fall of 2008, prompting concerns that that the investment activities of these once hometown-focused banks might move elsewhere over time. The acquisitions by Wells Fargo and Bank of America raised questions about Charlotte's future as a financial center.

SHOCKS, DOWNTURNS, AND RESILIENCE. The Charlotte region experienced nine economic shocks over the time period we examined. Four of these included national economic downturn shocks in 1981, 1989/1990, 1999/2000, and 2008, each of which resulted in a downturn in the Charlotte economy, although the region was resistant to a 1984 national industrial shock to the textile mills industry. With the exception of the most recent case in 2008, the Charlotte region never lost more than 1.3% of its employment and proved resilient to the shock within three years. The textile mills industry also had an industry shock in 1981 that was piggybacked on top of the national economic downturn shock. At no point did the region experience chronic distress.

STRATEGIES, POLICIES, AND RESPONSES. Over the broad time period of our study, the local (and regional) public sector appeared to play little role in attempting to transform the Charlotte regional economy. Partly this resulted from a business-oriented culture that included, in the language of one participant we interviewed, a general understanding that there was a "bright line" between public and private sector responsibilities. Some public officials acknowledged being taken off guard by the sudden unwinding of textile manufacturing, and there were no deliberate public policies to confront the economic loss. Conway et al. (2003) contend that such programs could have helped larger textile and apparel firms integrate production into the international supply structure, reach out beyond core competencies, and develop services to upstream suppliers and downstream users. With respect to the public sector, state government policies designed to positively affect economic development throughout the state or, in some cases, in all urban and regional areas in the state, played a larger role than did local or regional ones.[2]

Within the region it was largely the private and the nonprofit sectors that took the lead in forming economic development polices and undertaking actions. As noted earlier, private sector activity by enterprising bank CEOs, who took advantage of the favorable state banking laws and laid the seeds for the region's growth, was the driving engine behind the region's transformation from a textile-based economy to one now rooted in banking and finance. Economic development leadership came from the CEOs of these same banks (North Carolina National Bank and First Union) which, as a result of their aggressive bank expansion strategies, would transform into the nationwide financial institutions Bank of

America and Wachovia, both headquartered in Charlotte. A frequent refrain heard during our interviews was that it was the leadership of these bank CEOs, along with that of the CEO of Duke Power (a regional energy company), that was responsible for the region's (and the city's) economic vitality as well as its physical transformation. These private sector leaders envisioned and implemented a strategy to transform Charlotte and, particularly, its downtown. One interviewee stated that their contribution "could not be oversold" and that this triumvirate practiced "a perfect blend of strategy and execution."

To serve the employment needs of the major employers, actors in the region implemented an amenities-based development strategy. The leadership of the two rapidly growing banks believed there was not a sufficient pool of skilled workers in the region to meet their needs and that Charlotte would have to attract such workers from outside of the region. This was made difficult, however, by the city's image at the time. During the 1970s, the area that would become the downtown neighborhood was home to brothels, liquor stores, and drug stashes. One resident described it as the place "where people would go on a Saturday night if they really wanted to get killed. . . . How do you recruit talent to a city that is perceived to be life threatening?" Private sector leadership then encouraged community development investments to provide a set of amenities that would help attract and retain talent that was not available in the region.

Early efforts were directed toward encouraging downtown residential housing through the creation of a community development corporation (CDC) to spur downtown residential housing construction. This was done at the behest of the Bank of America. The CDC was established in the late 1970s and provided mortgage funds for moderate-priced housing downtown via the Charlotte/Mecklenburg Housing Partnership, a financial intermediary. Using their relationships with city officials to forge public-private partnerships, the CEOs of Bank of America, Wachovia, and Duke Power assumed a role in implementing housing production, commercial construction, and regional marketing. The completion of a series of public spaces in 1992, including a performing arts center, a corporate center, and a shopping center, brought people into the city, while new mixed-use condominiums appeared downtown, developing a positive street life of sidewalk cafes and public plazas.

There were also new stadiums constructed for the professional football and basketball teams and a branch of Johnson and Wales University (a hospitality and culinary arts college) opened, further boosting the local tourism and hospitality industry and expanding the pool of labor for this sector. One long-time resident described the process: "We totally renovated this city in the late 80s. We tore up streets. We put in infrastructure under the streets—power lines, and internet cables. Banks gave the city land to build the bus station. The city put in bus benches. There was a $100 million of redevelopment of downtown. It added to our ability to start building condos. We went from fewer than 1,000 people living downtown to close to 16,000 people living in the downtown area." The foresight shown by private sector leaders in pursuing massive downtown demolition and redevelopment was pointed to as enabling a rate of growth to be realized that otherwise would have been impossible had the city of Charlotte remained the place that it was in the early 1970s.

According to our interviewees, an increasingly revitalized downtown enabled the banks to attract the talent it needed—especially recent college and business school graduates—from outside the region. That in-migration enabled the financial industry to mitigate the effects of a lack of skilled administrative workers in the region and of a public education system that may have otherwise prevented the banking sector from obtaining the number and level of educated workers that it required.

The nonprofit sector (whether acting alone or in public-private partnerships) took the lead on developing policies specifically to deal with economic concerns in the region, particularly creating and restructuring a set of economic development organizations whose major efforts were to engage in regional marketing and industry recruitment strategies and to provide assistance to firms in the region. There were several efforts to identify and develop policies targeting various clusters for marketing and recruitment purposes, although these efforts were sporadic and relatively weak compared to those of other case study regions described in this chapter. The Charlotte Chamber of Commerce identified nine clusters of importance (film, health, defense, aerospace, energy, finance, motorsports, international business, and tourism), while the Charlotte Regional Partnership identified three preexisting clusters (financial services, transportation and distribution services, and high growth manufacturing) and three in emerging industries (innovative technology, professional services, and travel and entertainment services). Both organizations touted the region's job growth in energy and biotechnology and promoted the region as an emerging leader in these fields.

The Chamber also took the lead in providing assistance to firms, creating the Manufacturers Council in 1987 as a response to problems with local regulatory issues (onto which later were added advocacy of manufacturers' interests) and to facilitate the exchange of best-practices through online discussions, Chamber member visits to firms around Charlotte, and periodic electronic communications.

In 1999, Advantage Carolina was launched as a regional strategic planning arm of the Chamber after community-wide involvement in an economic analysis; it eventually started fourteen initiatives. In 2006, Advantage Carolina was restructured after a study clarified roles between the Charlotte Regional Partnership, the Charlotte Chamber, other agencies such as the Public Library of Charlotte and Mecklenburg County, and Advantage Carolina. Advantage Carolina then refocused on strategy rather than program management, while the Partnership provided assistance to firms in a sixteen-county area. The services included marketing the region to corporate leaders and advisors worldwide, serving as a mediator around issues of regional competitiveness, such as air quality, and regularly convening county economic development agencies.

There was, however, a lack of policies to support entrepreneurs, which was partially attributed to the difficulty of attracting venture capital. Perhaps due to the region's concentration of banks and that industry's generally "conservative" outlook (as one interviewee labeled it), there was concern expressed by some of our interviewees about the availability of start-up funds for entrepreneurs: "Venture capital is primarily invested in businesses next door. They're not going to give $10 million unless they can look at you every day. Charlotte has not had large numbers of wealthy people, which is what it takes to get venture capital. The region has not had the kind of start-up businesses in the past that would have attracted their attention."

SUMMARY. Despite the precipitous decline of its major export industry—textiles—Charlotte's regional economy exhibited resilience by successfully restructuring without experiencing a period of chronic economic distress. It was also resilient in terms of its response to all but one of the shocks it experienced over the forty-year period we examined. Charlotte's economic transformation involved the establishment of banking and finance as the major export cluster. This successful transformation was primarily the result of business decisions made by the executives of two Charlotte-based banks. However, they made those decisions in the context of a critical state public policy. They had experience with branch banking under North Carolina's permissive within-state branch banking laws at a time when most other states were restricted to banks without branches. This provided Charlotte's banks at an advantage when the Supreme Court ruled that interstate branch banking was constitutional in 1985.

The public sector intervention that our interviewees most often mentioned in connection with the successful transformation of the metropolitan region's economy was an amenities-based strategy: the redevelopment of downtown Charlotte to make the city and region more attractive to in-migrants with the type of skills required by the newly emergent banking and finance industries.

From 1970 to 2010 employment in the Charlotte region (with constant boundaries) grew by 164% (compared to the national rate of 72.5%), gross metropolitan product (GMP) per worker nearly doubled, and the average wage per worker increased by 44%, nearly double that of the national increase. Charlotte's

TABLE 4.1 Charlotte-Gastonia-Concord MSA

VARIABLE	1970	2010	% CHANGE
Population	741,118	1,758,038	137%
Employment	307,468	812,700	164%
National employment			73%
Avg. wage per worker ($2005)	29,763	42,928	44%
U.S. avg. wage per worker	34, 818	42,295	22%
GMP (millions of $2005)*	24.3	99.6	310%
GMP per worker*	63.7	122.6	55%
National GDP per worker			135%
Manufacturing employment	109,127	65,567	−40%
Employment in textile mills (NAICS 313)	52,413	4,875	−91%
Employment in credit intermediation and related activities (NAICS 522)	6,881	35,165	411%

MAJOR SHOCKS	SHOCK-RESISTANT (Y/N)	DOWNTURNS	RESILIENT (Y/N)	TYPE OF SHOCK
National economic shock (1981) + National industry (textile mills) shock (1981)	N	1981	Y	Employment
National industry (textile mills) shock (1984)	Y	—	—	Employment
National economic shock (1989)	N	1989	N	GMP
National economic shock (1990)	N	1990	Y	Employment
National economic shock (2000)	N	1999	Y	GMP
National economic shock (2000)	N	2000	Y	Employment
National industry (credit intermediation and related activities) shock (2006)	N	2006	Y	GMP
National economic shock (2008)	N	2008	Unknown as of 2010**	GMP and Employment

CHRONIC DISTRESS (Y/N)	NUMBER OF CONSECUTIVE YEARS OF SLOW GROWTH	FIRST YEAR OF CONSECUTIVE SLOW GROWTH	RECOVERY (Y/N)	TYPE OF CHRONIC DISTRESS
N	—	—	—	—

* GMP data is for 1978–2010; GMP per worker 1970 uses 1978 employment and GMP data. ** We are unable to determine if regions were resilient to recent shocks due to our operationalization of the variable, as described in chapter 2.

successfully transformed from a mostly low-skill, low-wage economy to a growing and much more productive one.

Seattle

ECONOMIC HISTORY. The Seattle regional economy underwent continuous
but generally successful evolution over the past century, and proved quite resilient in the face of change.[3] Major export industries during that time included
shipbuilding, forestry and manufactured wood products, transportation equipment manufacturing, military employment, information technology, and publishing. The region's primary economic engine during most of the post-war era
was transportation equipment manufacturing, joined later as a major export sector by information technology. The transportation equipment manufacturing
sector consisted primarily of aeronautics and aerospace manufacturers and suppliers and was anchored by the Boeing Company, which has had its major production facilities in the region since 1916. In the latter part of the twentieth century,
information technology, including developers, manufacturers, suppliers, and
major users joined aerospace as one of the two major export industries. The IT
sector is anchored by software giant Microsoft, which moved to the region in 1979.

These industrial changes are reflected in employment changes in the region.
During the late twentieth and early twenty-first centuries, the region's wood products industries largely disappeared as an important export base. Jobs in transportation equipment manufacturing accounted for 10.2% of regional employment
in 1970, but had fallen to 4.9% of regional employment by 2010. The number of
jobs in publishing (most of which were in the software industry) grew ten-fold
from 1970 to 2010 and increased as a share of total regional employment by
2.4 percentage points, from 0.7% of regional employment in 1970 to just over
3% in 2010. One staffer in the local workforce board stated, "Once the IT industry came into play, Boeing became less of the be all and end all."

In general, Seattle experienced rapid growth of employment and near-
average growth of its average wage between 1970 and 2010. The average inflation-
adjusted wage rose by 32%, well above the national average of 22%. The total number of jobs in Seattle region rose by 162% during 1970–2010, more than double the
national average job growth rate of 73%.

SHOCKS, DOWNTURNS, AND RESILIENCE. Although the Seattle region
experienced nine shocks, all but one of which also resulted in downturns, it was
quite resilient. It was also resistant to the 1998 local transportation manufacturing industry shock. The Seattle region did not have any periods of chronic
distress that meet our definition.

Seattle's economic fortunes reflected three factors. The first was the absolute and relative decline in the importance of its most shock-prone major export industries, wood products, and aerospace. The aerospace industry experienced declines in its employment growth rate in 1980–1982, 1990–1993, 1998–1999, and 2002. However, their impact on the region as a whole became less severe over time as Boeing's share of the region's employment declined. The second was the absolute and relative rise in the importance of the software industry. As a newer industry built around a relatively new technology and lacking the high fixed costs of durable manufacturing industries, the software industry was less prone to job growth downturns than the other major export industries, and its downturns were less severe. Following the decline of wood products and aerospace employment and the rise of software, the region's export base became more diversified. (As our earlier quantitative analysis showed, a diverse export base contributes to regional economic resilience.) The third was the region's ability to incorporate in its economy industries at different stages of the product cycle: wood and wood products (declining), aerospace (mature), and information technology (a combination of incubating and maturing).

Both the region's overall export base and its aerospace suppliers have become more diversified since the 1990s. In the past Seattle's aerospace suppliers mainly supplied components to Boeing, but over time they secured an increasing share of their business from other aircraft manufacturers located outside the region and even outside the United States. Thus, the suppliers are now more insulated from downturns in Boeing's business than they once were.

Nonetheless, the 2007 and 2008 downturns (which our interviewees associated with the Great Recession) had a serious impact on the regional economy as reflected in the downturn of both employment and GMP growth rates from 2007 to 2009. The region's employment growth rate dropped from 1.0% annually from 2000–2007 to –4.8% between 2007–2008 and –1.5% from 2008–2009; its annual GMP growth rate declined from 2.3% over the prior eight year period to –2.1% from 2007 to 2008 and 1.4% from 2008 to 2009.

STRATEGIES, POLICIES, AND RESPONSES. Given its historic and continuing dominance by large firms, the economic development problem in the Seattle region was usually cast in terms of the need for economic diversification. After the severe early 1970s recession, policymakers perceived a need to diversify the region's economy away from its strong reliance on aerospace manufacturing in general and Boeing in particular. In 1971, local government and business leaders created the King County Economic Development Council, known from 2005 through January 2013 as Enterprise Seattle, to recruit new firms to the region.[4] In 2008, the state established the Economic Development Commission, an independent, nonpartisan commission charged by the legislature with promoting an innovation-based economy that was less dependent on Boeing and Microsoft.

Diversification of the region's export base occurred, but more because of a historical accident rather than as a deliberate policy or strategy: Bill Gates moved Microsoft to the region in 1979. Other information technology-intensive firms (e.g., Starbucks, Amazon, and Costco, as well as their suppliers and Microsoft's suppliers) sprang up subsequently, in part to take advantage of proximity to Microsoft and the large pool of information technology workers that it attracted to the region. Additional local information technology companies were then founded by former Microsoft managers or engineers.

Nonetheless, the Seattle region remained reliant on big firms such as Boeing and Microsoft. The region's policymakers continued to focus on the aerospace industry, largely because the region is already competitive in the industry. The Seattle metropolitan area has the highest concentration of aerospace jobs in the world, and there are approximately 650 related companies located in the state, including aerospace manufacturing, commercial maintenance repair and overhaul, manufacturing of parts and tools, composite manufacturing, sub-assembly, and other functions (Aerospace Futures Alliance of Washington 2008). According to 2006 estimates, Washington's aerospace industry accounts for $36 billion (15% of Washington's gross state product) and 209,300 in direct and indirect employment (Aerospace Futures Alliance of Washington 2008).

In 2007, the governor commissioned a Governor's Council on Aerospace to identify a strategic plan for aerospace jobs in Washington. In addition to the state government's policy to support aerospace industry, at least three membership organizations support the industry. In 2006, the Prosperity Partnership created the Aerospace Futures Alliance, an organization that provides networking and advocacy for the aerospace companies and suppliers in the state. The Pacific Northwest Aerospace Alliance is a trade association for aerospace industry that provides its members with information, business networking opportunities, and industry advocacy. The Center for Advanced Manufacturing Puget Sound is a similar membership organization that was founded in 2008 with specific goal of helping small- and medium-size manufacturers (primarily in aerospace) succeed in the face of international competition. It emphasizes information and services related to innovation, business development, and supply chain positioning.

Given the centrality of Boeing in the region's economy, many interviewees told us that the biggest threat to Seattle's economy was the possibility that Boeing would increasingly move production to lower wage parts of the United States or abroad. The move of Boeing's headquarters to Chicago in 2001 and a recent history of strained union-management relations at the company exacerbated fears that Boeing would leave the area. When Boeing considered the possibility of building some of its new 787 airplanes outside the state, local governments and economic development agencies lobbied the governor and state legislature for a tax incentive package (of up to an estimated $3 billion) to retain production of the new aircraft. The incentives included tax rate reductions for the aerospace industry, tax credits for research and development, sales tax exemptions for the production for airplanes and their component and on new construction or improvement, and further property tax relief on new facilities and equipment in the state. The package was enacted into law, but Boeing nevertheless decided to build some of its 787s at a newly acquired plant in South Carolina. The state also offers tax incentives to the IT and biomedical industries, with recipients that include Microsoft, Intel Corp., Immunex Corporation, and Zymogenetic.

Some of our interviewees thought that the region was still too dependent on Boeing and Microsoft. One former business executive in the region said that their dominance was a "potential source of problem." One interviewee said, "The aerospace industry could trip up the future success of the region. These are high wage jobs. This area is still vulnerable to that." A manufacturer we interviewed thought that "the region's God-given right to aerospace also affects the health of [the] supply chain in the industry." Because manufacturing suppliers had depended solely on Boeing for a long time, the challenge that local composite suppliers faced was to diversify their products and customers. According to an executive from a local nonprofit organization, many supplier shops successfully diversified to other aerospace firms, such as Lockheed Martin and Airbus. In his view, "the hardest thing has been to diversify to other sectors—automotive or medical devices." Washington state has about 650 to 900 aerospace suppliers, and 35% of them have ten or less employees. Many supplier shops started after layoffs from Boeing and those people who were laid off started making parts.

Cluster initiatives were another response to the threat of Boeing's relocation of production and are closely related to the Puget Sound Regional Council (PSRC), the region's metropolitan planning organization, and the Prosperity Partnership, which was formed in 2003 as a joint initiative of the PSRC and the region's economic development district. The Prosperity Partnership is a coalition of more than 300 business, labor, education, and community organizations from King, Kitsap, Pierce, and Snohomish counties that conducts research on and planning for a common regional economic strategy. While the names of the clusters changed over time, as of 2012 there were ten clusters: aerospace, business services, clean technology, information technology, life science and global health, maritime, military, philanthropies, tourism and visitors, and transportation and logistics (Prosperity Partnership 2012). The partnership itself supports five of the industry clusters and activities. However, when we conducted our Seattle case study in 2009 and 2010, Seattle's cluster "policy" seemed to consist of sophisticated analysis and planning, with little implementation.

A positive legacy of the dominance of Boeing and technology intensive firms (such as Microsoft, Starbucks, Amazon, and Costco, as well as their suppliers) is the perception of the region as a haven for entrepreneurs, such as those that founded the above firms. One venture capitalist in the region stated, "Seattle is much more entrepreneurial; it was historically a strong angel network [kind of] place." Another local employee said, "It is okay to try something weird here. This is one of those places where people aren't afraid to fail. It is always been that way." The interviewee also pointed out the ethos of prosperity leadership in the region, which "makes people to stay interested, keep learning." This view is consistent with a local economic development practitioner, who said, "We do have a great innovative environment. . . . People grow up with messages of being an entrepreneur here."

The presence of both aerospace and information technology in the region may have also contributed to regional economic resilience by helping to spur the growth of new export industries such as medical device production. The two core export industries employ many mechanical and electrical engineers, some of whom formed new firms that applied their skills outside of the core industries. Layoffs of engineers from Boeing and, more recently, from Microsoft were a source of new firm formation. The wealth generated by the region's information technology industry helped support a local venture capital industry, which was a source of funding for these new firms.

In addition to policies and strategies designed to preserve or increase the region's economic resilience, Seattle has several economic development organizations that assist or target specific industries or engage in other activities in the regional economy, in addition to the Pacific Northwest Aerospace Alliance and Center for Advanced Manufacturing Puget. The Trade Development Alliance—jointly sponsored by local governments, the Seattle Metropolitan Chamber of Commerce, the Port of Seattle, and unions—promotes international trade in the heavily trade-dependent Seattle area by sponsoring trade missions for regional business and government leaders, promoting Seattle exports abroad, and providing local businesses with information about trade. The Washington Technology Industry Association, founded in 1984, is the regional trade association for high-technology businesses (initially software companies, but later also telecommunications and medical device firms) and engages in lobbying at the state and federal levels and provides members with business networking opportunities and discounted services. The Technology Alliance, founded in 1996 by Bill Gates, Sr., is a statewide organization that advocates for state-level public policies to improve K-12 and higher education, research capacity, technology transfer and commercialization of inventions, and the entrepreneurial climate.

The Seattle region's higher education system was frequently cited as another driver of economic development in Seattle region, although the exact impact and the extent of influence are unclear. A local journalist stated, "The University of Washington created its own sub-economy, especially technology and bio-sectors. There have been spin-off firms in the region." In case of biotechnology industry, the creation of the biotechnology complex depended heavily on spin-offs from the University of Washington and from other research institutions (Haug 1995). Higher education was also at the heart of the Seattle region's 2012 Regional Economic Strategy, with the goal of increasing production of bachelor's degrees in high demand fields, such as computer science, engineering, the sciences, and medical research. This built on an earlier state effort to fund and promote more students in higher education. However, the Regional Economic Strategy report indicated that the region continued to lack sufficient higher education capacity to meet regional needs, with "a growing mismatch between secondary education capacity and employer needs [that] is one of the single greatest economic development challenges facing the region" (Prosperity Partnership 2012, 47).

The Seattle region, with its technology-related jobs, has been an attractive magnet for highly educated and well-trained workers, including younger workers. The city's high level of amenities encouraged these trends. One local elected official with whom we spoke noted, "We think we know what makes the city attractive. Arts, culture, the environment are very important." In this regard, efforts to revitalize the downtown commercial area undertaken by the city in collaboration with the local Chamber of Commerce, the Downtown Seattle Association, and the Metropolitan Improvement District, while not adopted explicitly as an economic development strategy, nonetheless have been seen as contributing to the region's attractiveness.

Even with the existence of a regional planning organization, the PSRC, some of interviewees told us that regional fragmentation was a problem in pursuing regional economic development. Nonetheless, one staff member at a regional planning organization observed, "This region is lucky. It doesn't have a choice but be a region. For example, Boeing is located in Everett and Renton. There is no choice but to think regionally."

Regional economic development policymakers and practitioners perceived the Great Recession as the region's most severe economic downturn since the early 1970s. A staffer at a local labor organization said, "This recession is not just an aerospace or technology industry recession. The things that people took for granted are being reassessed." A local business journalist observed, "This recession has been felt very dramatically. The fall in 2008 was when it really slid off a cliff." The problem is "really bigger than anything that economic development agencies can do." Microsoft, the region's largest information technology employer, laid off workers for the first time during the Great Recession. Moreover, from 2007 to 2010, employment in the transportation equipment manufacturing industry—which in Seattle mostly consists of aerospace—fell by 1.5%.

It appears that no public or private organization had undertaken or planned any policy or strategy to restructure the regional economy in response to the Great Recession. Our interviewees did not think any such restructuring was necessary. Rather, they felt that they, in the words of one interviewee, "need to be focused on incubating the next big giant" in the region. One of our interviewees argued, "Incubators are not going to do it, tax policy won't do it. You need money, people who want to start business, and ideas."

SUMMARY. The Seattle regional economy is an example of an economy that restructured successfully, adding and diversifying to its existing economic base and, in the longer term, shedding older slow-growing industries for new and growing ones. Total employment grew by over 1,000,000 jobs (162%) from 1970–2010, and average wages per worker increased by 32% during that period, more than 10 percentage points higher than the national average. Employment in transportation equipment, its single most important industry, increased by 25% (nearly 17,000 jobs) between 1970 and 2010. During the same time the regional economy diversified by adding IT and publishing (i.e., software), the latter of which was nearly nonexistent in 1970, but grew by nearly 50,000 jobs, a ten-fold increase, by 2010. However, the propelling force for this increase was not public policy, but the idiosyncratic location choice made by Microsoft to locate in the region in 1979, a dramatic example of what has been termed "place luck." Despite the diversification, many in the Seattle region observed that the region remains too dependent on aerospace, and particularly Boeing.

The region has a large number of cluster organizations devoted to its main export industries as well as the usual set of local economic development organization. In addition, its regional development organizational infrastructure is probably more developed than that of most other regions. The Seattle region fostered a reputation for entrepreneurship, and its perceived high amenity levels and quality of its higher education institutions served as a magnet for the in-migration of highly educated and highly skilled workers, particularly in the IT industry. Many of the IT firms or their employees serve as a source for spinning off new entrepreneurial ventures.

TABLE 4.2   Seattle-Tacoma-Bellevue MSA

VARIABLE	1970	2010	% CHANGE
Population	1,836,949	3,439,809	87%
Employment	656,762	1,719,901	162%
National employment			73%
Avg. wage per worker ($2005)	38,630	50,863	32%
U.S. avg. wage per worker	34,818	42,295	22%
GMP (millions of $2005)*	61.9	209.0	238%
GMP per worker*	72.3	121.5	68%
National GDP per worker			135%
Manufacturing employment	135,490	166,988	23%
Employment in transportation equipment manufacturing (NAICS 336)	66,945	83,354	25%
Employment in publishing industries (except internet) (NAICS 511)	4,785	54,118	1031%

MAJOR SHOCKS	SHOCK-RESISTANT (Y/N)	DOWNTURNS	RESILIENT (Y/N)	TYPE OF SHOCK
Unidentified shock	N	1980	N	Employment
National economic shock (1989)	N	1990	Y	GMP
National economic shock (1990)	N	1990	Y	Employment
Local industry (transportation equipment manufacturing) shock (1998)	Y	—	—	Employment
National industry (publishing industries, except internet) shock (1999)	N	1999	Y	GMP
National economic shock (2000)	N	2000	Y	Employment
National industry (publishing industries shock (2007) and national economic shock (2008)	N	2008	Unknown	GMP
National economic shock (2008)	N	2008	Unknown	Employment

CHRONIC DISTRESS (Y/N)	NUMBER OF CONSECUTIVE YEARS OF SLOW GROWTH	FIRST YEAR OF CONSECUTIVE SLOW GROWTH	RECOVERY (Y/N)	TYPE OF CHRONIC DISTRESS
N	—	—	—	—

* GMP data is for 1978–2010; GMP per worker 1970 uses 1978 employment and GMP data.

Grand Forks

ECONOMIC HISTORY. Grand Forks provides an opportunity to examine a regional economy that does not have a history of manufacturing; rather, agriculture, the U.S. Armed Forces, and state government (including the University of North Dakota) were the largest industries in 1970.[5] The region's economy is relatively diversified among these sectors, but its historic reliance on them made it extremely susceptible to outside shocks (specifically, cuts in federal and state spending or bad weather and crop damaging pests). Further, it provided few levers for regional actors to respond to economic shocks. However, the Grand Forks region became substantially more diversified over time. In 1970, the military (19.3%); farming, forestry, logging, and hunting (16.3%); and state government (12.6%) constituted 48.2% of the region's total employment. By 2010 those same three sectors accounted for 21.5% of employment, with military employment having fallen drastically to 3.6% and farming, forestry, logging, and hunting to 5.5%.

One of the leading employers in the region, Grand Forks Air Force Base (GFAFB), was established in 1955 and reached its peak force strength of 15,000 service members and civilian employees in the 1960s. With the end of the Cold War and the restructuring of the U.S. Air Force to meet new missions, GFAFB saw a decline in its operations, with employment reduced to 2,105 in 2010. Throughout its history, the command at GFAFB played an important role in the region, as both an employer and a civic member. An economic development specialist said, "While some communities build their houses up to the base gates and then complain about the noise, our county commission asks, 'do we have the right ordinances in place so we don't impact what GFAFB needs to do?'"

Public employment is high in Grand Forks because of the presence of both the state University of North Dakota (UND) and the state-owned grain mill and elevator. UND employs over 4,200 people, 2,800 of whom are employed full time (Grand Forks Region Economic Development Corporation 2012; University of North Dakota 2010). The university grew from 10,000 students in the late 1990s to 14,000 in 2010 and is a center of export activity in terms of students, research, and training. The North Dakota Mill and Elevator Association, the only state-owned milling facility in the United States, has an annual payroll of $7,000,000 and contributes over 50% of its profits to the North Dakota State General Fund (North Dakota Mill and Elevator Association 2012).

Employment in the Grand Forks region increased by 74% from 1970 to 2010, which is approximately the national average. However, gross metropolitan product increased by only 33%, less than one-quarter of the national rate, and average wages increased only 8%. The Grand Forks economy, while it continued to produce jobs, is clearly producing jobs with lower productivity and wages than it previously did.

SHOCKS, DOWNTURNS, AND RESILIENCE. The Grand Forks region experienced fifteen shocks to either employment or GMP from 1978 and two instances of chronic distress beginning in 1986 and 1998. It was resistant to six of the shocks, including regional industry shocks to farming, forestry, and fishing in 1978, 1983, and 1985.[6] However, eight shocks caused downturns in separate years. Given its small economy, however, the downturns caused by "shocks" to which the Grand Forks economy was not resistant reflect smaller absolute impacts on the economy—for example, a 2% employment decline means 1,200 people lost their jobs, not tens of thousands as in the other regions. The region was resilient, by our definition, to most of the shocks it experienced. However, it was not resilient to two: in 1989, when it experienced a national industry shock affecting the military, and in 1996 when it experienced a local industry employment shock and a GMP shock of unknown origin that was then reinforced by a spring-time flood of the Red River in 1997. The region's most recent shock-induced downturns occurred to employment in 2007 and to GMP in 2008. The region was resilient to the GMP downturn, but as of 2010 was still not resilient to the employment downturn, which caused a decline of employment of 2.6% between 2007 and 2010. Grand Forks experienced two periods of chronic GMP distress, only one of which it was able to recover from by achieving annual average GMP growth equal to at least 75% of the national rate for seven consecutive years. Indeed, the region's real GMP per worker was actually lower in 2010 than it was in 1970.

The shocks that the Grand Forks region experienced beginning in 1996, "a one-two punch," were such that Grand Forks did not recover quickly enough to be considered resilient. Between 1996 and 1999, employment at GFAFB decreased by 35%, as a result of the end of its mission in support of the Minutemen missiles as part of the Strategic Arms Reduction Treaty.[7] In April 1997, the region experienced a flood that damaged 83% of homes and 62% of commercial units in the city of Grand Forks and all but eight homes in East Grand Forks, resulting in almost $2 billion of damage in the greater Grand Forks area. The agricultural industry suffered distress, presumably related to the flood, particularly with the spring wheat crop.[8] Prior to the 1996 shock, the Grand Forks region's average annual eight-year employment growth rate was 2.6%. In 1997, the annual growth rate fell to −2.2%, remaining negative or under 1% until 2002, when the annual employment growth rate was 1.3%.

The last shock to the community that was recorded in our database was the loss of the last tanker group at the Air Force Base as part of the 2005 Base Realignment and Closure (BRAC) process and its replacement with an Unmanned Aerial Systems (UAS) mission that included Predator and Global Hawk unmanned aerial vehicles for both the military and the Customs and Border Patrol. More than the impact of the jobs lost, the region was affected because of how much it had invested in its relationship with the base.

STRATEGIES, POLICIES, AND RESPONSES. According to many of those we interviewed, the main positive response to the series of shocks and downturns that Grand Forks experienced was increased collaboration among communities and stronger and more effective leadership that resulted in greater resilience. This finding from the fieldwork contradicts the statistical results derived from our methodology. Surviving the flood, rebuilding the infrastructure of the downtowns of Grand Forks and East Grand Forks, and using the flood protection system as a residential amenity, along with two rounds of BRAC cutbacks was viewed local as a monument to civic, if not economic, resilience.

Many people in the region viewed the flooding of 1997 as a catalyst that changed their own image of the region. "We now believe we're able to take on practically anything and make it come out well," said a high-level city employee. When asked how they perceived the region after 1997, interviewees consistently responded that the region was better. Two reasons were identified: increased collaboration among the different groups in the area, particularly between the business community and the local government in the city of Grand Forks as well as improved interactions between Grand Forks and East Grand Forks and, relatedly, a belief that, working together, they can improve their community. An economic development professional told us, "Since the community was literally forced to cooperate, collaborate, and work together on the task in front of them, and the task was so significant, they learned how, by necessity, to work together."

Leadership was seen as particularly important. The people we interviewed believed in the need to have the right leader at the right time. "Mayor Pat [Owens] was the mayor Grand Forks needed through the flood. She was the mayor people could put their arms around. . . . According to another interviewee, "Pat Owens was very good at being the leader we needed at the moment."

A third reason mentioned was the huge influx of money, primarily from the federal government, which enabled new investment in the region.[9] The reliance on federal funding, which typically takes several years to disburse, may be part of the explanation for a recovery time frame that exceeded our "resilience" definition.

An examination of the activities the region's economic development policymakers and practitioners undertook in the ensuing years enables us to evaluate the residents' perceptions. The flood resulted in the destruction of the downtowns of both cities. The major immediate response was thus downtown redevelopment, pursued more as community development or as amenity building rather than as an explicit economic development strategy. Nonetheless, downtown redevelopment was also seen as necessary for the long-term economic health of the region. Interviewees noted that one of the region's major problems was the need to attract workers to the area to sustain economic growth. Employers in the isolated region, with its harsh winters, had a difficult time recruiting the skilled workers they need; some manufacturers reported moving certain functions, like marketing or technology, to Minneapolis or other large cities because of an inability to find workers with the necessary skills. Others in the financial and medical industries found greater success in recruitment by focusing on the region's facilities and community life. One interviewee noted, "It's challenging. You have to work hard at telling your story and showing people what we have here." Downtown redevelopment was seen as one means of responding to this concern.

In Grand Forks, the vision for a revitalized downtown was driven by the then-publisher of the *Grand Forks Herald*. In addition to convincing the city to invest in the downtown, he committed to maintaining the newspaper in its downtown location, although production occurred elsewhere in the city. Brownstones and condominiums were built and occupied, adding a residential population that had been missing prior to the flood. Additional development following the flood included the construction of three sporting and events complexes, a hotel and waterpark, and a public golf course. A defining attraction is the Greenway, developed to prevent future flooding, which has twenty-two miles of trails for biking, running, and cross-country skiing. Downtown East Grand Forks was transformed from an industrial downtown, populated by old railroad tracks and dilapidated warehouses, into an area for retail, restaurants, and a movie theater. According to one city official, "We turned an area that previously had $0.5 million in taxable value to $12 to 15 million." Recovering from the flood likewise required actors in the region to reinvest themselves. Another city official said, "We did about twenty years of redevelopment in five years" in Grand Forks. Similarly, a city official in East Grand Forks told us, "That flood did in a week what urban renewal couldn't do in forty years."

The flood recovery was a small piece of a larger, longer term economic development approach in the city of Grand Forks, in which leaders sought to pursue growth through diversification. Economic development leaders undertook activities to encourage entrepreneurship and firm start-ups and to provide firm assistance in clusters related to the area's perceived competitive strengths. An important vehicle for accomplishing these objectives was the Grand Forks Growth Fund, which was created in 1988 and funded in part by 0.25% of the retail sales tax.[10] The Growth Fund provides gap and business support financing for new or expanding businesses and covers initial construction costs (land, buildings, and infrastructure), capital equipment, working capital, or seed funding (Grand Forks Region Economic Development Corporation 2013).

The Growth Fund Committee approved loans to a wind turbine manufacturer, a company that makes testing equipment for aircraft and missiles, and another company that produces metal components for military vehicles and contributed $500,000 toward the Research Enterprise and Commercialization Center (REAC), a level 3 laboratory. (Although that sounds like a small sum for many cities, we were reminded by the head of one economic development organization that we had to account for the size of the city and region. Grand Forks is a city with a population of 50,000.)[11] The lab is operated and funded by the UND Research Foundation, which assists UND in the advancement and commercialization of university innovations, discoveries, and partnerships with private companies. The UND Research Foundation also owns the Center for Innovation, which manages two tech incubators, provides small business innovation research outreach to the state's tech community, and formed three angel networks, one in each of the state's cities (Grand Forks, Fargo, and Bismarck). In early 2015 the Center reported that it had fostered over 670 start-ups employing more than 6,000 people and attracted over $140,000,000 in investment.[12]

TABLE 4.3   Grand Forks MSA

VARIABLE	1970	2010	% CHANGE
Population	95,537	98,461	3%
Employment	33,532	58,266	74%
National employment			72%
Avg. wage per worker ($2005)	28,279	30,545	8%
U.S. avg. wage per worker	34,818	42,295	22%
GMP (millions of $2005)*	2.9	3.9	33%
GDP per worker*	74.4	66.2	−11%
National GMP per worker			135%
Manufacturing employment	1,828	3,506	92%
Employment in military (NAICS MLA)	6,461	2,105	−67%
Employment in state government (NAICS GVS)	4,222	7,200	71%

MAJOR SHOCKS	SHOCK-RESISTANT (Y/N)	DOWNTURNS	RESILIENT (Y/N)	TYPE OF SHOCK
Local industry (agriculture, forestry, fishing and hunting) shock (1978)	Y	—	—	Employment
Local industry (military) shock (1980)	N	1980	Y	Employment

(Continued)

TABLE 4.3 (Continued)

MAJOR SHOCKS	SHOCK-RESISTANT (Y/N)	DOWNTURNS	RESILIENT (Y/N)	TYPE OF SHOCK
National industry (farming, forestry, logging, and hunting) shock (1983)	Y	—	—	Employment
Local industry (agriculture, forestry, fishing and hunting) shock (1985)	Y	—	—	Employment
National industry (military) shock (1987)	N	1987	Y	GMP
National industry (military) shock (1989)	N	1989	N	Employment
National economic shock (1989)	Y	—	—	GMP
National industry (military) shock (1990)	Y	—	—	GMP
Local industry (rail transportation) shock (1992)	N	1992	Y	GMP
National industry (military) shock (1994)	Y	—	—	GMP
Local industry (religious, grant-making, civic, professional, and similar organizations) shock (1996)	N	1996	N	Employment
Unidentified shock	N	1996	N	GMP
Local industry (military) shock (2007)	N	2007	Unknown as of 2010	Employment
National industry (rail transportation) shock (2007) and national economic shock (2008)	N	2008	Y	GMP

CHRONIC DISTRESS (Y/N)	NUMBER OF CONSECUTIVE YEARS OF SLOW GROWTH	FIRST YEAR OF CONSECUTIVE SLOW GROWTH	RECOVERY (Y/N)	TYPE OF CHRONIC DISTRESS
Y	8	1986	N	GMP
Y	7	1998	Y	GMP

* GMP data is for 1978–2010; GMP per worker 1970 uses 1978 employment and GMP data.

Tourism was also targeted as a potential economic growth industry. In particular, leaders in Grand Forks tried to position it as a destination city to attract Canadian visitors from Winnipeg; a city of 800,000 located 145 miles north. In his 2003 State of the City address, the mayor stated: "My vision is that we become a 'destination city.'" A former city official observed that, "having lived in Grand Forks my entire life, I never thought I'd hear Grand Forks and destination city in the same sentence." The notion of a visitor destination strategy can perplex an outsider until the role that Grand Forks and other market towns play in rural agricultural areas becomes clear—it is a retail and entertainment center that has a large geographic reach. In addition, visitors from Canada are drawn by the different and more competitive retail environment that exists south of the border. The region reaps additional benefits when the U.S. dollar is priced low relative to the Canadian dollar, which was true when the fieldwork was conducted.

Part of the destination strategy built on vacation-oriented cheap air service offered by Allegiant Air to Orlando, Phoenix, and Las Vegas. Airplane tickets are significantly cheaper in the United States than in Canada because of the Canadian national tax, so the Grand Forks International Airport worked with local hotels and attractions to keep Winnipeg residents in Grand Forks for a day or two before or after their flights to other destinations. Although the airport's boardings in 2010 exceeded those in prior years, the impact of the destination city strategy had not yet been evaluated as of that year. Mainline air service is provided by Delta's commuter flights out of Minneapolis, which gives the region the disadvantages shared by other rural metropolitan areas that live under a monopoly hub and spoke system. The challenge is one of fares but, more important, frequency of service.[13]

The strength of the social capital built up over the past fifteen years in the Grand Forks metropolitan region was on display during the national competition to locate test facilities for UAS. Grand Forks was selected to be one of six test sites in the nation at the end of 2013 by leveraging its rural location, fixed asset in its air force base, and a long tradition of education and training in aeronautics at the University of North Dakota's Odegard School of Aerospace Sciences. Work was under way in 2010 to prepare for its bid for the designation as a test site and also to house Unmanned Aerial Vehicle (UAV) missions for both the military and the Customs and Border Patrol. Leaders across all sectors and in both states understood that there was a cluster of activities around flight that made them a competitor for the development of an unmanned aeronautical systems industry. The UAS mission builds on the region's competitive advantage in energy research (conducting cold weather testing, renewable energy, and tactical fuels), engineering (developing payloads and sensors), and pilot training programs. The bid was enhanced by North Dakota state government investments in 2013 to establish an industrial park associated with the base, a specialized industrial authority, and an UAS research and test facility associated with the university. Minnesota's community college helped the effort by starting a technical degree program in UAV maintenance. Altogether $6.5 million was invested to improve the position of the bid. These investments responded to the Defense Department's desire to have a robust set of facilities operational soon after their designation was received (Aasheim 2014; Hageman 2013).

Although Grand Forks was nonresilient to its 1996 shock based on our methodology, people we interviewed in the region viewed themselves as resilient, having ultimately recovered from the flood and other shocks of 1997, with population, employment, and GMP all having surpassed their pre-1997 levels. Furthermore, the region of Grand Forks weathered the Great Recession economic environment well. During that recession, the Grand Forks region's unemployment rate hit a high of less than 6% in 2009 (U.S. Bureau of Labor Statistics 2013) and maintained a GMP growth rate of at least 2.2% each year. "We bounced back, then went beyond," a former city official said.

SUMMARY. Grand Forks experienced a gradual transformation of its economy from one in which nearly half of its 1970 employment consisted of military, farming, forestry, logging, and state government jobs to one in which barely more than 20% of its jobs were in these industries in 2010. During the late 1990s it also was hit by a substantial drawdown of armed services employment and by a major flood that devastated the economy of the region. Actors in the region responded with a range of collaborative activity, much of which was directed more toward community development and downtown redevelopment rather than economic development. A variety of traditional economic development programs were also enhanced or put in place.

By our statistical criteria, the region proved resilient to some shocks and non-resilient to others. In terms of employment, the region never recovered its prior rate of growth. However, it emerged from the more recent of its two periods of chronic economic distress. Indeed, its performance during the 2007–2010 national economic downturn was quite good. For the overall 1970 to 2010 period, employment in the Grand Forks region increased at about the same rate as the national average. However, GMP per worker was actually lower in real terms in 2010 than it was in 1970, and average wages per worker rose by only 8%, an indication that the region moved toward a more low-wage, low-productivity economy.

Despite the data, the people we interviewed repeatedly said that the region's economy had been resilient and had recovered. Using the statistical definition of resilience that is shared across this research the Grand Forks economy was not economically resilient. Subjectively, looking at its recovery from a devastating flood and two rounds of BRAC cutbacks at the Air Force base, our interviewees considered the region both socially and politically resilient and economically successful.

Conclusion

The six regions we chose for case studies (Charlotte, Cleveland, Detroit, Grand Forks, Hartford, and Seattle) and discussed in chapters 3 and 4 encompass a variety of economic experience over the time period of our study. The regions were chosen to reflect different kinds of shocks, experience with chronic distress, and different degrees of resilience in response. Cleveland, Detroit, and Grand Forks experienced cyclical shocks; Charlotte, Cleveland, Detroit, Hartford, and Seattle had industry shocks; and Grand Forks had a major natural disaster shock and military base closing. Cleveland, Detroit, Grand Forks, and Hartford all suffered from at least one period of chronic distress. The regions also differed in their degree of resilience with high resilience in Charlotte and Seattle and some resilience in Grand Forks to a lack of resilience in the 1980s in Hartford and, since 2000, in Cleveland and Detroit.

We found little difference in the strategies and policies of the three relatively resilient regions compared to the three that were less resilient, although there was greater rhetorical emphasis placed on the need for diversification in the less resilient regions. We also found that the strategies and policies regional actors pursued in periods of economic shock or chronic distress were generally no different from standard local and regional economic development policies they pursued during better times and that were being pursued elsewhere, with the exception of more vigorous efforts in marketing and recruiting. In the areas facing shock or chronic distress, there was also substantial organizational creation and restructuring of economic development institutions, in particular focusing them on a wider regional level (Cleveland especially, through the Fund for Our Economic Future and other initiatives that incorporated all of northeast Ohio). Organizationally, there was also increased participation by nonprofit institutions, particularly major hospitals, universities, and foundations. While this third-sector participation was a clear trend virtually everywhere, it was especially noticeable in several of our regions as the large businesses that had formerly dominated the local economies played a diminished role or, in some cases, disappeared or were bought by those headquartered elsewhere.

Particularly in areas facing chronic distress (Detroit and Grand Forks), there was a renewed emphasis on economic diversification, though this was usually pursued through traditional economic development strategies. Economic development strategies in many regions articulated explicit clustering strategies (e.g., Grand Forks, Hartford, and Seattle), although in most cases it was difficult to determine how they were implemented in practice other than through greater targeting of marketing and recruitment efforts. In some cases efforts were made to establish cluster associations or networks as a means of encouraging cluster development as well as economic development through entrepreneurship. Indeed, all of the regions had a variety of programs to encourage entrepreneurship and small firm start-ups as well as programs providing financial, technical, and other types of assistance to firms (e.g., TechTown in Detroit, Magnet and

JumpStart, Inc., in Cleveland). Nearly all of the regions engaged in downtown development efforts, sometimes, but not always, as explicit economic development strategy (although Charlotte's was). All of the regions had active workforce development programs, and several had made substantial efforts to integrate community colleges into their economic and workforce development systems. The regions all had, in other words, the normal range of economic development programs.

ASSESSING THE EFFECT OF RESILIENCE POLICIES DIRECTED TOWARD BUSINESS AND INDIVIDUALS

In chapters 3 and 4, we discussed the various attempts in each of the case study regions to engage in conscious activity to respond to shocks and/or chronic distress. In this and in the next chapter we ask whether these intentional efforts to bring about recovery through public policy or civic action make a difference. Or, alternatively, were they merely symbolic window-dressing derived from a mistaken, though understandable, belief that public officials and civic actors have some ability to affect their regional and/or local economies. How can we assess the effects of the various efforts in our case study regions?

In this chapter we examine policy actions that were focused primarily on businesses and individual entities (tax incentives, industry targeting, technical assistance to private sector firms, and entrepreneurial assistance and promotion). In chapter 6 we turn to actions that focus on the provision of public goods (human capital, infrastructure, amenities), on institutions (organizational restructuring), and on leadership. These chapters do not attempt to evaluate the effects of the particular policies, strategies, and tools that were brought to bear in each of the regions; nor, given limits to our resources, could we have done so. Furthermore, many of these policies are longer term efforts and would likely not show results in the shorter time frame we are examining. Instead we focus here on the likely effects of the various policies and engage in a variety of efforts to determine their likely impacts. First, we set forth and discuss the logic underlying the policy, that is, why and under what circumstances the policy might be (or might not be) expected to have an effect on regional economic resilience or development.

We then summarize the existing research literature that evaluates the specific policies and over what time frames they are likely to occur.

From among many possible approaches to bringing about economic resilience, we have identified nine that policymakers in our regions commonly pursue. In this chapter we focus on

- Tax incentives
- Industry targeting and cluster policy
- Technical assistance to private sector firms
- Entrepreneurial assistance and promotion

Tax Incentives

Tax incentives (or lower tax rates) designed to attract firms by lowering the operating costs of doing business within the area are a common economic development tool. Although state and/or local governments in all of our regions used tax incentives, few of our interviewees mentioned them as playing a large role in bringing about recovery from the shock or chronic distress, at least in the short term. Indeed, these programs were in most cases a traditional and ongoing economic development activity rather than put in place as a response to either shocks or chronic distress.

The Logic of Tax Incentives as an Economic Development Policy

State and local taxes are part of the operating cost of private firms, and, as such, a profit-maximizing firm will, ceteris paribus, want to minimize its tax cost. The extent to which reducing tax costs for locating in a region will actually affect firm location and investment decisions, however, will clearly depend on the importance of other factors which, in the real world, are never held constant. However, it is worth noting at the outset that taxes are typically a small percentage of total firm operating cost; indeed, Ady (1997), after reviewing databases from Fantus, a well-known site location firm, estimates that taxes accounted for only 4% of operating costs for the typical manufacturing firm.

There is widespread agreement, based on both theory and empirical research, that differences in taxes play a much more important role in choosing where to locate *within* a region (*intraregional location decisions*) than in choosing which region to locate in (*interregional location decisions*). With respect to interregional locational decisions, differences among metropolitan areas in labor cost and quality, transportation cost and access to inputs and markets, and energy costs play a dominant role.[1]

It is within a region, where there is relatively little variation in cost of and access to labor, transportation, and energy, that factors that do vary across local governments, such as taxes and services, have a greater impact on firm decision making. However, since our concern is with the *regional* economy, tax incentives offered by an individual local government within the region, even if they resulted in greater employment within the local government's boundaries, would only have an effect on regional employment if the incentive attracted a firm *into the region* that would otherwise not have been there. So this drives us back again to whether intermetropolitan differences in taxes—or the use of tax incentives to achieve such advantageous differences—is likely to make a difference.

In addition, it is important to recognize that taxes are not simply a nuisance imposed on business. Taxes are a cost of doing business. Public services—which are funded by those taxes—are benefits to the state and community in which a business is located. Some of these public services benefit business directly (such as infrastructure provision and maintenance, police protection, and trash disposal) while others, such as education and health care, have indirect benefits. Taxes are a deterrent to business location and economic growth, while a high level and quality of appropriate public services are an attraction.[2] But, as is widely recognized but not always taken into account, taxes pay for public services and, therefore, cuts to taxes may mean cuts in desired public services.

What Is Known about the Effectiveness of Tax Incentive Policies?

Substantial literature exists on the effect of tax incentives (and a related literature on the effect of differences among areas in tax and service levels[3]) and their effects on firm location and employment levels (see, e.g., Anderson and Wassmer 2000; Bartik 2007; Cohen 2000; Lynch 2004). A review of this literature provides a substantial amount of information on the probable effect of these programs. Given the above discussion on taxes and public services, it is not surprising that the vast literature on the role of public sector fiscal policy on an area's competitive advantages can be summarized quite succinctly. If the level of spending and quality of public services are held constant, *increases in taxes* negatively affect employment and economic activity, while, if the level of taxes is held constant, *increases in the quantity and quality of public services* positively affect employment and economic activity. Put another way, for any given level of taxes, an area that can provide services more efficiently and/or more appropriately for the needs of business will have a competitive advantage over other areas; for any given level and mix of services, a community that can provide these at a lower tax burden to business will have a competitive advantage over other areas. Both of these effects have a much larger impact on the competitive advantage of municipalities relative to one another within a metropolitan area than they do on the competitive advantage of a metropolitan area relative to other metropolitan areas.

Based on existing studies, Bartik (1991, 1992, 2007) concludes that the long-run elasticity of a metropolitan area's business activity with respect to local taxes is between –0.2 and –0.3. Thus, a 10% increase in taxes across a region would reduce the region's economic activity by approximately 2–3%. He suggests that these effects are not large.[4] However, he then emphasizes (2007, 107, emphasis added) that these estimates are for an entire state or metropolitan area: "Research suggests that a business tax cut by an *individual* suburb within a metropolitan area, holding the taxes of other jurisdictions constant, has much larger effects, perhaps 10 times as great per dollar of incentive. That is, a 10 percent cut in an individual suburb's business tax . . . will increase that individual suburb's business activity by 20 percent, largely by capturing business activity from other jurisdictions in the same metropolitan area."[5]

Bartik's estimates of the effect of tax incentives on both inter- and intrametropolitan levels assume no resulting reduction in public services. Indeed, he notes explicitly that if public services are reduced significantly, the result may actually be a reduction in job growth. With respect to intrametropolitan tax reductions, he also notes that his conclusion of a 20% increase in jobs resulting from a 10% decline in taxes assumes not only that all other communities leave their property tax rates unchanged, but that there is not an offsetting decrease in local spending (Bartik 1994, 853). Again, the caveat that all things must remain equal to realize these results is not a realistic assumption when local governments within a metropolitan area are likely to engage in interjurisdictional competition.

However, the fact that the effect of taxes and services on firm location and employment is likely to be greater within a metropolitan area than it is between them does not necessarily mean that tax differences among regions, whether brought about by incentives or otherwise, have no effect. The initial set of research on tax differences did indeed come to that conclusion. However, more recent research (see Bartik 1991; Newman and Sullivan 1988; Phillips and Goss 1995) suggests that the employment effect of lower taxes might well be positive (i.e., increase employment), though probably not large (for a review of this literature, see Bartik 1991; Peters and Fisher 2004; Thompson 2010; Wolman et al. 2008; Wasylenko 1997). Others contest this finding.[6] After a review of the literature, Peters and Fisher (2004) conclude, "The upshot of all this is that on this most basic question of all—whether incentives induce significant new investment on jobs—we simply do not know the answer." Ady (1997, 78) goes further and observes that the question, as posed in general terms, is unanswerable: "Location criteria are different for different business sectors and different companies within any sector, as well as at different stages of the site search. This greatly complicates any effort to discern causal relationships between any given location criterion, such as tax levels, and economic activity and growth. Indeed, what might be a direct relationship for one situation or set of studied circumstances might be quite different for another."

Even if the employment effect of tax incentives is positive, it is not necessarily the case that all regions would benefit equally from a similar tax incentive. Goss and Phillips (2001) also find that the positive effects of local business incentives are likely to be greater in high-income, low-unemployment areas than in areas suffering from low economic performance, that is, tax incentives are likely to have the greatest impact in areas where they are least needed and the least impact on areas where they are most needed.

To summarize, *tax incentives offered by a local government* will have an effect on regional business activity *only* if they result in attracting business activity to the *region* that would not otherwise have located there. Note that there are few significant region-wide taxes on business property or activity in the United States, so reducing the tax rate throughout the region, through incentives or otherwise, is not usually a feasible alternative. Of course, a business will locate not in a nominal place with the regional average tax structure and rate, but in a specific location within the region, with a specific structure and rate. It is possible, if other attributes of that site are competitive with those outside of the region, that a tax incentive available for locating in that jurisdiction will attract a firm into the region that would otherwise have not located there.

In general, however, the most likely way to increase the competitive advantage of a region is through lowering taxes via a reduction of state, not local, taxes or through a tax incentive provided by the state. Indeed, this is the approach that the states in which our regions are located appear to have pursued. We also conclude that the effect of any tax reduction, whether local or state, will be mitigated, if not eliminated, if it results in service reductions of greater cost to businesses than the benefit of the lower taxes.

Nonetheless, following Bartik, we conclude that there are conditions under which tax incentives can increase employment, other things (such as levels of public services) being equal. These conditions include "a more democratic process with full information, a budget constraint on incentives, better benefit-cost analysis, incentive designs that target new business activity that brings social benefits, and performance requirements" for incentive programs (Bartik 2007, 103). If tax incentives do have an effect, it would likely be in the medium- and long-term rather than as a short-term strategy to respond to an economic shock. Thus, they are more plausible for regions experiencing long-term stagnation than for regions responding to an exogenous shock. Of course, this does not imply anything about whether they are more effective in such regions than other policies that promote recovery from long-term stagnation.

Industry Targeting and Cluster Policy

Industry targeting has a relatively long history as a local economic development strategy. It reflects a more sophisticated approach than the more indiscriminate "smokestack chasing" and a more systematic and less opportunistic approach than attempting to attract a specific firm when it demonstrates an interest in the area. The goal of targeting is "matching industry competitive requirements with regional economic comparative advantages" (Buss 1999, 339). After identifying specific industries as targets, usually through analysis of location quotients and/ or shift/share analysis, economic development officials work to attract firms in the targeted industries through strategies keyed to those industries. Such strategies directed specifically at the target industries include marketing and promotion, tax incentives, infrastructure development or redevelopment, workforce training, and other approaches relevant to the targeted industries.

Cluster policy is a more recent and sophisticated version of industry targeting, in which policymakers encourage the development of interconnected businesses across industries in a geographic area. Although definitions of clusters vary by analysts (Martin and Sunley [2003] identify ten separate definitions of cluster), probably the most commonly used definition is that of Porter (1998, 78), who defines clusters as "geographic concentrations of interconnected companies and institutions in a particular field, linked by commonalities and complementarities." In most cases, these clusters include not only firms in a specific industry but also the suppliers to and customers of those firms, institutions providing services to the cluster industry (e.g., community colleges, trade associations, universities), and other organizations that have some relationship to members of the cluster.

Economic development policymakers and practitioners in all of our regions engaged in some form of targeting or cluster analysis and policy. In most cases these were efforts to build upon their historic legacies, although in some cases there were efforts to target new industries with growth potential in light of the area's characteristics. In some cases the identification of targeted industries or clusters resulted from a formal analysis of the region's economy.

The Logic of Targeting and Cluster Policies

Industry targeting and cluster policies serve as a practical method for areas to maximize their limited economic development resources by focusing on a subset of potential export-related industries or clusters that they wish to grow.

The logic of industry targeting is that specific industries can be identified, usually through some form of area economic analysis, for which the region has or can easily develop a competitive advantage. Economic development efforts, including marketing and promotion and the full array of other economic development policies, can then be directed to those specific industries, basing the exact measures on an understanding of the specific needs of each industry. The success of an industrial targeting effort thus depends on accurate identification of industries for which the area has a competitive advantage, an understanding of the locational considerations of that industry in view of its production and distribution needs, and the application of effective policy directed to the specific needs of the industry.

Although the effect of industry targeting thus relies in the end on the efficacy of the various economic development efforts applied, many of which we discuss in this chapter, it is nonetheless useful to examine whether and how specific industries (usually at the three-digit North American Industry Classification System [NAICS] level) for which the area has or can develop a competitive advantage can be identified. The identification procedure can be as informal as common knowledge (e.g., the Detroit region has had a competitive advantage in motor vehicle production; Seattle in aeronautics; Charlotte in banking and finance) or anecdotal (e.g., "have you noticed the number of firms in industry X that have begun to locate within the region?").

However, more formal analysis is usually applied. The most common types of such analyses are location quotients (LQs) and shift/share analysis. Location quotients are a measure of the specialization of a regional economy relative to some larger economic geography—usually the nation, Typically the LQ measures the share of an industry's employment in the region's economy relative to the share of employment in that industry in the national economy. Thus, if an industry has 10% of employment in a region, and that industry also comprises 10% of national employment, its location quotient is 1.0. If it has 30% of employment in the regional economy but only 15% in the national economy, its LQ is 2.0, whereas if it has only 3% of employment in the regional economy but 6% in the national economy, its LQ is 0.5.

Typically, industries with LQs much above 1.0 are considered export industries, since there is usually little reason to believe that a region is consuming locally a greater share of that industry's product than the national average, and interregional differences in labor productivity within an industry are typically assumed away. The exact LQ numerical threshold used to include an industry in a region's economic base, or traded sector, is subjective. Studies use thresholds of 1.2, 1.25, 1.5, 1.6, 1.8, and 2.0. In chapters 1 and 2 of this book we employed a threshold of 1.8, meaning that employment was 80% greater than the national average.

LQs are most frequently calculated with employment data because those data are more commonly available and employment change is the public policy variable that is most often of interest. However, other measures can be used. In our work LQs are frequently calculated in terms of gross product as well as for employment. This is particularly helpful when employment is dropping in an industry while productivity is increasing due to technological change in the production process.

Although LQs present, by definition, a picture of the region's industrial structure relative to the nation and also provide an indication of those industries that constitute its export sector, they do not logically identify a region's current or future competitive advantage. First, unless the region's industrial structure is exactly the same as that of the nation, there must, by definition, be some industries with LQs greater than 1.0. But this does not necessarily establish a competitive advantage in those industries or a potential for those industries to grow. In fact, an industry with an LQ of 1.2 may reflect an industry in the process of losing its competitive advantage if its LQ ten years prior was 1.5. Even if that industry had maintained an LQ of 1.5, it would not necessarily suggest growth potential for the area if that industry were declining nationally. Maintaining a steady share of a declining industry is better than losing it altogether, but is not a recipe for economic growth.

Decomposition methods such as shift/share analysis[7] correct for some of these problems. We utilize a variation of shift/share analysis to identify those industries whose rate of growth in the region exceeds the rate of growth in that industry nationally. For any particular industry, this method projects the region's predicted growth in employment over a specific period of time assuming that industry had grown regionally at the same rate it grew nationally and then compares the actual growth of the industry's employment in that region to the predicted growth. If actual growth exceeds predicted growth, then the region is presumed to have some competitive advantage for that industry.

There are some problems with shift/share analysis as well. First, the attribution of a regional comparative advantage is a leap of logic. What can be said in more precise terms about an industry whose actual employment growth in the region exceeded its predicted growth is that there is something related to the region that explains its positive shift. That something may not be related to the region's characteristics, and particularly those characteristics that are amenable to policy. For example, a region's employment growth in an industry may be due to a single firm whose location in that area is an historical accident or it may be due to the age of the plant and equipment. In addition, a shift/share analysis provides information about what has happened in the past, not what is happening in the present and certainly not what will occur in the future. Even *if* an industry with real growth potential is identified through shift/share, the technique provides no information about *why* it is growing or what the area can do to increase its growth.[8] This is why shift/share analysis is frequently accompanied by interviews in the industry and more extensive quantitative analysis of the industry and region.

Shift/share analysis also does not identify or establish relationships across industries by NAICS code. For example, employment in professional services industries (such as engineers, lawyers, and accountants) in a region may have far exceeded the rate of growth nationally (and may have, in addition, a high LQ). However, if professional service employment is dependent upon the presence of a manufacturing industry in the region to make use of these professional services, its growth potential may be largely derivative and tied to growth of the manufacturing industry.

It is largely because of these problems—and particularly the rigid strictures that classification by NAICS code imposes—that industrial targeting is increasingly being supplemented or replaced by cluster strategies and policies. Cluster strategies attempt to identify sets of firms (clusters) that interact across industries and are often mutually dependent upon each other (Cortright 2006). The focus may be on relationships between input-supplier firms and producers, between producers and distributors, among similar firms in the same industry or that employ sets of similar occupations.

Cluster policy has the same logic as industrial targeting discussed above in terms of identifying a subset of economic activity as its focus. But, there is an additional economic logic that supports cluster strategies. It is contended that the colocation of these interconnected firms and institutions results in "agglomeration economies" to firms in the cluster. Agglomeration economies take two very broad forms. One is that the colocation of many firms in the same industry can lead to increased sales by attracting more customers to the location. A classic example is New York City's diamond district, where the colocation of firms makes comparison shopping on the part of wholesale and retail buyers easier. Another example occurs in Southeast Michigan, where the interaction between the engineering staffs of the Detroit Big Three and those of auto parts suppliers, made possible by the colocation of the companies' research and development operations, leads to increased sales by the suppliers.

A second form of agglomeration economy reflects real cost savings to individual firms that are external to their individual operations, instead resulting from many firms locating in geographic proximity to each other. These cost savings, which may take the form of reduced input costs, increased productivity, and/or other forms of innovation, increase as the density of firms increases. They include the existence of large numbers of workers with specialized skills related to needs of firms in the cluster, more efficient worker-firm matching (more workers and firms mean better matching), input-sharing (making it more likely that input suppliers will locate within the region, thus reducing transportation costs), supplier specialization through the growth of supplier and subsidiary industries, development of a common infrastructure, reduction in transportation costs, and the transmission of tacit knowledge through geographically based social networks (see Wolman and Hincapie 2015).

The knowledge transmitted through informal networks of individuals across firms (and also across other related institutions such as trade associations, universities, research institutes, and labor organizations) can lead to more rapid productivity growth (as ideas spread more quickly among firms) as well as to more rapid innovation in products, production processes, work and business organization, marketing, and research. These "knowledge spillovers" occur largely as a result of unplanned and/or informal personal relationships brought about by individuals engaged in a cluster being thrown together rather than through the existence of formal networks. Or they occur as people and contractors move from firm-to-firm in the industry.

Thus, for example, Huxham and Vangen (1996, 12) suggest that few of the networks or community collaborations "seem to be convened in any sort of thoughtful way; instead membership tends to be created out of existing contacts and evolves in a rather unplanned way as new issues suggest new partners or new contacts become drawn in." Networks allow actors to learn from one another and to share resources. Successful network relationships can also lead to future cooperative efforts as trust among the parties is built (Feiock, Tao, and Johnson 2004).

The logic of cluster policy is similar to, but also extends beyond, that of industry targeting. As with industry targeting successful cluster policy requires identification of the cluster, understanding of the needs of the cluster, assessment of how likely it is that the area can meet those needs, and appropriate policies to strengthen the clusters health and viability in the area. Each of these links is to some extent problematic.

Cluster identification is conceptually and operationally much more difficult than is identifying target industries, though many efforts at cluster analysis rely as their base on the NAICS industry classification, which is organized by discrete industries. Porter (2003, 2009) and others have developed sophisticated techniques for identifying clusters, but these rely on relatively aggregated NAICS industry classifications because they are designed to be uniform throughout the nation. For this reason, they are not especially useful in identifying the specific relationships among economic functions that exist in particular metropolitan areas and, as a result, are not very useful for identifying clusters within any given metropolitan area (Clark 2013). Even when clusters are identified, important interpretation problems exist similar to those in industry targeting. First, while all regions have clusters, not all clusters produce high growth. Indeed, if a region has a cluster consisting of industries with low or declining product demand then its contribution to regional economic growth is likely to be small, no matter what other institutions are connected to it. Second, even within a cluster consisting of the same components (industries, research facilities, educational and training institutes, etc.), a cluster in one region may be more effective than the same cluster in another area at producing economic growth. Some of the differences may, of course, be due to inherent differences in the economies of the different regions. Some may be due to clusters that are in different stages of the product cycle for output that is at the core of the cluster. But some may be due to the quality of the clusters: the interaction of cluster members or the way in which clusters are organized or embedded in institution and area cultures (Wolman and Hincapie 2015).

There is widespread agreement among thoughtful proponents of cluster policy that it is not possible to create clusters where there is not an initial base for the cluster to grow on. There is less agreement on whether it is possible to identify "emerging clusters" or whether clusters can only be identified "in the rearview mirror," that is after they already exist. Cortright (2006, 48) writes that most researchers agree that, "No set policy prescription emerges from the cluster literature." In particular, the silver bullet of creating new clusters seems unattainable. As he notes, "The tantalizing paradox of clustering is that it implies that the location of economic activity is not preordained and that, therefore, public policy . . . can make a difference. Yet at the same time it is virtually impossible to say what it takes to successfully create a new industry cluster in a particular place."

A review of the literature (Wolman and Hincapie 2015) provides a set of cluster policies, strategies, and lessons that are relevant to economic development practitioners:

a) Learn how businesses interact and clusters work;
b) Support clusters based on their economic dominance, strategic importance, or leadership and potential;
c) Improve technical support services;
d) Support cluster expansion through recruiting companies that fill gaps in cluster development;
e) Develop and organize supply chain associations;
f) Support entrepreneurs through assistance for start-ups and spin-offs;
g) Encourage labor market pooling through providing labor market information and specialized training;

h) Encourage knowledge-spillovers and networking through public sector research and development support;

i) Facilitate market development through joint market assessment, marketing, and brand-building; and

j) Represent cluster interests before external organizations such as regional development partnerships, national trade associations, and local, state, and federal governments.

Most of the individual policies described above have existed long before there were intentional and explicit "cluster-based" economic development policies. The difference, to the extent a difference exists, is the target of the policies—that is, an identified cluster rather than a single industry sector or sectors or individual firms—and the way the policies are combined.

In addition, whatever the logic of both industrial targeting and cluster policy, both can be the result of political, rather than or contrary to, economic logic (Bartik 1996; Buss 1999). This may take the form of policies to retain or support traditional industrial manufacturers in the Rust Belt or to build up newer industries focused on green or high technologies or the health field. It may also result in wishful thinking as regions focus on leading clusters that exist elsewhere and decide that they would like one of those too (e.g., a bio-tech or a health-tech cluster), without any sense of the area's capacity to support such a cluster or an understanding that the same cluster cannot exist in every area.

What Is Known about the Effectiveness of Targeting and Cluster Policies?

Once target industries are identified, attracting the targets typically relies on traditional policies and practices we review elsewhere: incentives, reducing operating costs in various ways, customized workforce training, land and infrastructure subsidies of one form or another, and accelerated permitting. In this section we focus on cluster policies and related efforts to enhance or build business networks that are hypothesized to provide sustained sources of competitive advantage.

The assumptions that lie behind cluster policies are that agglomeration economies and informal networks promoting knowledge spillovers produce economic growth. There is a substantial research literature on this topic. (For reviews, see Cortright 2006; Wolman and Hincapie 2015.) However, there are challenges in finding a causal impact of clusters on economic development. Partly this is due to two conceptual concerns, the first of which is the lack of a common definition of and metric for a "cluster." Without this, it is both difficult to measure clusters[9] and to compare analyses of what different analysts term clusters. Second is a circularity question—do clusters influence economic development or does economic development influence the development of clusters (i.e., firms and entrepreneurs are drawn to strong economies, which then gradually centralize around specific industries)? Or is it an instance where both situations occur—in which case, how are the effects distinguished?[10]

Several literature reviews of the empirical econometric literature provide broad agreement that the agglomeration component of the cluster concept does have positive effects on various measures of regional economic performance (see, e.g., Glaeser and Gottlieb 2009; Rosenthal and Strange 2004). However, Duranton (2009, 31–32) argues that the effects estimated in the literature are very modest and that even these modest effects may exaggerate the true causal benefits of clustering on productivity. He notes that most studies fail to control for possible reverse causation or simultaneity, for example, the possibility that clustering may not lead to high local productivity and wages, but instead that high local productivity and wages may lead to clustering. If causation is in the latter direction, then most results from the literature would be biased, exaggerating the magnitude of clustering effects.

The most relevant of these studies focus directly on the concept of clusters rather than on proxies for agglomeration. O'Huallachain (1992) identifies eighteen geographic clusters consisting of related two-digit industries and examined the relationship between the strength of each of these clusters and regional employment and income growth for the 150 largest metropolitan areas in the United States. He finds that five of the eighteen clusters studied—high-order services, high-tech manufacturing, state and local government, textiles and construction, and insurance—had a positive effect on both employment and per capita income growth. Conversely, Feser, Renski, and Goldstein (2008, 343) attempt to assess the effect of technology clusters in the Appalachian Regional Commission region and conclude, "We found little evidence that technology industries in spatial clusters in Appalachia created more jobs than the same industries in noncluster locations."

Delgado, Porter, and Stern (2012) evaluated the role of regional cluster composition in the economic performance of industries, clusters, and regions, by examining both the impact of agglomeration among related industries and simultaneously accounting for convergence (declining output growth rate in a region-industry due to diminishing returns) within a given industry. They find that industries participating in a strong cluster have higher employment growth, growth of wages, number of establishments, and patenting. They also find that new regional industries tend to be created where there is a strong cluster environment. In a related paper, Delgado, Porter, and Stern (2010) find that regional industries located within a strong cluster experience higher growth in new business formation and start-up employment, and they also matter for the formation of new establishments of existing firms.

The above studies are mostly concerned with the agglomeration economy component of the cluster concept, although in some cases this also incorporates the knowledge spillover. However, knowledge spillover or the networking component of the concept is not directly tested in these studies. The studies that attempt to focus more directly on "knowledge spillovers" are mostly intensive case studies of specific areas and are based primarily on interviews and surveys of respondents. These studies (see Wolman and Hincapi 2015, for a review) tend to confirm that ideas flow freely in each of these clusters. Saxenian's intensive case study, for example, compared Silicon Valley and Route 128 in the Boston region and asked, "Why has Silicon Valley adapted successfully to changing patterns of international competition while Route 128 appears to be losing its competitive advantage?" She concluded:

> Silicon Valley has a regional network-based industrial system that promotes collective learning and flexible adjustment among specialist producers of a complex of related technologies. The region's dense social networks and open labor markets encourage experimentation and entrepreneurship. Companies compete intensely while at the same time learning from one another about changing markets and technologies through informal communications and collaborative practices. . . . The Route 128 region, in contrast, is dominated by a small number of relatively integrated corporations. Its industrial system is based on independent firms that internalize a wide range of productive activities. Practices of secrecy and corporate loyalty govern relations between firms and their customers, suppliers, and competitors. (1994, 2–3)

In an influential comparative case study of Youngstown and Allentown, Safford (2009) contends that, although he cannot state a direct causal relationship between network structure and economic outcomes there is evidence that the density of the economic and civic networks in Youngstown and Allentown may have played an important role in shaping their economic fortunes. He argues that the highly dense networks found in Youngstown may have limited how new ideas were incorporated into new policy initiatives there, while the less dense but more diverse networks in Allentown may have allowed access to more policy ideas. By reviewing the history of the two cities and inspecting how the economic and civic networks of major organizations differed and overlapped, Safford concludes that civic ties can connect actors otherwise not linked economically, allowing for the diffusion of ideas among those who otherwise might not communicate. In addition, dense and interconnected networks linking the same individuals in the same ways may limit the transmission of new ideas. He argued that these networks might explain the differing trajectories of the two cities in the postindustrial era.

There is limited quantitative evidence about the effects of networks on economic development. Of the small number of quantitative analyses, Olberding (2009) finds that regional partnerships for economic development, presumably an effort to create a formal network, have a significant positive effect on employment and an insignificant positive effect on per capita income. By contrast, Ha, Lee, and Feiock (2010) find that networks either with only private organizations or with both public and private organizations have a positive, statistically significant effect on local economic development.

From a policy perspective, it would be useful to know the mechanisms through which agglomeration economies and networks produce growth in order to guide intervention efforts. Unfortunately, the empirical literature fails to separate out the effects on regional economic outcomes of the very diverse processes that lie behind agglomeration economies and knowledge spillovers. Rosenthal and Strange (2004, 2146) ask what studies on productivity have to say about the various microfoundations of agglomeration economies and answer "not much." Hanson (2000, 489) echoes this: "We have relatively little understanding of the precise type of externalities that contribute to agglomeration. . . . Individual studies find evidence consistent with human capital spillovers across workers, localized knowledge spillovers in the innovation process, and regional cost and demand linkages between firms." The conclusion that information transfer or knowledge spillover is the "process" behind economic growth in large agglomerations is based largely on indirect evidence. As Cumber and MacKinnon (2004, 964) write, "The importance of locally specific forms of knowledge circulating through the labor market has been identified as a key feature of successful agglomerations such as Silicon Valley (Saxenian 1994). Yet few detailed studies have sought to test this proposition empirically."

Thus far we have reviewed what is known about the effects of clusters on economic growth. What about the effects of explicit economic development cluster *policy* on economic growth? As Delgado, Ketels, and Zyontz observe (2012, 4), "So far there is little empirical evidence of the overall effectiveness of . . . different cluster programs." There are many case studies of specific cluster-based initiatives, most of which focus on the processes through which cluster-based policy is applied or operates. Very few actually undertake systematic evaluation of outcomes.

Rather than justifying a cluster approach in terms of its substantive effect, Cumbers and MacKinnon (2004, 962) observe, "In a regional context in particular, a clusters approach seems to provide development agencies with a new and compelling rationale for both identifying a limited number of sectors to support—generally those that are deemed to have the highest growth potential—and defending and justifying this to those interests that are consequently excluded." Observing Arizona's cluster strategy, Waits (2002, 39) concluded that "best practice is the use of cluster working groups to help policymakers better understand an industry, the challenges it faces, and the most valuable assistance government can provide."

Using a cluster framework suggests that economic development policymakers and practitioners should focus not solely on individual export sectors, but on the wider set of firms, actors, and institutions that form a cluster and help to determine the cluster's competitiveness, including export industry supply chains. Cortright (2006, 47) notes that a cluster framework suggests that regional economic development practitioners should work with groups of firms rather than with individual firms. He also argues that use of a cluster framework "will shift analysis from firm-level rent-seeking (subsidies, tax breaks) to more widely shared competitive problems."

However, use of a cluster framework does not directly lead to answers to the difficult questions for regional economic development. As noted earlier, there is widespread agreement that it is not possible to create clusters where there is not an initial base for the cluster to grow on. There is less agreement on whether it is possible to identify "emerging clusters" or whether clusters can only be identified "in the rearview mirror," that is, after they already exist.[11] But even if emerging clusters can be accurately identified, can they be built on and made more effective, and, if so, how? Given that the literature we have reviewed indicates that clusters develop naturally through market processes and individual actions of firms, workers, and residents (consumers), is it possible for direct and intentional intervention to improve cluster operations, and, if so, through what kinds of policies or practices? Cluster policies, as previously noted, appear to be mostly traditional policies focused on selected clusters rather than applied scattershot or only on specific industries as in industry targeting. Whether these policies work depend on the efficacy of the traditional policies. One important insight from the cluster framework is the importance of *informal* networks (developed at, for example, the trade shows, hobby clubs, seminars, and receptions in Silicon Valley that Saxenian 1994 describes). However, little other than anecdotal evidence shows that efforts to create *formal* networks or bolster informal ones are likely to be successful.

In short, adopting a cluster framework does not answer the question of how to proceed. Should policy be directed at specific clusters or at concerns that are the foundation of virtually every cluster such as, for example, human capital and public infrastructure? If a cluster-based policy makes sense, should the policy be targeted at specific clusters or to things that any promising cluster can take advantage of? If targeted, toward what kinds of clusters and how they should they be selected? To none of these strategic concerns, much less what specific policies to pursue, does utilizing a clusters framework provide definitive answers.

Moreover, a regional economic development cluster policy, whatever strategies it actually consists of, will exist in a competitive environment, and the same cluster specialty cannot be competitive everywhere. Although a very high proportion of regional cluster-based development plans focus on biotechnology, life sciences, and/or information technology clusters, it is just not possible for every region to have such a cluster. Some regions are simply better positioned to be competitive in a particular cluster than are other regions.

There is, however, more to cluster-based economic development policy than which clusters, if any, should be the focus of policy attention. The cluster approach, because it is premised on the existence of positive spillovers (in economic terms, externalities) between firms, suggests the possibility that private firms and markets may underprovide the activities (such as worker training or research and development) that are the subjects of those spillovers. Therefore, there is a role for public policy to identify and promote those activities regardless of the particular cluster in which they are found.

However, public policy must be sensitive to the particular circumstances of a region's economy. A flaw in cluster-based economic development theory and practice is that it does not incorporate product cycle theory and some of the observations about the structure of firms and industries in different stages of the product cycle provided by Markusen (1985). Firms face different constraints and opportunities at different stages of the product cycle. When industries are in the early stages of the product cycle they are frequently capital-constrained and are reliant on their supply chains for capital and technology, their workforces are titled toward engineering and technical talent, technologies are rapidly evolving, and workers frequently move between firms. Model cycles within the product cycle are rapid, barriers to entry are low, and, most important, markets are growing. This is an environment where cooperation between firms in a cluster has economic reward.

Economic incentives differ in industries with older products in the mature stage of the product cycle. Model cycles have slowed, technology development is modest, and, most important, growth rates have slowed. In this environment cost containment and process innovation trump the returns from product innovation. Firms are battling for market share and technical employees have been replaced with production workers and managers. If barriers to entry are high then firms act quickly to internalize positive externalities and are less likely to cooperate with other firms in their cluster. The cooperation that does occur

among mature firms in a cluster often takes the form of collective investments in
the regional labor market to respond to spot labor shortages.

Technical Assistance to Private Sector Firms

Governments employ a host of economic development tools that are meant to
assist individual firms or clusters of related firms with their needs. Although
these efforts are directed at individual firms, from the regional perspective the
objective of these programs is to contribute to area economic growth and development. In many cities and regions basic assistance to firms occurs through
broad-based federal programs such as the Department of Commerce's Manufacturing Extension Partnership and International Trade Assistance Centers, the
Small Business Administration's (SBA) Small Business Development Centers
(SBDCs), and SCORE (formerly the Service Corps of Retired Professionals).
There are also state and local efforts to provide assistance to private firms or specific industries through financing, consulting services, and provision of shared
space and incubators.

What Is the Logic of Technical Assistance to
Firms as an Economic Development Strategy?

It is possible that market failures of some sort have reduced the ability of specific
firms to be as productive or efficient as possible and thus have restricted their
ability to produce to their potential. Firms, especially small- and medium-sized
ones, may have inadequate knowledge of production technologies, management
techniques, the organization of work, business strategy, market studies, and/or
business-related activities such as accounting, legal assistance, and inventory
control. There may also be knowledge gaps in whom to use for help or assistance.
These kinds of information deficiencies are likely to be most prevalent in small
enterprises, but they may well occur in middle-sized ones as well. Since firm
assistance programs are voluntary, firms that might benefit from the program
must recognize that they need assistance, be motivated to seek it, and be willing
to pay the fee required of clients in most such programs. However, given these
requirements, it is possible that some of these firms already have a relatively high
likelihood of succeeding even in the absence of firm assistance.

Publicly provided (or publicly paid for) assistance might enable these firms to
become more competitive and thus increase the area's income and employment.
For this to occur, the firms receiving assistance should be in the region's export
sector or else their improved performance will likely simply be at the expense of
existing firms in the region. Indeed, even if the firm is in the export sector it is

possible that firms receiving assistance may increase sales partly at the expense of other firms in the same region producing the same goods or services for export. Large firms that are major drivers of a region's economy are much less likely to make use of firm assistance service programs, partly because they have the internal capacity to improve their performance (Jarmin 1999) and partly because they are more likely to make use of management consultants. Any important inadequacies that these firms have in terms of management, business strategy, and so on, that are not addressed internally or through consultants are not likely to be affected by public firm assistance programs, even though these inadequacies may have drastic effects on a region's economy.

The effective logic is thus that smaller firms, if provided with appropriate information and advice, have important potential to grow a region's economy. This is surely true over some period of time, since all large firms start out at some point as small firms,[12] but, of course, not all small firms become large firms.

Because the provision of this kind of assistance is nearly certain to be by voluntary request from a firm, there is an obvious question of how much scope there is for this policy within a regional program in terms of the ability to expand it to other firms that have not, for whatever reason, applied. The self-selection basis for participants also raises the concern that many of the applying firms may well be likely to succeed even without the assistance.

What Is Known about the Effectiveness of Private Firm Technical Assistance Policies?

The scholarly literature on assistance to firms is heavily descriptive and sparse in terms of evaluating their effectiveness. Many of these programs lack formal evaluation processes, which has likely limited the research conducted on their effectiveness (Duscha and Graves 2006; Shapira, Youtie, and Kay 2011). Even under the best of circumstances, firm assistance evaluation studies present difficulties in terms of collecting outcome data for participating firms, establishing a counterfactual or control group similar to participating firms but that did not participate in the program, and surmounting the selection-bias problem noted above.

Because the federal Manufacturing Extension Partnership (MEP) includes required formal evaluation processes, much of the systematic research on firm assistance has been focused on it (Bartik 2010; Dziczek, Luria, and Wiarda 1998; Ehlen 2001; Hill 2004; Jarmin 1999; NEXUS Associates 1999; Ordowich et al. 2012; Shapira, Youtie, and Kay 2011; Voytek, Lellock, and Schmit 2004). MEP is administered through the National Institute of Standards and Technology (NIST) and provides various services to small- and medium-sized manufacturers through regional centers across the country. MEP addresses the capital, training, and strategic needs of firms through services that include product development and commercialization assistance, workforce readiness, and strategic counseling (NIST 2012). MEP also tends to serve more mature, established firms rather than those at the early stages of the product life cycle. Most of the evaluation studies of MEP consist of a small sample of MEP programs operating within a specific state or region or of MEP programs in a small number of states. Although initial studies suffered from serious methodological limitations (see Jarmin 1999 for a discussion), some more recent work has been more rigorous.

The results are mixed. Early studies find weak or no effects on productivity (Dziczek, Luria, and Wiarda 1998; Luria and Wiarda 1996; Oldsman 1996), though Nexus Associates (2003) finds productivity increases between 3.6% and 5% over the 1989–1999 period for firms receiving services, and Luria and Wiarda find a positive and significant effect on sales and employment. Jarmin (1999), in a more rigorous study that controls for the likelihood of firms voluntarily seeking services, finds MEP services to be associated with labor productivity increase (ranging from 3–16%, depending on the model specification, over a five year period), though his earlier study (1998) found a much smaller (1% over the five-year period) effect.[13] Jarmin (1999) deals with the impact that self-selection into the program by firms has on measured impacts of the program. He finds that larger firms were more likely to select themselves into an MEP program than were smaller firms and that single unit establishments were more likely to seek assistance than were multiunit firms.

None of the evaluations of MEP attempts to measure anything other than the impacts of MEP services on the average manufacturer. The program may, however, have different impacts on firms that performed well (as measured by productivity, sales, or employment, or growth rates of any of these) prior to receiving services than on those performed poorly. One might judge the program to be successful if it improves the performance of previously low-performing firms by a large amount even if it has no impact on the performance of previously high-performing firms. Moreover, future analyses of MEP may need to focus on different outcomes; Luria has argued that available evaluations do "not address what should matter most: whether MEP makes U.S. manufacturing larger or clients more productive" (2011, 7).

Assistance to firms in terms of business strategy and technical advice is often delivered through entities such as the SBDCs in the United States or Business Link (BL) program in Britain. According to the SBA's website, in December 2012 there were over 900 SBDC service points in the United States and its territories, and these centers operated in collaboration with state and local governments, universities and community colleges, chambers of commerce, and other private sector organizations. SBDC programs are available to anyone starting or expanding a small business, although there are special services for specific populations, such as women, minorities, veterans, and those with disabilities. SBDCs offer assistance with "development of business plans, manufacturing assistance, financial packages, and procurement contracts."

Chrisman (2011), in a national study of SBDCs and their clients, finds that the centers provided almost 65,000 clients with more than five hours of services each in 2009; less than 40% of these clients had not yet established their business, and 89% of survey respondents considered the counseling beneficial. He also estimates that the assistance created over 61,000 full-time equivalent jobs and sales of $4.7 billion and saved over 69,000 jobs and $5.1 billion in sales.

The BL program, which has been the object of several evaluations studies, was a British government-supported entity that provided a variety of services to small- and medium-size enterprises through regionally oriented franchises. The services varied due to the program's decentralized design, but the provider organizations provided advice to small- and medium-sized firms as well as a variety of targeted interventions. As with MEP, data on the effectiveness of the BL program have been collected through a number of surveys with BL clients, allowing for evaluation of this program on a variety of levels (Bennett 2007; Bennett and Robson 2004, 2005; Mole et al. 2008, 2011; Robson and Bennett 2010). Mole et al. (2011) find that intensive assistance to a smaller number of firms had a large and statistically significant effect on employment (2.2%) and sales growth (4.0%), whereas providing limited services to more firms did not have a significant impact. An earlier study by the same authors (Mole et al. 2009) also finds a significant increase on employment from intensive services but that other, less intensive services did not have a significant impact.

In summary, the research, while mixed, suggests that firm technical assistance programs may provide support that results in modest increases in productivity to firms, particularly small firms that receive intensive services. However, it also suggests that medium-sized firms are more likely to self-select into using these services than are small firms. The logic of firm assistance also suggests that positive results, if they occur, will take place over a multi-year period. There may also be some spillover benefits as well by improving the performance of supply chains.

Entrepreneurial and Small Business Assistance and Promotion

The perceived importance of small business and the role of entrepreneurs is a persistent theme in American economic and political history. Particularly during times of national economic downturn and decline in the large-scale manufacturing sector, the focus on promoting small business entrepreneurship as a means of creating new jobs and economic growth receives wide attention, both nationally and locally. Economic development policymakers and practitioners in each of our case study regions pursued some type of assistance to entrepreneurs, although the mechanisms and reasons differed. In most of the study regions, our interviewees expressed some concern that the desired rate of entrepreneurship had been inadequate in the past (for different reasons) although there were currently efforts underway to support entrepreneurs.

What Is the Logic of Entrepreneurial Small Business Assistance and Promotion as an Economic Development Strategy?

Innovation in product and/or processes is a compelling force in bringing about economic growth. Innovation is often seen to be closely connected with entrepreneurship—the willingness to risk one's capital and labor to start a new business—although much innovation also still occurs within the traditional firm setting as a normal business activity.[14] Glaeser, Kerr, and Kerr (2012) show that entrepreneurship, whether measured by average establishment size or the proportion of employment that is in new firms, is associated with economic growth and provide evidence that suggests that entrepreneurship may be a cause of economic growth.

Many studies as well as more popular journalistic accounts sing the praises of small businesses and new start-ups. Fairlie (2012, 4) has calculated that in 2011 there were "approximately 543,000 new businesses being created each month." Stangler and Litan (2009, 2) find that, from 1980 to 2005, "without startups, net job creation for the American economy would be negative in all but a handful of years." The author also states that firms less than five years old were responsible for almost eight million of the twelve million jobs created in 2007.

Of course, these kinds of comments need to be viewed in context; after all, over a long enough period all job creation results from new start-ups. In addition, new start-ups and small businesses also fail at a high rate (Stangler and Litan 2009). Shane (2009) observes that a typical startup creates few jobs and generates little wealth and also notes that the typical new start-up firm fails within five years. Haltiwanger, Jarmin, and Miranda (2011) find that five years from birth about 40% of the jobs originally created by start-ups have disappeared as a result of firm failure. Furthermore, research suggests that it is not small businesses or start-ups in general that are responsible for creating large numbers of new jobs, but rather a few relatively new small firms that grow quickly (so-called gazelles; see Haltiwanger, Jarmin, and Miranda 2011; Shane 2009).

Hurst and Pugsley (2011) review the small business literature, asking: "What do small businesses do?" They demonstrate that most small business owners are not interested in managing a high-growth business, bringing a new product or service into the marketplace, or to innovate in any way. Most small businesses are concentrated among the crafts and trades, restaurants, small shopkeepers, and local service providers in industries where local knowledge is important and barriers to entry are low. Hurst and Pugsley conclude that different sets of policies are relevant to the small business community, where social spillovers dominate, and for entrepreneurs, who are interested in building high-growth disruptive businesses. They conclude that for many industries scale economies are small and for many owners "the existence of nonpecuniary benefits of owning a small business, such as increased flexibility and control, may induce individuals to forgo some natural benefits of increased scale in exchange for higher utility rates" (2011, 112)

From the perspective of regional development, it is possible that the likelihood of entrepreneurship, particularly the kind that results in "gazelles," varies across metropolitan regions. Glaeser, Rosenthal, and Strange (2010) suggest why this variation might occur—differences in returns to entrepreneurship across regions, differences in the availability of inputs required for innovation (including the availability and capability of entrepreneurs in the region as well as financing and nearby suppliers of intermediate inputs), differences in the supply of innovative ideas, and cultural differences among regions. Entrepreneurship assistance programs assume that one or more of these differences can be positively affected through specific programs to encourage entrepreneurs and new businesses. However, clearly some of the reasons for low entrepreneurship are more easily addressed than others. In particular, differences in the availability of inputs are more susceptible to policy intervention in the short and medium term than cultural differences or differences in the supply of innovative ideas.

The logic of entrepreneurial assistance programs is that the services they provide compensate for information failures on the part of potential entrepreneurs and funders of new businesses, including the link between idea and commercialization; these information failures result in fewer start-ups in a region than would be socially desirable. Entrepreneurship programs at the metropolitan level vary substantially in the kinds of services they provide and may consist of a wide variety of approaches, mostly related to input availability and most of those related to entrepreneur education, training, and assistance. Other programs designed to encourage entrepreneurship such as the provision of credit and venture capital and incentives to promote the commercialization of university research are often funded by the state and/or federal governments.

What Is Known about the Effectiveness of Entrepreneurial and Small Business Assistance?

Governments, nonprofit organizations, and even for-profit businesses have devised various policies to help new and small businesses. The ultimate goal is for residents to start small businesses that employ a few local residents and that later turn into larger companies with more local employees and greater revenues.

Entrepreneurial assistance (or education) programs offer a wide range of aid.[15] These may include assistance in: developing a business plan; learning how to run a business (from the basics of different types of accounting software to contracting with business service providers such as lawyers, accountants, or health care providers); accessing venture capital, loans, or other funding sources; participating in government procurement programs; networking; and mentoring. Many programs to build entrepreneurism also have an awareness component to encourage entrepreneurial ideas or access to entrepreneurial assistance programs, as well as programs to build entrepreneurial awareness and skills among youth (during K-12 education), college students,[16] or the unemployed (through Unemployment Insurance [UI] or Workforce Investment Act programs).

Sometimes these programs are offered through nonprofit or for-profit business incubators or accelerators. These usually offer office space that rents on flexible leases at below market rates and provides shared spaces such as conference rooms and kitchens as well as business resources such as shared fax machines, wireless internet, and administrative assistants. Despite the popularity of business incubators as a local economic development tool over the past thirty years, the systematic research on their results and effectiveness is relatively sparse. Partly this may be due to the difficulty in determining the effects of the incubators, including what jobs were actually created directly due to the incubator that would not have been created otherwise (Hackett and Dilts 2004; Lewis 2001; Udell 1990). Yet another factor may simply be the political issues involved. Many of the cities and other jurisdictions that are employing the incubator methodology are responding to dramatic downshifts in their economic climate, and so political actors must be seen as doing something to encourage business creation. Incubators fit that need well, especially with their emphasis on entrepreneurship. In addition, relative to many other economic development programs (e.g., location incentives, worker training), the budgetary costs of incubators are often much smaller, which likely leads to less emphasis on accountability.

Stokan et al. (2015, 314) review several studies of the effects of business incubators on firm employment and revenue and conclude, "What emerges is a portrait of measurable yet unassuming job and revenue growth for incubated firms." However, they also note that even that conclusion is called into doubt because most of the studies do not take into account selection problems, that is, that the firms most likely to grow may self-select themselves into incubator programs. Their own research did attempt to take selection problems into account through use of propensity scores and found that the association between business incubator participation and job growth continued to exist even after selection bias was accounted for.

Studies of incubator effectiveness focusing on technology incubators seem to yield even more positive results. A survey of Maryland technology incubators (RTI International 2007) finds that the state's technology incubators increased employment by 14,044 new employees, gross state product by $1.2 billion, and state and local tax revenues by $104 billion. Moreover, every $1 in funding provided by the Maryland Technology Development Corporation to the state's incubators resulted in an $1,800 increase to the gross state product. Older studies find similar positive results. Molnar et al. (1997) find that technology incubators had an average annual sales increase of over $250,000, an employment increase of 2.6 full-time and 0.9 part-time positions per year from 1990 to 1996 and that twenty-three incubated firms generated local tax revenues of $402,000 in 1996. Markley and McNamara (1996), meanwhile, find that employees at companies in an industry and technology incubator in Illinois had a total of direct salaries and wages of $22.5 million while the companies had gross sales of $127.5 million from 1987 to 1993. Other studies rank the value that incubator firms place on the services provided (Campbell and Allen 1987; Mian 1996), although these studies do not attempt to monetize the impacts. Further, these studies were of technology incubators, which may have seen higher sales, salaries, or investment yields (due to the nature of that industry) than incubators that served other types of clients. (Detroit's TechTown, for example, serves entrepreneurs starting a wide variety of companies not limited to those interested in high-tech products.)

The federal government invests in many entrepreneurship development and assistance programs, with some offered by the SBA and others through the Department of Labor via the unemployment insurance program or programs of the Workforce Investment Act and others through various federal research and development programs.[17] Two of the largest of these programs with federal funding are the SBDCs and the Small Business Innovation Research Program (SBIR), both overseen by the SBA. Eleven federal agencies operate their own SBIR programs, under an overall mission "to support scientific excellence and technological innovation through the investment of Federal research funds in critical

American priorities to build a strong national economy" (SBIR 2012).[18] SBIR is a three-phase program (with each subsequent phase building on the prior one), and only U.S. small businesses that meet a series of criteria can apply for the competitive funding.

Although such programs are popular among entrepreneurs and policymakers, there has been a lack of robust research on the effects of many of these policies, especially when offered as whole programs. Recently, however, the Employment and Training Administration of the U.S. Department of Labor and the SBA-hosted Project GATE (Growing America Through Entrepreneurship), a large-scale demonstration program that operated in seven sites in Maine, Minnesota, and Pennsylvania from 2003 to 2005. Potential participants needed to meet a few general criteria (eighteen years of age or older, legally eligible to work in the United States, a resident of one of the three states, and interested in starting or expanding a legal business) and needed to attend an orientation meeting at a One-Stop Career Center to be considered eligible. If they met the requirements, they could complete an application for Project GATE, with applications randomly assigned to either a treatment or control group. Those assigned to the treatment group could choose to use all or none of three services: a meeting to determine the entrepreneur's needs and potential providers to help them meet those needs; training courses including general business, accounting, legal, human resources, and specialized courses; and one-on-one counseling sessions. Those in the control group were ineligible to receive any of these three services through Project GATE, but they could access these types of assistance or other help elsewhere, which means that any results found in Project GATE were only about adding Project GATE services to those already available.

Although there were some positive findings from the program, its overall impact (measured by comparing mean values for each outcome) was not substantial (Benus et al. 2009). Project GATE recipients were more likely to start a business, more likely to start their business sooner, and more likely to have that business last longer than members of the control group, but, by sixty months after random assignment, both groups had the same likelihood of business ownership. With regard to job creation, Project GATE had only a short-term increase in the probability of self-employment and no likely impact on total employment. In addition, program participants also often experienced a short-term negative impact on their wage or salary earnings (as the opportunity cost of devoting time to their new business). The program also had only a short-term impact on receipt of unemployment insurance benefits and no impact on public assistance receipt or the income of the participant's spouse. In a cost-benefit analysis, Benus et al. (2009) find that the costs of the program exceeded its benefits for participants ($718), nonparticipants ($989), and for society ($1,707), although when examining the costs and benefits of those who were receiving UI benefits, the benefits outweighed the costs for both participants ($4,523) and for society ($2,192). Because Benus et al. label the methodology of their cost-benefit analysis "uniformly conservative," they ultimately decide that "our overall conclusion is that the benefits of Project GATE exceed its costs" (2009, ix).

There are few other evaluations of entrepreneurship assistance programs using random assignment. In their review of twenty-two peer-reviewed studies of small business assistance programs, Gu, Karoly, and Zissimpoulos (2008) argue this is because of the difficulty of finding a comparison group to those who received the services. They find only one other evaluation of entrepreneurship assistance using random assignment (of demonstration programs in Massachusetts and Washington in the early 1990s and which found generally positive results). Their review finds some positive impacts of the assistance programs, although they cite many methodological limitations to the studies that could put even that assessment into doubt.

In general, entrepreneurial assistance programs seem to be popular among those accessing the services. For example, a study by Yusuf (2010) uses the Panel Study of Entrepreneurial Dynamics to learn that, while entrepreneurs who accessed support services frequently found a disconnect between the services they wanted and the services they received, those entrepreneurs were also mostly satisfied with the services they received.

Most evaluations rely on cost-effectiveness or cost-per-job-created, rather than full cost-benefit analysis. With regard to public subsidies, a survey conducted for the National Business Incubation Association finds that the cost per job created ranged from $1,109 to $2,218, depending on how many jobs are credited to the incubator (Molnar et al. 1997), while Lewis (2001) surveys the literature and finds that costs per job at technology incubators ranged from $3,000 in Maryland to $11,353 in a national random sample. Both Molnar et al. and Lewis also note that it is important only to compare the results at incubators with similar missions, since different types of incubators have different effects.

There are also programs at the federal or state level to make it easier for entrepreneurs to access the capital they need to support their fledgling business. This is especially important as credit markets continued to be tight and housing values remained low after the Great Recession.[19] Some entrepreneurial assistance programs help the entrepreneurs make contact with venture capital firms or "angel" investors, while others (especially at the federal level) provide capital or loan guarantees for the new business. Using data on all MSAs from 1993 to 2002, Samila and Sorenson (2011, 338) find that venture capital does have an effect on the number of start-ups. Their findings show that if venture capital firms invested in one additional firm in a region, it would lead to "the entry of two to twelve establishments—in other words, more new firms than actually funded. A doubling in the number of firms funded by venture capital also results in a 0.22% to 1.24% expansion in the number of jobs and a 0.48% to 3.78% increase in aggregate income." In comparing venture capital backed entrepreneurship, Gompers et al. (2006) find that venture capital funding only has an effect on the success of new firms whose owners were unsuccessful in previous entrepreneurial ventures, suggesting that the venture capital firms provide new competences that help the entrepreneurs develop their businesses (and that previously successful entrepreneurs already know). While not specifically examining the performance of entrepreneurial firms, Kortum and Lerner (1998) also find that venture capital has a positive impact on innovation, as measured by the number of patents.

Despite the lack of robust evidence on the effects of entrepreneurship assistance programs on the local or regional level, the literature on these programs generally suggests that they can play a positive, if modest, role in promoting regional economic growth. They do so by addressing limitations on the information that potential entrepreneurs and funders of start-ups have about the prospects for entrepreneurial success in a region. However, these are not the only barriers to entrepreneurship and innovation. Glaeser, Rosenthal, and Strange (2010) argue that embedded cultural values may make some regions more likely to produce entrepreneurs than others. Saxenian (1994) attributes interregional differences in entrepreneurial success to differences in social structure. She finds that the differences between interpersonal and interorganizational networks in Silicon Valley and those in the Route 128 area near Boston allowed firms and entrepreneurs in the former to adapt, create, and deploy new innovations better than in the latter. She also shows how social structures can change over time, as relationships became calcified in Silicon Valley in the 1970s but then reverted to being more flexible once again in the 1980s.

Conclusion

All of the business- and individual-oriented responses discussed in this chapter have shown some degree of positive results in some circumstances. They should, therefore, be included in the toolbox of economic development policy. However, these policies, by themselves, are not likely to be effective in responding to either short-term economic shocks or chronic distress. None of the policies has the potential to be put in place and have an impact in the short term in response to economic shocks. In the longer run, even when the effects are positive, they seem far too modest to have a major impact on moving a region out of chronic distress. Potentially more powerful policies to deal with chronic distress are examined in the next chapter.

ASSESSING THE EFFECT OF RESILIENCE POLICIES DIRECTED TOWARD PUBLIC GOODS, INSTITUTIONS, AND LEADERSHIP

In this chapter we turn to policies related to public goods, institutions, and leadership:

- Human capital, education, and workforce development
- Infrastructure
- Amenity improvement/creation
- Organizational restructuring
- Leadership

Human Capital, Education, and Workforce Development

It is now widely accepted in the economic development policymaking community that human capital—the skills and abilities that workers bring to their jobs—is an important if not critical component of an area's ability to compete in the global economy. Policymakers' and practitioners' recognition of the relevance of this connection for responses to economic shocks and emergence from chronic distress is greatest with respect to workforce development and community college training, less so for other components of the formal education system (higher education and elementary and secondary education), and much less so for preschool education.

The Logic of Human Capital, Education, and Workforce Development as an Economic Development Policy

Human capital is the set of skills embodied in labor, a critical factor of production for most economic activity. The higher the amount of human capital per worker, the more able the worker will be able to engage in complex tasks and operations, adapt to changing circumstances, and participate in problem-solving. In short, higher human capital should lead to greater productivity and economic growth. Human capital is a product of a series of informal and formal processes. The former consists of a combination of individual endowment, informal education, and value transmission provided through the family, transmission of cultural values through family and peer group, and knowledge gained from labor force participation and on the job experience. Formal processes include preschool development programs, elementary and secondary education, higher education, and workforce development and training programs.

Many studies have shown a link between the level of human capital of an area's residents and the amount of economic growth in a city, region, or country. (Human capital is usually measured by educational attainment, since human capital is not directly observable and other dimensions of human capital are more difficult to measure.) Glaeser, Scheinkman, and Shleifer (1995) find that area population and income growth are both positively related to the level of initial schooling of the area's residents. Bell et al. note, "The most consistent finding in the empirical literature is that human capital (education and skills of the area labor force) is positively related to economic development" (2005, I; see also Barro 1992; Glaeser and Shapiro 2001). Others note that areas with more highly skilled or educated workers are the areas attracting new skilled or educated workers (Berry and Glaeser 2005; Moretti 2003). These tendencies—as well as the desire of policymakers in many urban areas to shift their industrial base from low-skill manufacturing to higher skill manufacturing (e.g., green technologies, robotics, advanced medical devices) and nonmanufacturing (e.g., information technology, professional services) businesses—make human capital development a priority for urban regions. Part of the obvious benefit of having more highly skilled or educated workers in a region is that these employees tend to earn higher incomes (Moretti 2003), which allows them to consume more and also provides a higher tax base for local governments (Dudensing and Barkley 2011). They may also contribute to higher levels of entrepreneurship and innovation in a region (Mathur 1999).

Highly skilled and educated workers also make important *indirect* contributions to regional growth. Mathur (1999, 210) calls this a "knowledge multiplier effect" and relates it to the benefits of workers clustering and of agglomeration economies. In addition to increasing their own productivity, the presence of educated and highly skilled workers may also increase the productivity of those with whom they work. Moretti (2004) finds that a higher level of college graduates in an MSA results in higher wages for less educated workers, with the benefits greatest for coworkers with the least education. He finds that, a 1-percentage point increase in the number of college graduates results in a 1.9% increase in wages for high school dropouts, a 1.6% increase for high school graduates, a 1.2% increase for other workers with some college, and a 0.4% increase for other college graduates. In another paper, Moretti (2003) also notes that there are other less obvious benefits of more education, including less crime (and other negative behaviors) and more voting and other political activities (see also Lochner 2011).

What Is Known about the Effectiveness of Human Capital, Education, and Workforce Development Programs?

Policymakers pursue efforts to increase human capital through both the formal education system (higher, secondary, and elementary education and preschool programs) and through workforce development programs, although these systems often interact through the community college and vocational training systems. Increasing human capital through improvements to the formal education system is generally a long-term endeavor (fifteen to twenty years), both because of the time it takes to put in place and implement changes and because of the long pipeline that children entering the system must traverse. Nonetheless, research suggests that the payoffs may be substantial. To get some sense of the benefits that accrue from investment in various levels of the formal education system, Hungerford and Wassmer (2004) cite studies that find:

> Cutting statewide public K–12 expenditure by $1 per $1,000 state's personal income would (1) reduce the state's personal income by about 0.3 percent in the short run and 3.2 percent in the long run, (2) reduce the state's manufacturing investment in the long run by 0.9 percent and manufacturing employment by 0.4 percent. Cutting statewide public K–12 education per student by $1 would reduce small business starts by 0.4 percent in the long run. Cutting statewide public K–12 expenditure by one percentage point of the state's personal income would reduce the state's employment by 0.7 percent in the short run and by 1.4 percent in the long run. (vi; see also MacEwan 2013; Weiss 2004; Hanushek and Woessmann 2004)

Bartik (2011) also finds positive returns (as measured by state resident per capita earnings) of two to three times the costs for three early childhood programs, and specifically that "a high-quality universal pre-K education increases the present value of state residents' earnings by $2.78 per dollar of costs" (80). Furthermore, research has also consistently shown that the returns to education for individuals are positive and large. High school dropouts earn less over their lifetime than do high school graduates; those with community college degrees earn more than do those with no more than a high school education; and those with four year degrees earn even more.

WORKFORCE DEVELOPMENT PROGRAMS. Unlike the formal education system, workforce development programs have a shorter time frame and, assuming they work, promise a more immediate effect. As a result, regional publicly funded human capital policies often look to workforce development to improve the skills and training—and thus the employment opportunities and wages—of residents.[1] Within a much shorter policy time frame, there are a wide range of publicly funded workforce development programs funded by all levels of government. At the federal level, the Government Accountability Office (2011) identified forty-seven programs offered by nine agencies (the Departments of Labor, Education, Health and Human Services, Interior, Agriculture, Defense, Justice, and Veterans Affairs, and the Environmental Protection Agency).[2] These programs include job search assistance, classroom training, on-the-job training, subsidized public sector employment, and subsidized private sector employment. They vary in their target groups, including youth, adults, displaced workers, and social program recipients whose participation is required as a condition for receiving services.

In a meta-analysis of workforce programs in developed western countries, Card et al. find that "job search assistance (JSA) and related programs have generally positive impacts, especially in the short run, whereas subsidized public sector employment programs are less likely to yield positive impacts. Classroom and on-the-job training programs are not particularly likely to yield positive impacts in the short-run but yield more positive impacts after two years. Comparing across different participant groups, we find that programs for youths are less likely to yield positive impacts than untargeted programs" (2007, 3).

The federal government's primary vehicle for workforce development funding is the Workforce Innovation and Opportunity Act (WIOA) of 2015, which—like its predecessor Workforce Investment Act of 1998—was designed to provide flexibility at the local and state levels in order to better respond to economic conditions and the needs of businesses and residents in those areas (rather than a "one size fits all" federal program).[3] Within each state, the governor and a state-level workforce development board (WDB) generate a five-year strategic plan (which is submitted to the federal Department of Labor) that provides information on statewide workforce programs, including how local workforce activities support the state plans. The governor, with assistance from the state WDB, also monitors workforce activities in the state and reports outcomes to the federal government. Local and regional WDBs and elected officials are responsible for local or regional workforce development planning and operations and report to the governor and the state WDB. Private sector employers must comprise at least half of a WDB's members. WIOA funds a variety of services to workers, including job search assistance, initial skills assessments, labor market information, and training. Furthermore, WIOA services are supposed to be provided in "one-stop" centers ("American Job Centers") so that customers do not have to access multiple sites for job assistance; these one-stops can also house other federal, state, and local assistance programs, including Employment Service, Temporary Assistance for Needy Families, and vocational rehabilitation.

Since WIOA programs are overseen at the state level (by the state WDB and governor), operated at the local level (overseen by the local WDBs), and supposed to be able to respond to local economic conditions, there is substantial diversity among the services available to the workforce nationally. This range is one of the challenges of assessing the impact of federally funded workforce development program. The so-far limited evaluation literature on WIA is generally positive, certainly more so than earlier federal workforce programs (the Comprehensive Employment and Training Act [CETA] of 1973 and the Job Training Partnership Act [JTPA] of 1982), and finds that the program generally met its federal goals (King and Heinrich 2011).

Heinrich, Mueser, and Troske (2008) use administrative data from twelve states to compare the earnings of WIA participants to those of demographically similar workers within the individual state and local workforce areas. Their goal is to provide an "average impact" for WIA participation in those twelve states, but they maintain that the results may be valid for many other states. For WIA programs serving disadvantaged adults, they estimate an earnings effect of WIA participation of $500–$600 per quarter for women and a brief decline (for three quarters) in income followed by an increase of approximately $400 per quarter for men. They further break down WIA adult participants into those who received only job search, placement, initial skills assessments, and/or labor market information and those who received some training through WIA. They find that, "The short-term effects are greatest for individuals who do not receive training services, although the benefits that accrue to them tend to degrade over time. Those who obtained training services have lower initial returns, but they catch up to others within ten quarters, ultimately registering larger total gains" (Heinrich et al. 2008, 58). They estimate that, at about two and a half years after training, disadvantaged women who received training eventually earn an additional $800 per quarter while men earn $500–$600 more.

With respect to dislocated workers—those who are probably most obviously adversely affected by downturns resulting from economic shocks—their results are less encouraging. Dislocated workers who received training under WIA typically saw their earnings fall when they began receiving services (possibly due to the opportunity cost of participating in the training) and minimal long-term benefits from the training. However, dislocated individuals who received only job search, placement, initial skills assessments, and/or labor market information usually did not experience a drop in earnings and ultimately saw a small increase in quarterly earnings (although these individuals also utilized WIA services for less time than individuals who received training).

Hollenbeck (2009b) analyzes WIA programs in Washington, Virginia, and Indiana and finds that WIA job training resulted in a short-term quarterly earnings impact ranging from $146 to $711 and that these earnings differentials did not decrease over time. He also conducts a benefit-cost analysis of the programs (excluding Virginia) and finds that the social rate of return for the programs was positive, especially over the long run due to the greater tax payments WIA participants paid on their increased earnings.

In general, the findings for WIA are more positive than those for its predecessor programs, CETA and JTPA. Evaluations of voluntary programs under both CETA and JTPA (as compared to federal mandatory training programs such as the Work Incentive Program or its successor, the Job Opportunities and Basic Skills Training Program) generally produced positive and significant outcomes for adult women but less consistent outcomes for adult men (Friedlander, Greenberg, and Robins 1997; King 2004; Stanley, Katz, and Krueger 1998).[4] In the studies reviewed by Friedlander, Greenberg, and Robins, for example, participation in CETA's voluntary programs resulted in an annual wage effect for men ranged from –$3,342 to $1,634 and for women from $28 to $2,815. Further, for participation in JTPA's voluntary programs, the average annual effect for men was $970 (since they only include one study) and for women ranged from $771 to $1,103. In addition, Stanley, Katz, and Krueger highlight the finding by Bloom and colleagues (1997) that increased earnings for JTPA participants usually resulted from additional hours worked, not from higher wages.[5] Lafer (2002, 90) finds evidence "that JTPA has failed to achieve its goals. Furthermore, this failure reflects the structural constraints of job training policy rather than the difficulties of program implementation." He also questions positive impacts of all job training programs, due to two concerns. First, that there would not be enough well-paying jobs available if all those eligible for a program were actually served. Second, those who participate in training programs are simply taking jobs that would have gone to other qualified workers and leaving those other workers unemployed instead.

WIOA and WIA differed from the previous iterations of federal workforce development programs principally by shifting more of the oversight and administration of the programs to the state level and offering training via vouchers, which allow recipients to choose a training provider (although this choice may be limited due to a WIOA and WIA requirement that states create lists of eligible training providers). In addition, there is a greater emphasis under WIOA and WIA on the role of community colleges (O'Leary, Straits, and Wandner 2004).[6] Another significant difference is that federal funding under WIOA and WIA is less than was available under JTPA or CETA.[7]

COMMUNITY COLLEGES. Community colleges have always had a role in the nation's higher education system (by providing an alternative to or preparation for a traditional four-year baccalaureate program) and job training, but there is a new emphasis on the roles of community colleges in economic development and workforce training.[8]

Community colleges offer a number of different educational opportunities, including two-year associate degrees, shorter term credential and certificate programs (which typically differ based on the number of credits required and the type of education), and noncredit programs. Compared to those with only a high school diploma, each of these programs generally increases an individual's earnings (although they still typically earn less than those with baccalaureate degrees). Using data from the National Longitudinal Survey, Kane, and Rouse (1995, 601) found that "the average person who attended a two-year college earned about 10-percent more than those without any college education, even without completing an associate's degree." Using administrative data from Kentucky, Jepsen, Troske, and Coomes (2009) also found that completing a community college program resulted in both an increase in earnings and an increase in the probability of employment, although the return decreased as the type of program changed from degrees to diplomas to certificates. In all cases, though, the returns were higher for women than for men.[9] Important for regions struggling with changing economic conditions and resulting unemployment, both Jacobson, LaLonde, and Sullivan (2005b) and Leigh and Gill (1997) found that displaced workers and returning workers, respectively, saw increased earnings from a community college education.

Because many students enroll in community college programs without completing a degree or other credential, it is also important to note that there are generally positive returns to simply receiving some credits from these programs. Kane and Rouse (1995) find that completing two semesters at either a community college or a traditional four year college or university resulted in generally the same increase in hourly and annual earnings (approximately 4–6%).

Gill and Leigh (2003) also observe that enrolling in a training program at a community college increases earnings (by 31.1% for white males and 45.0% for black males) by as much as enrolling in, but not graduating from, a four-year school. However, in his review of the literature, Grubb (2002) concludes that the returns to those completing less than twelve credits would be less than 5% and may even be zero. An additional consideration is that, as Marcotte et al. (2005) and Jacobson, LaLonde, and Sullivan (2005a) note, at least some of these increased earnings may be the result of increased hours worked rather than increased wages.

For some occupations, earning an associate degree has also been shown to result in higher earnings than baccalaureate degrees in less well-paying fields. Grubb (2002, 313) explains, "Men can earn more by getting an Associate degree in engineering, public service, or vocational/technical subjects than they can from a baccalaureate in the humanities or education; women can earn more with an associate degree in business or health than with a baccalaureate in vocational/technical subjects, the humanities, or education." This leads to what Grubb terms "reverse transfer," in which those with baccalaureate degrees enroll in community college programs to obtain the skills or credentials for higher paying fields.

There are also typically varying returns for the same degree or credential earned in different fields. Jepsen, Troske, and Coomes (2009), for example, find that both men and women typically received the highest labor market returns from a degree or diploma in the health field, while men had negative returns for both degrees and diplomas in the humanities and services fields and women had the smallest returns (although still positive) in these fields.[10] Jacobson, LaLonde, and Sullivan (2005a, 272) find, "On the one hand, we estimate that an academic year of more technically oriented vocational and academic math and science courses raises earnings by about 14% for men and 29% for women. On the other hand, we estimate that less technically oriented courses yield very low and possibly zero returns." King and Heinrich (2011) also review the findings of several sector-specific workforce training programs, which produced greater returns to individuals in particular fields. These differing returns and the limited results of earlier training programs have led to more demand-side training, which is designed to meet the needs of the labor market and link training in specific skills or industries to the needs of businesses in the region (Giloth 2000; Holzer 2009). This is in contrast to training that would seek simply to improve the residents' general skills and education without any direct linkage to possible job.

In addition to the training that they provide, community colleges can also serve as an intermediary between businesses and workers to serve the needs of both groups (Garmise 2009; Lowe, Goldstein, and Donegan 2011). Although many different types of institutions may serve as intermediaries, community colleges are often well suited to this role since many already provide customized training to local businesses.[11] These intermediaries can perform roles including analyzing local labor market conditions, providing training, and linking businesses and jobseekers in different networks.

ELEMENTARY AND SECONDARY EDUCATION SYSTEM. There is a massive literature on strategies, policies, and approaches to change local elementary and secondary education systems so that they produce better educated and more workforce ready students (for reviews, see Jacob and Ludwig 2009; Ladd 2012; Murname 2009). We do not review that literature here. Although there are enthusiastic advocates for a wide variety of educational approaches, we think that it is fair to say that there is little consensus as to which is best.

Research suggests that better schools and teachers make a substantial difference, but there is no real agreement on what the characteristics of good schools or teachers that make a difference are. More recent research also indicates that smaller class size, particularly in earlier grades, matters (Loveless and Hess 2007; Schanzenbach 2007). However, a growing body of evidence suggests that many students growing up in high-poverty areas enter the formal school system already substantially behind and that public interventions must be made at the preschool level (Ladd 2012). Although a vast amount of research shows that the amount of money spent by schools per student, by itself, has little or no relationship to student outcomes, changes that will make a difference—better teachers, smaller class sizes, more and better preschool developmental education—will cost more money (see Burtless 1996; Grubb 2009b; Hanushek 1997).

In addition, from a regional economic development point of view, improving the preschool and elementary and secondary education system may not fully benefit the region that produces the improved results. If the region is not producing sufficient jobs, the benefits of the improved human capital will be mitigated to the extent that some of the recipients will migrate out of the region in search of better job opportunities elsewhere. Nonetheless, Bartik (2011) suggests that these benefits, at least at the state level, are substantial at every level of education, even after accounting for out-migration from the state, and are equivalent to those of business incentive programs. He also finds that long-term benefits for preschool education programs are highly positive even at the metropolitan level, a geography where out-migration by very young beneficiaries over time is likely to be high.

To summarize, there is little disagreement on the importance of human capital development to regional economic growth and development. Although the effects are long-term, the benefits to be derived from increasing the high school graduation rate and increasing the participation rate of an area's students in community college and higher education are significant. (In many areas, however, the benefits of increasing the higher education participation rate would be mitigated to the extent that local students moved out of the region after completing their education.) Improvements in formal education systems also would likely have a high payoff, although how to accomplish that has been a continual matter of national debate for the past several decades and remains unclear. Expansion of high-quality preschool developmental education would almost certainly also have a high payoff but would be very expensive.

By contrast, shorter term workforce development programs are in many ways more attractive as programs in response to economic downturns and the resulting distress. They have a short timeframe, rarely taking longer than a year. Their clients are identifiable, and their needs are visible. The payoffs are, if not immediate, relatively quick. Furthermore, as the research we have reviewed suggests, the payoffs are positive. However, it is worth pointing out that, while positive, they are rather modest, certainly not enough to move the average participant into the middle class or, from the regional economy's perspective, turn a relatively poorly skilled regional labor force into a highly skilled one. To accomplish that, some combination of improvements in the formal education system and the in-migration of more educated workers from outside of the region would be required. The institutional nexus where the short and long-term perspectives may well meet is at the community college level, particularly to the extent that community colleges can tailor the education and training that they provide to industry-specific job needs of employers in the region or who may be interested in moving into the region.

Despite the generally positive returns to many human capital and workforce development programs (especially when considered over the long term), one of the biggest challenges is the lack of integration of the different types of education and training available to workers. Instead of one system that provides different services from literacy assistance to advanced degrees, workers usually must seek out different providers depending on their needs. Greater coordination of such programs would be better able to reflect and aid the workforce needs of businesses. A more coordinated system would also benefit individuals who need better or different skills for advancement in their careers (rather than entry level jobs). Successful advancement would also have the added effect of providing additional job openings for other workers as those currently holding the positions advance (Persky, Felsenstein, and Carlson 2004).

Infrastructure

Infrastructure investment and public works are among the most common economic development policies pursued in developing nations and lagging regions (such as Appalachia) in developed countries. Yet we found few instances of infrastructure investment as a response to either shock or chronic distress in our case study regions, other than airport expansion in several regions, infrastructure incidental to downtown development efforts, and rebuilding associated with a major flood.

The Logic of Infrastructure Investment as an Economic Development Policy

Infrastructure investment and public works spending have two different rationales depending upon the time horizon. In the short term, particularly as a response to a cyclical shock, spending on public works acts as a stimulus to the regional economy, resulting in employment of unemployed workers in the construction industry with attendant stimulus provided through indirect and induced multiplier effects throughout the regional economy.

However, there are concerns to be considered in using public works spending as a short-term stimulus policy. First, the time between planning and actual construction may be substantial, and the actual stimulus may take place too late to have the desired effect. Thus, as in the federal American Recovery and Reinvestment Act (ARRA), there is usually an emphasis on "shovel ready" projects. From the point of view of local or regional projects, the logic suggests reprogramming already approved projects (i.e., projects that have already been determined worthy), moving them forward for immediate implementation. Alternatively, if providing an immediate response is not as important a criterion, new projects can be planned and supported through issuance of bonds, thereby transferring expenditure to the present and revenue raising necessary to pay for the expenditure to the future.

The effect of public works investment as a stimulus for a region's economy will also be mitigated by the extent that the stimulus funds are spent outside of the region. Carlino and Inman (2013) estimate that at the state level a 1 standard deviation increase ($390) in public works spending per capita by the largest state in the region (e.g., Illinois in the Midwest) would generate about 107,000 jobs in the region. However, nearly 40% of them would be spillovers to surrounding states as a result of purchases of inputs from them and subsequent reduced multiplier effects. These spillovers are even larger in a smaller geographic unit such as a metropolitan region. Carlino and Inman also estimate that the effects would be transitory and that most would dissipate after a year. There is also the possibility that public works funds spent in the short term primarily for stimulus purposes will be spent on projects that are inefficient or difficult to justify as long-term investments.

In the longer term, the logic of infrastructure investment is to generate regional growth through improvements in productivity brought about by the infrastructure itself or by augmenting the efficiency of private inputs employed by firms such as labor or private capital (Eberts 1990). Of course, without some level of basic infrastructure, the functioning of a modern economy is virtually impossible. However, once beyond the basic provision of transportation (roads, bridges, etc.), water treatment and distribution systems, electricity, and energy distribution, how much do marginal improvements to infrastructure produce additional jobs, income, and economic growth? Romp and de Haan (2007) note that the principle of diminishing returns suggests that an increment of public capital stock should have a smaller effect on output in areas that already had a substantial capital stock than on areas that had a smaller preexisting stock.

Public infrastructure investment can substitute for private investment or it can complement it through increasing the productivity of private capital. The desirable effects of public infrastructure investment will be reduced to the extent that it displaces some portion of private investment. And, of course, if the relationship is complementary, there is the question of causality: does public infrastructure investment generate additional private investment or does private investment call forth new public infrastructure investment? Romp and de Haan (2007) review a set of studies at the national level that differ in terms of their findings. Eberts (1986) finds that public investment in metropolitan regions is a complement rather than a substitute to private investment, while Munnell (1990) finds the same at the state level. Eberts and Fogarty (1987) find a significant association between public infrastructure outlays and private manufacturing investment in thirty-three of forty metropolitan areas between 1904 and 1978. After observing which came first, they note that the causal direction goes both ways but that public capital investment preceded private investment in the majority of cases. They note, "Private investment is more likely to influence public outlays in cities located in the South and in cities that have experienced tremendous growth after 1950. Public outlays are more likely to influence private investment in cities that experienced much of their growth before 1950" (25).

Romp and de Haan also note that the overall effect of public infrastructure investment will depend on how it is financed, observing that "an increase in public capital stimulates economic growth only if the productivity increase of public capital exceeds the adverse impact of higher taxes" (2007, 9). They also note that new infrastructure may have a "perverse effect if it draws scarce government resources away from maintenance and operation of the existing capital stock."

Despite these caveats, most economists have stressed the importance of infrastructure (see Romp and de Haan 2007 for a review), and recent theory has particularly stressed the critical nature of transportation infrastructure as a means of making the movements of inputs to producers and finished goods to consumers quicker and less expensive and thus making a region more productive.

What Is Known about the Effectiveness of Infrastructure Policies?

In the short term, infrastructure investment creates jobs through direct employment of those involved in the infrastructure construction and through induced and indirect multiplier effects resulting from these jobs. Thompson (2010) estimated that investment by state government (in New England) would produce thirteen jobs per $1,000,000 invested when all direct, indirect, and induced effects were included, and this would be increased to fifty-two jobs per $1,000,000 of each state dollar invested when federal dollars leveraged through the state expenditure were included. Carlino and Inman (2013) note that the effect of a short-term infrastructure investment by a state would vary by state and estimate that an increase of $390 per capita by Massachusetts would generate 35,000 jobs in that state at a cost of $72,000 per job. The same increase would result in 108,000 jobs in California at a cost of $90,000 per job. Feyrer and Sacerdote (2011) find that at the state level, each $1,000,000 in ARRA stimulus funding created 5.4 jobs within the state, while at the county level, each $1,000,000 in stimulus created 1.5 jobs. They also find that ARRA spending for infrastructure had job creation effects that were higher than these averages.

The long-term effects of infrastructure investment on jobs and economic growth should result from increased productivity—and consequently reduced costs—that the new or improved infrastructure generates for economic activity in the region. Although some early studies find little or no support for the impact of public investment on private productivity (Garcia-Mila, McGuire, and Porter 1996; Holtz-Eakin 1994; Sturm and de Haan 1995; Tatom 1991), more recent research generally supports this expectation (for reviews, see Eberts 1990; Munnell 1990; Romp and de Haan 2007; Thompson 2010). Aschauer (1989) finds that a 10% increase in the public capital stock increases output in the private sector by 3.3%. Other scholars also find significantly higher rates of return from public investment (Lynde and Richmond 1992; Munnell 1990, 1992). Henderson and Kumbhakar (2006) find that 10% increase in a state's stock of public infrastructure increases total economic output in the state by 1.2%. Munnell (1990b) finds that an additional $1,000 per capita spent for public infrastructure in the initial period contributes roughly 0.2% to the average annual rate of employment growth. She also finds that the major impacts on output from public capital come from investments in highways and water and sewer systems. She concludes,

"The evidence seems overwhelming that public capital has a positive impact on private sector output, investment, and employment" (Munnell 1990b, 26).

There are relatively few studies on the effect of public capital investment at the regional (metropolitan) level. Eberts (1986) finds that the marginal product of public capital is positive. In another work, Eberts (1990) estimates the relationships between local public capital stock and regional manufacturing output, inputs, and productivity. He finds that 1% increase in public capital stock is associated with a 0.49% increase in total factor productivity (i.e., the increased productivity not accounted for by increases in the amount of labor and private capital) and a 1% increase in public capital stock is associated with 0.70–0.76% increase in growth of combined inputs. Haughwout (2002) finds that the stock of public capital, including roads, parks, sewer systems, and public buildings, not only raises productivity but it also has important consumption benefits in a region.

Eberts and Duffy-Deno (1991) estimate the effect of public capital stock on regional income growth and find both public investment and public capital stock have a positive and statistically significant effect on per capita personal income. A 10% increase in public investment outlays increases personal income per capita by 0.37% or 1.1%, depending on the model specification. Also, a 10% increase in pubic capital stock is associated with 0.94% increase in per capita personal income. This study suggests that public capital stock is an important input into the regional production process. Improving public capital has long-run consequences for enhancing a region's productivity, and thus its competitive advantage.

To summarize, over the short-term public infrastructure expenditures can have a positive effect on a regional economy through the immediate employment of workers in constructing the infrastructure and the consequent multiplier effects. However, as a means of responding to a shock, such investments will have the desired short-term effect only if made quickly, which suggests they must be made through reprogramming already approved projects. Since the effects of these expenditures are likely to last no more than a year, they are not an effective response to chronic regional economic distress.

Over the long term, the strategy of investing public capital, especially infrastructure, seems to be an important component to a region's economy because it can alter the productive capacity of a region. In general, both theory and empirical research support the growth-enhancing effect of public infrastructure investment. However, marginal effects are likely to be lower, often considerably lower, for incremental investments in regions that already have serviceable levels of infrastructure than for those that clearly have poor infrastructure capacity. As Romp and Haan (2007, 33) conclude, "the larger the stock and the better its quality, the lower will be the impact of additions to this stock."

Amenity Improvement/Creation

Efforts to improve an area's amenities are a common approach by local officials and civic elites to encourage economic growth. Although some amenities are clearly not susceptible to policy intervention (e.g., climate, geographical location, topographical features), others may well be (e.g., downtown characteristics, architectural features, the arts, parks, nightlife, spectator sports, and recreational activities and facilities). Moreover, unlike efforts to increase economic activity and employment through other means, many of these amenities are within the direct control of local officials and are often supported by the local citizenry. Many local officials and members of the civic elite appear to believe that amenities are an important factor in attracting economic activity, and even if amenity creation or improvement should prove to play little or no role in economic recovery, an amenity strategy can provide public consumption goods that existing residents may value.

The Logic of Amenity Improvement/Creation as an Economic Development Policy

Amenity improvement/creation is often seen as a community development rather than an economic development tool. In order for it to be a successful regional economic development strategy, it would have to attract economic activity to the region that, in the absence of the amenity improvement, would not have located there. Thus, to affect the regional economy, downtown development, for example, would have to attract economic activity into the region, not simply redistribute it from other areas in the region to its downtown.

How might this occur? If new or improved amenities attract residents to the region who have the kind of skills that employers desire—particularly highly educated and highly skilled labor—then firms may find these regions more attractive as a place to locate and existing employers, such as the banks in Charlotte, would more easily be able to grow. This is the case not only because the desired labor will be available, but also because the existence of valued amenities will enable employers to pay lower wages to workers who enjoy an amenity premium by locating in the region. Furthermore, if new or improved amenities attract the kind of individuals who are more likely to be entrepreneurial, the region may spawn new small businesses that would not otherwise have been there.

It is worth noting that amenity creation as a regional economic development strategy is thus largely a story about in-migration (or deterring out-migration) with the expectation or hope that the improvement will attract people with skills that are either absent from the regional labor market or very scarce. But will amenity improvement/creation attract new in-migrants in the absence of available jobs? For regions in which jobs are available but qualified labor for those jobs is in short supply (e.g., Charlotte in our study), improving amenities was a strategy supported by existing firms concerned about filling positions. Would the same strategy work to attract in-migrants to an area of high unemployment and current job unavailability, such as Detroit?

Furthermore, the strategy may not benefit a region's existing residents. If in-migrants simply take jobs from existing residents[12] or if lower wage rates occur due to an increased supply of labor, do the results still qualify as regional economic development? If the strategy works to increase in-migration but additional jobs for existing residents do not follow, it is possible that the region's original residents may be worse rather than better off.

The popular version of an amenity-building approach to economic development is often associated with Richard Florida's (2002) *The Rise of the Creative Class*. Florida's book makes the argument that if cities (or regions) are to succeed, they must aim to attract the kind of workers who are central to the economy of the twenty-first century, namely creative types who can generate new ideas. In order to attract these workers, Florida argues, policymakers should focus on creating a hip downtown area that will cater to a Bohemian, gay-friendly crowd. He finds a positive relationship between his "creativity index" and regional economic growth. Glaeser (2005), however, is unconvinced, concluding that there is no evidence to suggest that there is anything to the argument for diversity or Bohemianism once human capital is controlled for. Yet investments in place making have gained in popularity.

Peck (2005), in a generally critical review of Florida's work, points out that the appeal of theories such as Florida's is that they put the goal of urban redevelopment in reach, even for "ordinary places." With such development theories, the policy prescriptions are concrete and easy to follow, with the delivery of most of the components of this strategy feasible within the parameters of local election cycles and fiscal constraints. The creative cities script is also mobilizing in that it is framed as an imperative: cities either remake themselves or they cannot thrive. Peck underscores the argument that government officials cannot create things like a local arts scene artificially and that such environments are often the product of private sector wealth.

Although the argument is enticing, a variety of questions still exists, the most obvious of which is whether the targeted "creative" population group or groups can make or stimulate more than a minor marginal contribution to the region's economy. Even if the processes claimed are actually at work, will they be as transformative as the creative class argument suggests? Scott (2006, 11) observes, "Any city that lacks a system of employment able to provide these individuals with appropriate and durable means of earning a living is scarcely in a position to induce significant numbers of them to take up permanent residence there, no matter what other encouragements policy makers may offer." Similarly, Storper (2013) argues that the location decisions of employers, which lead to the creation of jobs, rather than interregional differences in amenities, are ultimately responsible for the migration of workers between regions.

There are other concerns as well. An amenity is not an undifferentiated good. Glaeser, Kolko, and Saiz (2001, 28) identify four different types of local amenities that they term particularly critical: 1) a rich variety of consumer and service goods such as restaurants, theatres and performance venues, shops, and an attractive mix of social partners; 2) a region's aesthetics and physical setting, including climate and natural features; 3) good public services, particularly quality schools and low crime; and 4) speed or easy access to these amenities as well as to employment sites.

As this implies, there are many different kinds of amenities, some of which (art and music venues, for example) may be attractive to highly educated and skilled labor, while others (such as bowling alleys and bingo parlors) may not. Even within more highly educated groups, amenity preferences are likely to be heterogeneous. Markusen (2006) uses a study of artists to illustrate the tenuousness of the notion that artists will attract high-tech activity and suggests that it is misleading to lump together many of the different groups that Florida describes as making up the creative class, such as scientists, managers, engineers, and lawyers.

Even if amenity preferences of targeted creative class groups can be identified, can local public policy affect the presence of those amenities in the region? Some kinds of amenities, such as downtown development, may be relatively easily within the control of local or regional actors to improve, while others, such as climate or natural features, may be much less so or impossible to affect. In between are amenities such as the presence of ethnic restaurants, a "music scene," and/or cinemas featuring foreign and independent movies. These types of amenities are not usually the product of public policy (though the availability of low-rent or subsidized premises may make them more likely); instead they usually result from market demand. Scott (2006) and Markusen (2006) both question the direction of causality under the creative class hypothesis. If the answers to all these questions do not come out right, then "creative class" amenities is unlikely to work as a local economic development strategy in general, although they could work for particular industries in particular places (e.g., Charlotte).

What Is Known about the Effectiveness of Amenity Policies?

The existing literature is focused mostly on the first part of the question—do amenities attract in-migrants—rather than on the question of direct concern, which is does amenity improvement result in additional permanent economic activity. These migration studies are based on the relationship between changes in population, income, or wages, and housing prices and assume that the value of amenities or disamenities will be capitalized into wages and housing prices. Positive amenities will result in lower wages since workers will receive psychic benefit from the amenities that will compensate for lower wages. However, amenities will also be capitalized into higher housing prices, so that the existence of amenities will be reflected in both lower wages and higher housing prices. But productivity gains that provide no independent benefit to workers are also capitalized into higher wages. As a consequence, it is necessary to examine the movement of the three variables separately in order to assess the effect of amenities on population change (see, e.g., Beeson and Eberts 1989; Roback 1982). As Glaeser and Gottlieb (2006, 1277) explain: "High wages accompanied by stagnant housing prices and rising populations suggest an increase in productivity. Housing prices that rise faster than nominal wages suggest that consumption amenities are increasing."

These migration studies generally show that amenities that are broadly valued by many people do have a positive effect on population in-migration at the regional level (Graves 1980; Greenwood and Hunt 1989; Liu 1975; for reviews of the literature, see Gottlieb 1994; Greenwood 1985). Most of the empirical research literature on economic growth does not include amenity variables, either because the researchers do not consider them theoretically relevant within their model or because variables for regional level amenities are not available. The major exception is climate as measured by average temperature at some period or annual snow- or rainfall. Studies frequently find a strong relationship between pleasant climate and economic growth (see, e.g., Blumenthal, Wolman, and Hill 2009; Gabriel, Mattey, and Wascher 1999; Glaser and Saiz 2004; Green 2007). Although changing to a more pleasant climate is not available to economic development policymakers as an approach to improving their regions' prospects, these findings nonetheless indicate that amenities more under the control of policymakers may affect economic performance. As support for this, Carlino and Saiz (2008) employ tourist visits as a measure of a metropolitan area's amenities and find that employment growth was 2% higher for a metropolitan area with twice as many tourist visits as a similar metropolitan area.[13]

It is also possible that amenities might directly influence owners of businesses in making their location decisions. Evidence on the possibility of such an effect is available mostly from surveys of executives. Gottlieb (1994) reviews a number of surveys of business executives conducted between 1962 and 1992 on the choice of region or state. He observes, "Amenities are clearly viewed by executives as an important locational factor, with the aggregate phrase 'quality of life' frequently ranking in the top half of all factors" (1994, 271). He also notes that this preference is particularly strong among high-tech firms.

A policy that invests in amenities can reposition a specific part of the metropolitan area within a region's housing and labor market. This can result in tax revenues flowing to the benefiting municipal jurisdiction. It can have social benefits if service sector jobs are created that can be accessed by people with modest educational attainment who would otherwise be unemployed, although it can harm less-educated workers if it results in the displacement of higher paying manufacturing jobs from locations accessible to those workers.

However, an amenities-based policy is not likely to lead to region-wide economic development unless it facilitates the attraction or expansion of employers in a regional export industry. This is what happened in Charlotte, where downtown residential and retail development in the traditional central city attracted the young MBAs that the region's banks sought to employ. Cleveland's downtown development had very different consequences. In Cleveland the downtown population was 7,000 in 1970 and approached 15,000 in 2015. Less educated individuals could access service jobs due to public transportation access. Yet at the same time the region's population was largely stagnant and the city's overall population was declining. Although this repositioning of part of the city can have fiscal and social benefits, it is not generative economic development for the region.

In general we conclude that an amenities improvement/creation strategy is a tenuous one. We question in particular whether it will work for a region with current high rates of unemployment and low job availability and the extent to which the benefits of such a strategy will accrue to current residents or to in-migrants. Furthermore, there are many different kinds of amenities, and the literature provides little guidance on whether downtown development, the most common amenity policy undertaken by our case study regions, will have an important effect. Regardless, any likely impact of amenity improvements on the economy, given the lag between project inception and completion and the corresponding in-migration response, is likely to occur in the medium- or long-term rather than in the short-term and is thus more relevant for regions suffering from chronic distress than for those experiencing sudden shocks.

Organizational Restructuring

A common response to regional economic downturns or chronic distress among our regional case studies was to restructure or create new organizations for economic planning and development. In many cases the response involved expanding the scope of economic development activity so that it encompassed a region or larger area rather than simply a single local government. The goal of the realignment is to have the geographic scope of the organization better match that of the region's labor market.

The Logic of Organizational Restructuring as an Economic Development Policy

Although regional development institutions do exist in most regions, most economic development organizations, regardless of whether they are part of the formal government structure, a quasi-independent economic development financing entity, a private organization such as a local Chamber of Commerce, or a public-private association, are specific to an individual municipal or county unit of government. Their mission is to bring about economic growth and development within the boundaries of their individual jurisdiction, usually in order to take advantage of the fiscal returns of development, rather than in the region as a whole. Local economic development organizations thus reflect the same degree of fragmentation that exists in the entire region. Does this fragmentation adversely affect regional economic performance?

Logically such uncoordinated local government efforts might have three possible results. It might increase regional growth, if gains made by an individual jurisdiction do not come at the expense of another part of the region, but come instead from attracting economic activity from outside of the region or generating new activity from within the region. It might have no effect on regional growth, either because the efforts of these organizations are not successful even within their own boundaries or because their gain comes at the expense of the loss of some other jurisdiction within the region.[14] It might decrease regional growth, if the lack of a regional approach puts a region at a disadvantage compared to regions that do have such an approach or because regional resources are deployed to no effect.

Many scholars, planners, and regional advocacy groups contend that individual local government actions at best are likely to have little or no positive effect on the regional economy and are simply a wasteful expenditure of public funds. Some go further and argue that fragmentation serves to actually reduce regional economic growth and that reorganization to incorporate a more regional approach would enhance regional economic performance (see, e.g., Barnes and Ledebur 1998; Bartik 2003; Cigler 2008; Katz and Bradley 2013; Pastor, Dreier, Grigsby, and Lopez-Garza 2000; Peirce 1993; Rusk 1993). Bartik (2003) contends that local government independent economic development activity rather than regional activity is likely to result in overinvestment in activities that bring high fiscal returns to individual jurisdictions and sub optimal employment and income benefits to the region's residents and that for many economic development functions, coordinated regional efforts are likely to be both more efficient and more effective. He observes, "Marketing an area to attract new branch plants is more effective if done in one unified campaign. Job training programs will work better if they train individuals from throughout the labor market for jobs throughout the local labor market. The firms in a "cluster" will be located throughout a local area, and so cluster strategies will need to be areawide" (Bartik 2003, 39). For those economic development actors in a region who share this concern, the restructuring of existing economic development organizations (or the creation of new ones) to reflect a more regional interest is an obvious response.

There are reasons why the optimal structure for the best practice of metropolitan regional economic development includes regional as well as local organizations. Some market failures have a regional geographic scale while others have a local scale. The demand for an overarching regional organization is based on information failures and regional-scale externalities and public goods that are very difficult to overcome simply through cooperation of independent local jurisdictions within a region. Demand for information on labor markets, transportation infrastructure, utilities, sites, and the location of potential suppliers and customers is regional—roughly the geographic scope of the labor market. Industry clusters, with their accompanying externalities and industry-specific public goods, are often regional in scale, or at least their geographic scale typically exceeds those of municipal and county governments.[15]

The implicit assumption underlying the logic of organizational restructuring is that 1) reorganization of these organizations or creation of new ones will result in making the existing activities of the set of development organizations more effective, and/or 2) newly or reorganized institutions will engage in activities different and more effective with respect to outcomes than the ones previously undertaken. It is seldom noted, however, that there may be costs as well as benefits from such reorganization. The literature on organizational restructuring suggests the possibility of short-term costs that may make organizational restructuring problematic for shock responses. Andrews and Boyne (2012, 297) note that the positive changes that accompany reorganization may take some time to emerge and that there are very real short-term "disruptive effects" that often accompany reorganization, including lower staff morale, greater organizational turnover and loss of organizational memory, work overload, and distraction from core service functions.

Moreover, theory suggests that fragmentation does not necessarily have to lead to zero-sum or even negative regional results. First, action by an individual local government may attract a firm and its jobs into the region that would, in the absence of the local activity, have located in some other region. This would be a gain to the entire region. Second, local governments engage in large numbers of formal and informal agreements with one or more other local governments, and these agreements may achieve common objectives.[16] Applying an institutional collective action framework, Feiock, Steinacker, and Park (2009) have explored, both theoretically and empirically, the conditions under which local governments will enter into arrangements with each other through interlocal agreements or joint ventures in pursuit of economic development. Such arrangements will be entered into when the benefits accrued through the arrangements exceed the transaction costs of establishing and maintaining them. In addition, some economists argue that fragmentation and the existence of many local governments result in competition among these local governments to provide services more efficiently and at lower tax costs (for a review of the literature, see Oates and Schwab 1991; Wallace 2008).[17] As we discussed in the earlier section on tax incentives, if a region can lower its average tax cost without lowering its level or quality of services, it will have a competitive advantage over other regions.

What Is Known about the Effectiveness of Organizational Restructuring?

Existing empirical literature does not provide much guidance. There is little other than descriptive case studies on organizational restructuring with respect to membership (see Hanson et al. 2010), board-staff relationships, or organizational decision-making processes. There is a small empirical literature that provides evidence on the effects of regionalism, one of the more common institutional and organizational restructuring strategies pursued (and advocated) in the regions in our case studies. Nelson and Foster (1999, 310; see also Foster 2001) argue that prior case studies and aggregate studies show that "[e]mpirical evidence linking governance structures to income growth is scant and inconclusive." Foster (2001) concludes that the theory and empirical evidence on the effects of regionalism in achieving such metropolitan goals as equity, environmental sustainability, and regional economic growth paints a mixed and inconclusive picture. Swanstrom (2002, 484) agrees, observing that "the evidence that fragmentation hurts regional economic development is both weak and mixed."

Several studies look directly at the effect of fragmentation on regional economic outcomes such as employment, income, or firm births. Some studies find that fragmentation reduces regional economic growth (Hamilton, Miller, and Paytas 2004; Paytas 2001), but Stansel (2005) finds that fragmentation increases regional income growth. Carr and Feiock (1999) look at a specific type of regionalism, city-county consolidation, to test whether this rather extreme form of reducing fragmentation affects development patterns and efforts to attract new business to a metropolitan area and find no significant impact of consolidation on the number of business establishments. Others find that the results are sensitive to the way that fragmentation is measured. Grassmueck and Shields (2010) find that when local governments per capita is used as the measure of fragmentation, the more fragmented a metropolitan area is, the lower its regional employment growth, whereas using a measure that adjusts for the relative importance of various local governments produces results showing that fragmentation increases regional employment (see also Nelson and Foster 1999).

Despite the prevalence and importance of jurisdictionally based economic development institutions, regional economic development institutions do exist. Nearly all regions have one or more regional public institutions with some economic development responsibilities (usually planning and data collection), often tied to federal program requirements or funded through small amounts of federal money (such as Economic Development Administration-funded economic development districts). However, these regional organizations often are not capable of, nor are they designed for, undertaking major regional economic development initiatives or bringing disparate actors in a region together in such an endeavor, although they may offer a forum for regionally focused policymakers to meet. There are also generalist regional organizations such as metropolitan area Councils of Governments (COGs), for which regional economic development may be a peripheral or one of many regional concerns, and Metropolitan Planning Organizations (MPOs), whose dominant concern is area-wide transportation planning and which have some degree of power under federal law to affect the regional transportation system, a system that has an important impact on regional economic performance.[18]

Of much greater relevance are regional private or public-private partnerships or collaborative organizations devoted to economic development, such as the ones in place in several of our case study regions. Some of these organizations are general in nature and some are devoted to specific clusters (Olberding 2002a, 2002b, 2009). Such regional organizations take a variety of forms, including private sector organizations such as regional chambers of commerce, business-led CEO organizations, public-private associations (which might include non-profits, foundations, and major regional education and medical institutions), trade or cluster-related organizations, and loose coalitions of local public sector organizations.

Does the existence of these economic development partnerships and collaborations at the regional level improve regional economic performance? Would "stronger" regional development institutions make a difference?

The lack of strong public economic development institutions at the regional level and the difficulty in constructing and implementing regional policy across a range of jurisdictions and other institutions pursuing their own interests is widely recognized. These are themes noted not only in the literature, but by many major actors with a stake in the region such as leaders of major businesses and business organizations, foundations, universities, medical institutions, newspapers, and utilities. (We heard this refrain frequently during some of our interviews, especially in the Detroit region, which is relatively well-known for its intraregional animosities.) That leading actors recognize this as a problem is manifested by the increase in regional organizations and partnerships for economic development over the past several decades. Olberding (2002a) identifies 191 regional partnerships for economic development (groups formed voluntarily to enhance the economy of a multijurisdictional area) that existed in U.S. metropolitan areas as of 1998. Based on her survey of these organizations, she finds that the number of such organizations quadrupled from the 1970s through the 1990s. The average size of the governing board of these regional partnerships was twenty-seven, consisting of an average of eighteen members from businesses or chambers of commerce, six from city or county government, and three from other sectors.

Unfortunately, there is virtually no empirical research on the extent to which regional economic development organizations of any kind affect economic outcomes. The exception is Olberding (2009), who finds that the existence of a regional partnership organization, the number of such organizations, and the age of the organization were all separately positively related to the rate of a region's employment change between 1984 and 1996, but not to its income change. However, the effect sizes are small.

As we observed in our case study regions, one of the most immediate responses to economic shock or distress was the creation of new regional economic development organizations and/or the restructuring of existing ones. The question regional actors were addressing is what *kind* of regional organizations and what type of activities are most likely to enhance economic performance (we note that if regional activity is not effective in any case, then organizational creation or restructuring at the regional level is mostly symbolic). Differences in regional economic development effectiveness could relate to either or both aspects of the organizational structure and of the activities undertaken by regional organizations.

With respect to organizational structure—the number of organizations, their membership, the geographical area covered, the size and expertise of the staff, organizational decision making rules, and many other organizational aspects (i.e., the kinds of decisions that regional actors were dealing with)—there is almost nothing other than anecdotal information and reflection on the prior experience in the region that yields information on what kind of organizational setting and structure, if any, is likely to lead to more effective regional economic performance. Ha, Lee, and Feiock (2010) examine the effect of organizational network structure on economic development, but their dependent variable is the city's economic performance, not the region's. Nonetheless, their findings are suggestive: mixed organizational networks (networks connecting local government, quasi-governments, and nonprofit organizations) and private-oriented organizational networks (networks connecting local government with private sector organizations) are both more significantly associated with better economic performance than are public-oriented organizational networks (networks connecting only public sector organizations).

One way of assessing the possible effectiveness of regional economic development is to ask what regional economic development organizations do and whether these activities have been linked to economic growth. Even considering that policy activities are likely to vary across regional economic development organizations, there is very little information available on the most common kinds of activities in which they engage. Unfortunately, the only systematic information on this comes from research that is more than fifteen years old and not focused on all regional economic development activities. In her 1998 survey of regional partnerships (reported in Olberding 2002b, 2009), Olberding finds that the most common set of activities engaged in relate to marketing—publication of brochures and information gathering and dissemination. Other activities that more than half of these regional organization engaged in included developing a strategic plan, sponsoring workforce development programs, assisting businesses in acquiring tax incentives and acquiring regulatory relief, participating in trade shows, and lobbying government for infrastructure and workforce development programs. Nearly half also sponsored entrepreneurial assistance programs, a percentage very likely to have increased since then given the recent focus on entrepreneurship. Less than 20% were involved in funding infrastructure assistance.

In short, it appears that these regional alliances engaged in very traditional economic development activities with a focus on marketing and assisting businesses to locate within the region. Unlike local development agencies and private organizations in some other regions (e.g., the Chambers of Commerce in Scranton and Wilkes Barre, Pennsylvania; see Friedhoff, Wial, and Wolman 2011), they did not appear to—or have the legal authority to—offer tax incentives, grants, loans, land write-downs, and most other forms of subsidy. Thus, the extent to which regional economic development organizations and their activities are likely to be successful rests to a substantial extent on whether their activities are likely to create or enhance the networks among actors in the region or nurture other economic initiatives, that is the subject dealt with in the other sections of this chapter.

Despite the lack of evidence that regional organizations have had an important impact on economic growth, the restructuring of the set of regional economic development institutions or creation of new ones as a means of responding to economic shocks and long-term distress is hardly surprising. These are, after all, the institutions presumably responsible for economic performance and that the public and elected officials look to for accomplishing that end. The actors in the regions and at the state level who are committed to regional economic growth and who have established, participated in, and resourced the regional development institutions are likewise searching for an effective response. Their responsibility is not so much with policy (likely to be left more to the professional staff and the organizations' boards) as with the nature of the organizations themselves and their interactions with each other. If they perceive that the response of the existing set of institutions is not having or likely to have the desired effect, then institutional change is an immediate—indeed, often the only—response that these leaders can engage in. Indeed, Olberding (2002b) finds that economic need, as indicated by low rates of employment, is associated with the formation of regional economic development partnerships, a finding she notes is consistent with several case studies that she cites. However, it is difficult to avoid the conclusion that organizational restructuring is at least as much a manifestation and recognition of regional economic problems as it is a solution to them.

In contrast to many of the other economic development policies examined in this chapter, organizational restructuring may be the quickest to be implemented in times of economic shock or distress. However, it remains a challenge to create or reform such organizations at the regional (as opposed to the jurisdiction) level and there is little evidence to support (or counter) the effectiveness of such initiatives. Although reorganization may be a low-cost, symbolic way for policymakers to signal their commitment to stabilizing the local or regional economy, it often may simply function as a type of window dressing, neglecting more substantial and effective but also difficult policy changes.

Leadership

One of the most frequent motifs we heard in our interviews was the importance of leadership. We were frequently told that the success of many of the other strategies that regional actors undertake to improve their economic outcomes relies, in part, on leadership from the public sector, the business elite, foundations, and/or nonprofit groups and community organizations.

THE LOGIC OF LEADERSHIP AS AN ECONOMIC DEVELOPMENT PROGRAM. In public discussion, in our interviews, and in much of the research as well as popular literature, the importance of effective leadership as a key component of a successful economic development strategy is frequently stressed. But if leadership is a key factor in generating regional economic growth, what are the linkages that make it so? In order to begin to make sense of this question, some important prior questions need to be answered, the first of which is "What is meant by leadership?" Increasingly leadership has come to be seen less in terms of leaders and followers and more in terms of creating a vision and/or collaborating and negotiating among competing visions (see, for example, Kellerman 2012; Van Vugt, Hogan, and Kaiser 2008). In the context of regional economic development, Stimson, Stough, and Salazar (2009, 32) identify several different definitions and settle on leadership as "an expression or result of collective action." DeSantis and Stough (1999, 41) define leadership as "the tendency of the community to collaborate across sectors to enhance the economic performance or economic environment of its region."

If leadership is important for achieving economic growth, the term would seem to imply bringing together the appropriate actors in the region to craft and implement a strategy that will bring about economic growth.[19] Appropriate actors are those that can commit resources to craft and implement the strategy. Those resources include financial resources, expertise, the ability to bring about any required public sector action through laws and regulations, and sufficient community-wide support to assure that opposition will not prevent the leaders from moving ahead. Leadership may thus fail to be effective in bringing about economic development if the strategy is poorly conceived in that the measures taken are not able or sufficient to bring about economic development, because the strategy is poorly implemented, because it lacks widespread community support, or because it is poorly resourced.

In terms of regional economic development, "leadership" can refer to the actions of a public official or officials, a private individual, a group of individuals, one or more organizations, or a group of individuals and organizations who lead efforts to craft and implement a strategy that will bring about economic growth. The task of regional economic development is immediately complicated by a lack of formal government institutions at the regional level and the weakness of much of the quasi-formal and informal regional institutions; furthermore, given the competition among jurisdictions within the region, it is also unlikely that officials in local government will alone undertake the primary regional leadership roles. (This is why leadership, defined as orchestrating collaboration among diverse groups, may be especially important for regional economic development in the United States.) Therefore, regional leadership often is provided through nonpublic regional organizations or associations or more informal collaborative action among groups in the region. It is important to have the support of local public officials as well, since they have the power to commit public resources and to regulate land use and other actions critical for successful implementation of a regional strategy, vision, or plan.

Regional leadership appears to be particularly important when time is taken into consideration. Crafting and implementing an economic growth strategy is often a long-term enterprise, at least in terms of its expected payoff; there are likely to be difficulties if leadership has short-term time perspectives or is not committed for a substantial period of time. The relevant time horizon for the political calculations of elected officials is measured in electoral cycles and in most cases is unlikely to exceed a decade (and usually much less). In addition, elected officials commonly are less committed—or even opposed—to the plans of their predecessors and so may not expend the necessary political capital or budgetary resources to support the plan or strategy.

It is also likely that regional leadership needs may differ depending on the economic circumstances and the policy issues and options. Task-oriented leaders are effective where interests converge, while people-oriented leaders are more effective when the situation requires persuading people with diverging interests. Especially of concern to readers of this book, the traits that make a leader effective in responding to a sudden economic shock, such as a flood or industry-specific threat, may be different than those needed in a leader addressing long-term chronic distress.

Business executives historically have played major roles in urban and regional economic development (Hanson et al. 2010). While providing their own time and resources (including money and personal connections) to support regional economic development efforts, these individuals also provide staff and financial resources for planning and implementing major economic development efforts and sometimes funding of specific projects. However, changing corporate environments (e.g., corporate takeovers, movement or consolidation of headquarters operations, and an increasing emphasis on maintaining returns in globally competitive markets) have reduced the propensity and opportunity for publicly held corporations to play important leadership roles in civic enterprises such as economic growth efforts (Hanson et al. 2010). Their leadership role is now often fulfilled by foundations and nonprofit institutions such as major universities, hospitals, and research institutions. Although these institutions may have fewer financial resources to commit, they are more likely to have a stronger commitment to engaging in collaborative activities due both to previous collaborative experiences (whether informally or by contract with funders or other regional service providers or recipients) and to their relative inability or implausibility to move their operations out of the region.

This discussion still leaves unclear what the characteristics required for effective leadership in pursuit of economic growth are and whether those characteristics are innate, a product or regional cultures or institutions, or can be taught. In short, can effective leadership be promoted or developed (and, if so, how) as part of an economic development strategy as opposed to taken as given? Such a strategy would require the ability to identify and/or develop effective leaders or leadership-generating institutions. If this kind of effective leadership cannot be produced, than the argument that leadership is an important if not critical factor in successful regional economic growth and development is not very helpful as a policy prescription.

WHAT IS KNOWN ABOUT THE EFFECTIVENESS OF LEADERSHIP? Although leadership may well be an essential component for regional economic success, we have yet to find a body of empirical work that measures leadership and evaluates its role in economic outcomes at the local or regional level.[20] Nonetheless, a large body of case study literature attests to the importance of leadership. For example, Judd and Parkinson (1990) present a volume of twelve case studies of cities in North America and Europe, which examine the role of leadership in local economic responses of cities impacted by the restructuring of the global economy. Similarly, in a study financed by the U.S. Economic Development Administration (EDA), the Council on Competitiveness examined how five regions developed effective regional economic development strategies. They found that regional leadership, including the need for leaders from the private sector who recognized the need for regional collaboration, was a key component. Erickcek et al. (2008, 24) surveyed EDA field representatives and staff and found that "strong organizational leadership" was the most important of thirteen factors that influence the success of public works projects with 56.8% of respondents deeming it "essential" and another 32.4% calling it "very important."

One difficulty for leadership researchers is separating leadership qualities from outcomes—the tendency is to identify a good leader with the results. Nearly all of the literature that makes the case for the importance of leadership suffers from two critical defects related to this problem. It begins with "successful" economic development efforts, in which an identifiable leader or set of leaders is visible and concludes that the leaders and their characteristics played an important role in bringing about that success. Conversely, the literature sometimes focuses on unsuccessful efforts and makes the assumption that leadership was one reason for the failure (possibly for being unable to overcome other challenges, such as political infeasibility or resource constraints). In short, there is an unsupported assumption that the success would not have occurred without the leadership or the failure would not have occurred with better leadership.

Equally important, since these studies are usually analyses of single cases chosen to focus on specific economic outcomes, they cannot be generalized. Certain leadership characteristics (or lack thereof) may have an effect in one region but these traits may not be reproducible in other regions (essentially, the "so what?" question). Without such comparisons, it is virtually impossible to know the importance of leadership and leadership characteristics. If the same types of leaders, with similar characteristics and engaged in the same type of collaborative activity, are engaged in economic development efforts that failed as well as those that succeeded, than those characteristics are evidently not sufficient to bring about success. Even if the same leadership characteristics are present in failed as well as successful efforts, it does not necessarily mean that leadership is not important. It may instead mean that importance of leadership is contingent upon other factors, particularly the presence of adequate resources.

Obtaining good leadership is only a reasonable strategy if one can identify who is a good leader or which institutions produce good leaders. Unfortunately, there is a wide literature filled with many different conceptions of the attributes of leaders. Kellerman (2012, 193) identifies various attempts to distinguish and structure leadership qualities, including her own "seven essential competencies," Hill and Lineback's "3 imperatives for becoming a great leader," Gandz et al.'s "five things" good leaders do, Kouzes and Posners's "five key leadership practices," and many others.

Case studies show us examples of effective leadership but the context in which these people and organizations succeeded may be as critical to their success as the attributes of the leaders (i.e., they were in the right place at the right time). Furthermore, the few efforts in the literature to assess the effectiveness of activities resulting from collaboration among civic leaders have focused on outputs rather than outcomes. Although the activity may have been carried out (e.g., a crime prevention plan, an educational reform measure, or a city marketing scheme), the question whether the outcome to which these activities were presumably directed (reduced crime, improved educational performance, the attraction of more tourists, respectively) is seldom addressed with regard to the role of effective leadership.

Given the importance attributed to leadership, building leaders for regional economic development might be a reasonable long-term strategy if one could identify the necessary characteristics and how to produce such leaders. In fact, there are many such leadership development programs, but with the difficulty of even defining leadership or what effective leadership consists of, little reason exists to believe that these programs are producing effective regional leaders for economic growth and development. A book by Barbara Kellerman, the executive director of Harvard University's Center for Public Leadership, asks whether leadership can be taught and answered, "the truth is, we don't know" (2012, 177). Although more than $50 billion is spent annually on the industry of leadership training, "we don't have much better an idea of how to grow good leaders than we did a 100 or even a 1000 years ago" (xiv). In addition, even if these leadership development programs were to "work," it would also be necessary for those who participate to remain active in the region, rather than seeking more lucrative returns (e.g., salary, public role) elsewhere in order for the region to capture the benefit from the program.

Our research, as well as other research examining regional economic development, recognizes the importance of leadership. Yet the feasibility of pursuing leadership development as a regional strategy remains unknown.

Conclusion

Our examination in chapters 5 and 6 of the various strategies applied by regional actors as they attempt to respond to economic shocks and to emerge from chronic economic distress does not yield any magic bullets. The strategies differ both in terms of likely effectiveness, and, the time frame over which they are likely to have an impact. We were able to identify more strategies that were likely to be effective in the long term, as responses to chronic economic stress, than in the short term, as responses to shock.

None of the strategies appear to have a sufficiently large impact in the short term to have an identifiable effect on successful recovery from an economic shock. The exception is public works infrastructure spending as a means of providing construction and related employment through reprogramming of already planned projects or borrowing to fund new projects that can be quickly implemented. In the short term, policies that can have a desirable impact are those that attempt to cope with and cushion the effect of shocks on residents and communities. These include temporary income support and short-term increases in providing social services, including mental health, housing aid, and homelessness assistance. They also include the maintenance of an adequate "rainy day" fund for local government budgets in order to enable continued provision of important local services and avoid the necessity of serious expenditure and service reductions in the face of increased needs. It is also likely the case that, however politically difficult it might be, state and local governments would do less harm to the economies of their region by raising taxes and maintaining spending during an economic downturn than by cutting spending to match reduced tax revenues.

Long-term chronic economic distress, sometimes triggered by economic shocks, is a different matter. Our review of the empirical literature evaluating the various strategies and policies, combined with our own analysis of the logic undergirding the various strategies, does suggest that many of them may have a positive effect in the medium- and longer-term and thus can play a role in assisting regions coping with chronic distress. In particular, human capital strategies—such as improvements in the preschool, elementary, secondary, and community college formal education systems—can play an important role in improving an area's labor force skills and thus contributing to an area's economic growth. Although the literature also suggests that another human capital approach—"second chance" workforce training programs—does have positive effects, these effects are likely to be more modest and in any case are likely to occur only in the context of economic growth; they are unlikely to stimulate growth. Investment or reinvestment in major components of the region's public infrastructure (airports, bridges, transshipment facilities), particularly if the areas public infrastructure is lacking or of a low quality to start with, can also have a major impact. Firm technical assistance programs, programs directed toward stimulating entrepreneurship, and possibly state-level tax incentives, if well-thought out and constructed, show evidence of being able to yield positive, though modest, effects.

Some of the "strategies" that have received the most attention seem to hold less promise. There is little evidence that amenity improvement strategies on their own actually "work" as an economic development tool, despite the existence of a logic that, under certain circumstances, seems sound. At best, amenity strategies may be necessary for the growth of particular industries in particular places (e.g., the banking industry in Charlotte), and that growth may be an important contributor to regional economic growth in some of those places (as it was in Charlotte). However, amenity strategies are not a universal recipe for sustained economic growth.

Organizational change is a near universal response to economic shock and/or long-term economic distress. However, it is difficult to make broad generalizations about what kind of organizational structure is likely to "work" better than others, although in the context of a specific existing structure in a region it may be possible to identify that the existing organizational structure is not working and to put in place sensible changes to produce better performance. In terms of geographic scope, many economic development organizations are becoming more regional and, although this certainly makes good sense conceptually, the existing empirical literature is mixed in terms of its effect.

One of the most frequent prescription we heard as a lever for improving regional economies is the need for improved "leadership." Unfortunately, we find this prescription nearly useless in application. Good leadership is almost certainly contextual; leadership qualities necessary for one kind of situation will differ from another kind. We have even seen evidence that the leadership necessary for dealing with an economic shock is different from that that successfully deals with chronic distress, so that a "good" leader for one situation might be a "bad" leader in another. Not only do we not know the particular characteristics necessary for good leadership, we are unlikely to know how to produce them even if we could identify them. Under almost any conception, leadership without sufficient resources is likely to yield disappointing results. Although we believe good leadership is important—perhaps even vital—for economic revitalization, we do not think the constant repetition of its need or importance is going to produce it.

SUMMARY AND POLICY IMPLICATIONS

Can Regional Economic Development Policies Make a Difference?

The puzzle that we set out to solve in this book is why some regions are resilient in the face of economic adversity, while others are not. To address that puzzle we conducted research to explore the extent to which economic regions are indeed resilient in the face of adversity; the ways in which they are resilient, and the factors that underlie their resilience. We considered two different, though sometimes related, forms of economic adversity: shocks to regional (metropolitan) economies and long term chronic economic stress.

We also tried to examine and assess strategies that regions have employed in an effort to be resilient. Can intentional local public actions and policies help regional economies to recover from economic adversity? If the answer is yes, such strategies and policies could then become part of intentional economic development planning and practice at the regional level.

It is first important to set the question of the effect of intentional local and regional strategy and public policy on economic adversity in context. A metropolitan area economy consists primarily of private firms that exist in a market economy and compete in regional, national, and/or international markets. The strategic decisions made by important individual firms in the area, along with the ability of entrepreneurs to create successful new firms there, are the primary factors in determining a region's economic resilience or lack thereof. Individual firm decisions with respect to the introduction of new products, markets, technologies, marketing strategies, and so on, that either position firms for success in a changing economic environment or make failure more likely, are therefore critical. The aggregate of these private sector decisions by businesses in the region plays the major role in determining area resilience. Public policies, including fiscal, monetary, tax, subsidy, and regulatory policies, among others, can have large impacts on those decisions. Local and regional economic development policies are less important.

This does not mean that intentional public economic development policies and actions at the local and regional levels have no effect. Indeed, if money and time currently spent on public sector or quasi-public sector economic development activities reveals the beliefs of government and business leaders alike, then the answer to the question of whether such policies have an important effect is a resounding yes. Intentional economic development policies, planning, marketing, and investments are perceived to generate net benefits for a region. The extent to which these are truly net economic benefits is not known. However, the evidence that is reviewed in this book gives us pause and leads us to a much more nuanced and cautious set of conclusions about the extent to which local or regional economic development activities can help regions recover from economic shocks or long-term stagnation.

Our results show that in most cases metropolitan regional economies recover from shocks within a relatively short period of time, regardless of whether any explicit economic development policies are put in place to help them do so. Even in the Great Recession 79% of the 331 metropolitan areas that were adversely affected were resilient, that is, they returned to their prior eight year growth path within four years of the recession's onset. But there are enough cases of regions stuck in Myrdal-like negative path dependencies to pay attention to the importance of economic development policy as a means of promoting regional economic recovery. Where is the balance struck? How can we advise the formation of regional economic development policy and the practice of economic development?

Our findings provide some answers. Using our operational definitions of shock-resistance, resilience once adversely affected by a shock, and nonresilience, we found that from 1978 up to the onset of the Great Recession metropolitan regions were resistant to nearly half (47%) of the employment shocks that they experienced and more than half of the gross product shocks (56%). In other words, they did not experience a serious economic downturn as a result of them (see figure 7.1).

The Great Recession, however, overwhelmed metropolitan economies; more than 90% of these were adversely affected by the national economic downturn. When regions were adversely affected by the employment shocks they were resilient 65% of the time—they returned to their previous growth path within a four-year period. They were even more resilient to gross product shocks that adversely

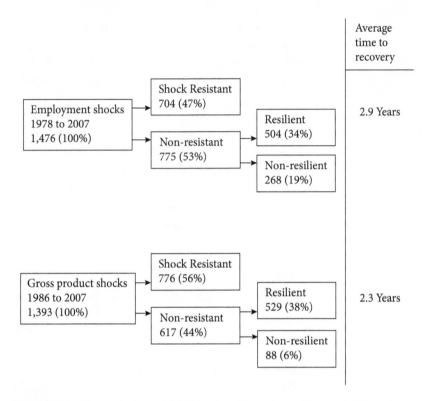

FIGURE 7.1 The experience of U.S. metropolitan economies to employment and gross product shocks. Percentages are the percent of all shocks in 361 U.S. metropolitan areas. Source for response to employment shocks: Table 1.2: Employment shocks by type and their effect on regions. Source for gross product shocks: Table 1.3: GMP shocks by type and their effects on regions.

affected them, recovering within a four year time period 86% of the time. Only 6% of all gross product shocks resulted in a nonresilient response. Nonresilience to employment shocks occurred in nearly 20% of the occurrences.

Resilience rates during the Great Recession were essentially similar to those during the prior period. From 1978 to 2007, the resilience rate for metropolitan economies that suffered gross metropolitan product (GMP) downturns as a result of a national economic downturn was 79%. The rate was exactly the same for metropolitan economies during the Great Recession. However, it took longer for regions to return to GMP resilience during the Great Recession, an average of 2.7 years compared to 2.3 years from 1978 to 2007.

Metropolitan regions returned to their prior *rates* of employment and GMP growth more rapidly than they returned to their previous *levels.* They also returned to their prior rates of GMP growth more rapidly than to their prior rate of employment growth, suggesting that resilience to shock was led initially by productivity gains, with employment gains following later.

We found no "magic bullets" that both insulate metropolitan area economies from the harmful impacts of economic downturns and help them recover quickly from downturns. We did find that certain characteristics of metropolitan regions and their economies are associated with shocks, shock-resistance, and resilience, although these relationships were complex and sometimes counterintuitive. For example:

- A region with a poorly educated population is more likely to suffer from an employment downturn, but is also more likely to be resilient in recovering from such a downturn.
- A high percentage of regional employment in the manufacturing sector makes it more likely to suffer from an employment downturn as a result of a shock, but more likely to quickly recover.
- Income inequality made a region *less* likely to have its GMP adversely affected by a shock, but more likely to be resilient and to return to its prior growth rate more rapidly.
- Income inequality made a region *less* likely to be resilient in terms of employment.

Other results are consistent with the commonly held beliefs. Export industry diversity, for example, made a region less likely to experience a shock and more likely to be resistant to a shock when it occurred, at least with respect to employment. The right-to-work variable, to the extent it measured wage flexibility and/or business climate, was positively related to regional resilience to both employment and GMP shocks.

During the 1978–2007 period, about one-quarter of U.S. metropolitan regions experienced periods of chronic distress. We define chronic distress as prolonged periods of slow growth relative to that of the national economy. Some of these cases are associated with an immediate or delayed response to an economic shock that is captured in our data: nearly 30% periods of chronic employment distress directly followed an economic shock to which the region was not resilient. Others were on courses of prolonged slow-growth that might have been triggered by an earlier shock that predate our data or are associated with an event that is not captured in our data (see figure 7.2). These later cases are involved in a negative path dependency.

A bit less than half (47%) of all of the metropolitan regions that experienced chronic employment distress recovered. The good news is that despite the fact that they experienced serious economic hardship, it did not last forever. Nonetheless, there were some regions that continued to be mired in chronic distress.

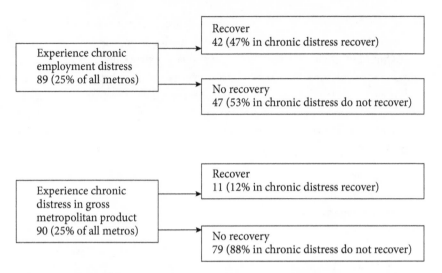

FIGURE 7.2 The experience of U.S. metropolitan economies experiencing chronic distress. Number reported is number of metropolitan areas that meet the condition from 361 U.S. metropolitan areas. Source: Table 2.1: Regional differences in the number of chronically distressed metropolitan regions.

Forty-seven metropolitan regions did not recover from chronic employment distress during the time period covered in our analysis. Thus, 13% of all U.S. metropolitan regions were involved in prolonged periods of chronic employment distress that had not ended as the nation entered the Great Recession. Twelve regions experienced ten or more consecutive years of chronic employment distress and did not emerge from that condition during the time frame of our study. (An additional thirteen regions experienced fewer than ten years of continuous distress but were still experiencing chronic distress at the cut-off point of our data.)

The results were less encouraging for metropolitan regions that experienced prolonged periods of slow growth in gross metropolitan product relative to the national economy. Again, one-quarter of all metropolitan areas experienced periods of prolonged below normal growth in GMP. What differs from chronic employment distress is in the proportion that recovers: only 12% recovered. Seventy-nine of the 90 metropolitan regions that experienced chronic slow growth in GMP did not recover between 1986 and 2007.

Nearly all of the chronically distressed regions that *were* resilient experienced positive restructuring where restructuring was defined as a change in the region's industrial structure so that its portfolio was better positioned for growth ten years after the onset of chronic distress than it was before. Resilience through restructuring occurs when existing resources are redeployed or adapted to new sources of demand; in other words, the product portfolio of the traded sector of the economy changes substantially as a response to decline.

Some of the regional characteristics associated with chronic distress are similar to those of our shock findings, while others are not. Regional chronic economic distress in terms of both employment and output was associated with low educational attainment in the region at the onset. Factor cost explanations also received some support. Controlling for regional industrial composition, high wages per worker were associated with the onset of chronic-distress. Regions whose population was less than 1 million and that were far away from a metropolitan area of that size were also more likely to experience chronic distress. Income inequality, in the form of a large gap between workers at the 80th percentile and workers at the 20th percentile was positively associated with the onset of distress. Economic diversification, often cited as a panacea for regional health, was unrelated to whether a region experienced chronic distress.

However, the determinants of emergence from chronic economic distress were not always the converse of those that predisposed regions to enter a chronic distress period. For regions that experienced chronic distress, those with a higher proportion of their employment in manufacturing were less likely to emerge (be resilient) from GMP distress, but were more likely to be resilient from employment distress (i.e., return to rates of total employment growth near to or above the national rate). The stickiness of high wages mattered as well: the longer high wages relative to other areas persisted, the longer it took a region to emerge from chronic distress. Income inequality, while, as noted above, appeared to predispose a region to chronic distress, was also positively associated with recovery—the greater the extent of income inequality the more likely a region was to be resilient to both employment and GMP chronic distress. And the number of major export industries, while not a factor in preventing a period of chronic distress, was positively related to resilience from GMP chronic distress.

Our case studies failed to find any local or regional public policies put in place during the shock period that were likely to have affected whether a region recovered from a shock or how long it took to do so. (National policies, such as the federal economic stimulus and assistance to the Detroit Three automakers during and after the Great Recession probably had much greater effects on the recovery of our case study regions from that shock but the full effects of these policies had not occurred during the time period of our visits to the regions.) Strategies and policies that were put in place, expanded, or revised in the case study regions were sometimes motivated by shocks but were mainly longer term efforts that could not have been expected to prevent shocks or cushion their negative impacts. These strategies included marketing and recruitment, business tax incentives; industry targeting and cluster policy; technical assistance to firms; entrepreneurial assistance and promotion; human capital, education, and workforce development; infrastructure improvement; amenity improvement and creation; restructuring of economic development organizations; and leadership

While none of the strategies are likely to have an identifiable effect on successful recovery from an economic shock, some of them are more likely to have a positive effect in terms of emergence from chronic economic distress. Human capital strategies, especially improvements in the preschool, elementary and secondary, and community college formal education systems, and, to a lesser extent, workforce development programs, may be able to help regions avoid or recover from chronic stagnation. Well-planned and well-implemented firm technical assistance programs, programs directed toward stimulating entrepreneurship, and possibly state-level tax incentives (if they do not result in reductions in public spending) also show modest promise in the context of chronic stagnation.

Public Policy and Economic Resilience

Within that context, what can we expect of explicit economic development policies as contributors to resilience? To address that question, we develop and utilize a temporal framework for assessing the effect of economic development activities. Economic development policy is usually envisioned as a time-undifferentiated menu of approaches, policies, tools, or practices from which economic development practitioners choose the mix appropriate to their situation. Evaluation of these actions, however, often ignores the time frame in which they are set. There are two time dimensions to this framework: implementation and impact.

The amount of time required to put different policies into a place will vary depending on legal changes that need to be undertaken, funding cycles, the number of jurisdictions and levels of government required to approve the policy, and the difficulty of building the program and the delivery team. Some policies, such as tax credit programs, may be put in place relatively quickly, even if their effect may not be felt for a substantial period of time. Other policies may take years to implement, though, once in place, their impact might—or might not be—nearly immediate (e.g., training programs).

The second dimension is time needed before the policy can either change the quality of a regional economic resource (such as the quality of labor or infrastructure) or affect the behavior of firms (such as a process or product innovation program). Policy effects are not instantaneous. In assessing policies, it is critical to do so within the time frame for which they can reasonably be expected to have a noticeable and significant impact.

This poses three critical distinct questions for policy makers facing economic shocks or chronic distress: (1) is the program expected to make a difference in economic performance? If there is no expectation that the program will make a difference, then putting it in place is a political or symbolic act though it may have economic or fiscal consequences; (2) when should the program be put in place; and (3), how long will it take for that program to have an impact?

We set forth a framework consisting of three time periods for examining economic development policies and their likely impact during each of these periods. Specific policies can be expected to have an effect within each of these time frames. In the short term the economic development activity that can be expected to have an impact, assuming the activity is effective, is limited mostly to managing, marketing, and increasing the utilization of the area's current factors of production, or what economic development practitioners frequently call assets or critical location factors—the current stock of labor, real estate, infrastructure, water, and access to customers and suppliers that are central to a firm's location or expansion decision. One focus of the near term is on transactions. An economic development policy or practice could help with the retention or expansion of existing firms and with marketing the area. Many of the activities revolve around providing information about the region's development assets and then lowering the risks and costs of engaging with the local development process, such as permitting, site approvals, utility hookups, and transportation access. A second focus of the near term is on promoting the full utilization of the region's assets, especially unemployed workers, by expanding the demand for the goods and services those assets produce. This generally involves increasing government purchases of goods and services, particularly through spending on infrastructure.

In the intermediate term programs and policies designed to improve the competitiveness of the region's existing firms and portfolio of products could be expected to have an effect. These include increasing research and development, increasing qualified workers through technical training through the community college system and vocational training programs, establishing cluster associations and relationships, and technical assistance around process and product innovation. Other activities include improving the quality and cost of transportation infrastructure and energy systems. If near-term activities are focused on selling a region's current stock of assets—land, labor, and infrastructure, then the intermediate term activities should result in improving the cost and quality of its stock of land, labor and infrastructure.

For the long-term, investments in education and major infrastructure components would be expected to have an impact as would the overall quality of public services and the efficiency with which they are delivered. Over the long run education, training, and infrastructure dominate the policy agenda.

Perhaps surprisingly to some readers, the literature review did not show that investing in place making, or amenities, had an impact on economic performance. Yet a good deal of professional and governmental activity focuses on providing and improving residential amenities. Our case studies in both Charlotte and Grand Forks indicated that amenities changed the position of downtown work and residential locations and, in the case of Grand Forks, its long-term viability under the reoccurring threat of floods. Can the literature and practice be reconciled?

Much of what is considered to be place making will not have regional economic development effects. There are two reasons for this. First, place-specific amenities will shift the competitive position of portions of the region in relation to other parts of the same region, redistributing economic activity within the region but not necessarily increasing the total amount of activity in the region. Second, community development investments are necessary preconditions for economic development. If an entire region is missing community assets, such as good schools, infrastructure, and residential amenities then development will not take place unless the region possesses assets that are in short supply elsewhere, such as natural resources or access to critical customers or suppliers. One should not confuse community development policies and investments with regional economic development policies and investments. In most developed regional economies community development is necessary but not sufficient for regional economic development to take place.

SHOCKS AND SHORT-TERM RESPONSES. Short-term outcomes in regional economies are principally determined by demand conditions in the markets for the traded, or export, products and services currently produced in the regional economy. In the short run the supply and quality of the factors of production are inelastic and the demand side of the market for the factors of production is derived from demand for the region's portfolio of export, or traded, goods and services. Consequently, most local policies designed to increase regional employment and income either take too long to put in place or too long to have an impact (or both) to make a difference in the short-term. While there are a few exceptions, they are difficult to put in place without federal or state assistance.

One such exception is public works infrastructure spending as a means of providing construction spending, since this will provide both construction-related employment and income, much of which will accrue to residents of the region.

Such a policy requires either reprogramming future planned spending for which funds are available into the present or raising new funds through bond sales, which in many states requires citizen approval through a referendum.

Increases in public sector employment are an even more direct way of providing short-term stimulus to the regional economy. However, economic downturns cause shortfalls in revenues for local governments throughout the region, resulting in layoffs of public employees, thus exacerbating the region's economic problems. Legal restrictions prevent most state and local governments from creating an operating budget with deficits. States can cushion the impact of a downturn by raising tax rates to keep tax revenue and, therefore, spending from falling, but it is often politically difficult for them to do so.

In addition, tax and expenditure limitations in many states, make increasing public employment as a short-term strategy impossible in those states unless funded by federal assistance—as was the case with American Recovery and Reinvestment Act, which permitted local governments to use funds received to support public employment during the Great Recession. Federal spending is not only critical to national economic recovery from a severe recession; it can also be critical to region-specific recoveries from region-specific downturns if the amount of spending can be calibrated to the depth of the regional downturn

Rather than economic development policies, the most important local policies to have in place as a short-term response to shocks are a social safety net that will be able to protect residents and serve as an automatic stabilizer to dampen the downturns that often result from economic shocks and a budgetary rainy day fund that will mitigate the need for sharp reductions in important local public services. These types of preshock planning should in principle be possible.

Our findings indicate that some types of regions are more prone to experience shocks and their adverse effects than others. In particular, regions that have high rates of manufacturing employment, lower levels of worker educational attainment, and less economic diversity are more at risk. Policymakers and planners in these types of regions should be particularly alert to the need to have adequate social and budgetary social nets in place. In addition, since our analysis indicates that regional economies that are more diverse are more likely to be shock-resistant, this suggests that prior strategies or policies that result in successful diversification have some protective value as a shield against the potential adverse impacts of shocks. However, that simply pushes the question back further—what kinds of policies will successfully result in economic diversification.

CHRONIC ECONOMIC DISTRESS AND MEDIUM-TERM POLICIES.
Long-term chronic economic distress, sometimes triggered by economic shocks, is a different matter. As time passes and it becomes possible to change and improve

the stock of factors that serve as economic development assets, the factor markets dominate the development path as the supply of assets becomes more elastic. Here public policy—particularly human capital and infrastructure investment policy—can play an important role in shaping a region's economic future.

Our research results in chapter 2 show that the regions most at risk for entering periods of chronic economic distress are those with high levels of manufacturing employment, low levels of worker skills, and high wages. These findings need to be interpreted with care. They do not imply that manufacturing or high wages per se cause chronic distress. Rather, regions with a high manufacturing presence and high wages in the last two or three decades of the twentieth century were often chronically distressed because they had cost structures that were uncompetitive and product portfolios dominated by old manufactured products with slow-growing product markets and diminishing margins. Regions such as Seattle, where manufacturing was important and also characterized by product innovation, did not become chronically distressed during our study period, and manufacturing-based regions where companies continue to produce new products are not likely to become chronically distressed in the future.

Similarly, high wages per se are not a problem. To the extent that labor costs matter for regional competitiveness (something that varies depending on the labor-intensity of the region's major export industries and the availability of lower wage alternative locations for those industries), they depend not on wages alone but on wages relative to productivity. Seattle can continue to support high-wage aerospace manufacturing because its aerospace companies are highly productive and the product continues to evolve, requiring engineers and other highly skilled workers. Thus, there are two ways to solve a regional wage-competitiveness problem: by lowering wages or by raising productivity.

It is important to think about what increased productivity means in this context. A commonly accepted measure of labor productivity is total value added divided by hours worked. Businesses often think of increasing productivity by reducing the number of hours worked to produce their existing products while keeping value added constant. Strategies to accomplish this include automating production, improving work organization ("working smarter") or—less sustainably over the long term—working harder or faster. However, it is also possible to raise productivity by increasing value added without necessarily reducing labor hours. This involves introducing new products, enhancing the value of the brand, and improving the effectiveness of sales and distribution. At the regional level, there is often a bigger productivity payoff to increasing value added than to reducing work hours because strategies that increase value added—especially introducing new products—are less easily copied by firms in other regions. That is why regions whose products that are old in terms of product cycle age often have lower productivity growth rates and, therefore, lower growth rates of gross product and employment as well.

The dynamics of the product cycle often play a critical role in regional economic change. This may be because, as in Detroit or Charlotte, the region's traded, or export, sector is dominated by a single industry. In such regions, the dynamics of the dominant export industry largely determine the medium-term. Or it may be because, as in Cleveland, a portfolio of regional export products may be in different industries but have similar economic ages. This means that they move through the same phases of their product cycles at the same time. As those products move from development to maturation and routinization, employment in their industries declines in the region and increases in areas with more competitive factors suited for routinized production.

In terms of the product cycle, successful regions are those that 1) are diversified (i.e., have a variety of products in various industries that are in different stages of the product cycle) and/or 2) are able to continue to regenerate through developing new products in the same or new industries (think Silicon Valley, New York, Boston, or Seattle). Unsuccessful regions enter a period of chronic economic distress when their portfolios become unbalanced and dominated by old products—no matter how technologically sophisticated or capital intensive.

The above discussion suggests that chronically distressed regions need to regenerate through diversification, entrepreneurship, and innovation. But these are more aspirations than strategies or policies. Our review in chapter 5 suggested that policies presumably designed to achieve these results (cluster policies, entrepreneurship assistance, small business technical assistance, and the like) have some potential but that potential is either limited or extremely difficult to execute. (This does not mean that those policies should not be pursued, just that they need to be very well planned and implemented and that they should not be regarded as panaceas for economic recovery.) At the heart of a region that has experienced chronic economic distress are problems that relate fundamentally to its assets.

LONGER-TERM POLICIES AND LONG-RUN ECONOMIC DEVELOPMENT. Policy efforts to improve the region's assets in the long run can play a critical role in changing the trajectory of a regional economy. As we noted in the previous chapter, our review of the literature strongly indicates that human capital strategies—particularly improvements in the preschool, elementary, secondary, and community college formal education systems—can play an important role in improving an area's labor force skills and thus contributing to an area's economic growth.

But the task of improving an area's human capital assets is not simply one of imparting higher levels of skills. Particularly in previously dominant manufacturing regions like Detroit and Cleveland, it may also require changes in expectations and attitudes. In chronically distressed regions, the region's labor market has seen its implicit social contract torn up, but a new one such as exists in the Scandinavian countries has not been put in place to provide benefits and protection for workers as well as for businesses and investors. What was once expected in terms of earnings, benefits, employment stability, career ladders, and political behaviors can no longer be sustained. This all too often means that workers, investors, and institutions sit back and wait for their traditional economic base to kick back into gear or they frantically attempt to reestablish the position of their traditional employers through political means. Trying to reestablish the jobs that they are trained for and to maintain the social contracts that they have come to expect is understandable, though almost certainly futile. Existing worker training and retraining programs provide limited assistance for the current lower skilled generation of workers unless the economy has already entered a growth phase. Under these circumstances, improvements in the performance of the formal education and training institutions for those currently engaged in them provides the best avenue for emerging from chronic economic distress and for long-term economic growth.

The quality of infrastructure assets is also a target for public investment. The form of the region will reflect the land use demands placed on the region by its traded sector and its residential pattern at the time of its fastest growth. The region's infrastructure will also reflect the transportation and communications technology of this same period. Once land use patterns and infrastructure technologies are locked in they become expensive to change. Finally, as infrastructure ages it needs to be maintained, upgraded, or replaced and these investments can be deferred for a period of time. When a region experiences decline, the real value of its tax base shrinks and the ability to make these expenditures also declines. And, as the quality of infrastructure declines and its operating expenses rises, the region's competitive position is further weakened. This is a perfect example of negative feedback that is not self-correcting.

IMPLICATIONS FOR ECONOMIC DEVELOPERS. At the beginning of this chapter we wrote that the evidence that is reviewed in this book gives us pause and leads to a much more nuanced, and cautious, set of conclusions about the economic payoffs from intervening in the functions of regional economies. It is clear that near term actions to intentionally strengthen the operation of regional economies on the part of local officials cannot offset the impacts of cyclical economic downturns or other forms of exogenous economic shocks. Rainy day funds, countercyclical construction employment, extended unemployment benefits and other actions to counteract the impact of a recession on regional economies are outside the purview of economic development agencies and beyond their budgets.

What does this mean for the practice of economic development? The answer largely depends on our expectations. Traditional economic development activity can do little to ameliorate economic adversity in the short-term. In addition to the reasons we have discussed why this is so, it is also important to realize that it comprises a tiny part of regional expenditure. As an example, we were able to obtain 2012 budget data on the economic development intermediaries operating in Northeast Ohio, which is roughly the Cleveland-Akron-Canton Consolidated Metropolitan Statistical Area and the Youngstown-Warren Metropolitan Statistical Area. The region's metropolitan chambers of commerce and the economic development intermediaries had a combined budget of $67.6 million. This figure does not include spending by the county and local government on their economic development staff and activities and it does not include the cost of any incentive payments. These funds included spending on attraction, marketing, entrepreneurship and incubators, the Manufacturing Extension Program, chamber of commerce services, and a small number of workforce activities. Gross Metropolitan Product for these same metropolitan regions in 2012 was $185.6 billion. Assuming that the trajectory of a regional economy of this size can be changed in the short term by spending 0.04% of GMP is not credible. Of course, adding infrastructure and educational spending and building an inclusive regional economic development budget would provide a different and holistic picture of the scale of a region investing in its own future.

Furthermore, decisions about the most important assets of a regional economy lie outside of the domain of an economic development organization. Education, training, sanitary and drainage infrastructure, communications, utilities, and logistics all exist outside of the scope of an economic development intermediary. At best, economic developers can inform government about the demand side of the market for these factors of production.

What then should guide the practice of economic development? We ask this question not in terms of the broad public policy investments, but in terms of how to structure the work of economic developers. The practice of economic development, the day-to-day operation of an economic development intermediary, takes place at the margin of the economy by making incremental investments. There investments either help diversify the region's portfolio of traded products through attraction and expansion activities, addressing management failures in the areas of process and product innovation, or through advocating for improvements in the quality and quantity of labor and infrastructure.

What are the market failures and transactions costs that practice can address? One critical market failure relates to information about the regional economy and available building sites, real estate, and the associated infrastructure. This information needs to be accessible at the scale of the labor market. As is true of any product—and in this sense the assets of the regional economy are a product—there needs to be a sales function associated with the activity both to businesses that are located within the regional economy for expansion and retention and to potential users, or investors, from outside of the region. This is usually done through commercial real estate brokers or site selection consultants and at times by working directly with the firm. However, a good deal of the information that is requested is customized: labor force availability, specific infrastructure requirements, utility availability, rail and road access, and permitting requirements.

The second major area of activity of economic development professionals is related to minimizing transactions costs and reducing investment risk. Most companies are not expert at opening up new locations or at expansion, and no matter how efficient a city's system of planning, zoning, permitting, and inspecting are, investors need guidance and support. There are genuine transactions costs that can be reduced by a good economic developer.

The third role of an economic developer is to minimize risks and costs that are inherent in any complicated project. The largest risk is that the facility will not open on time and the best way to reduce cost is to provide a workforce that is trained at the time a facility opens. This required coordinating with the region's workforce and education systems. Economic development, as a practice, consists of a series of activities that helps to build a regional economy one transaction at a time. Practitioners cannot expect, on their own, that their activities are the primary key to economic growth and resilience. But they nonetheless are an important contributor.

Conclusion

The quantitative portion of our work indicates that most regional economies in the United States do indeed bounce back from a shock, but some do not. Our finding also show that many regions that enter periods of prolonged economic distress nonetheless are able to adapt through restructuring and manage to exit from that condition.

We also identified cases of prolonged regional economic distress. Transactions costs, risk perceptions, distance, and social and institutional barriers can all inhibit recovery from chronic distress. These factors trigger negative path dependencies, or cumulative causation, in factor markets because they shape the stock of skills in a region. We also observe in our review of the regional economic histories we conducted for our case studies that these path dependencies are frequently rooted in product markets. Some regional economies are able to successfully adapt through generating new products, while others have been less able to do so.

Our own findings as well as our review of the research literature suggest that, while local and regional economic development policy has little role to play in the short-term as a response to exogenous economic shocks, it has a critical role in the longer term as a means of improving the area's assets and economic performance. Primary among these is increasing the human capital of the regional labor force through policies that improve the performance of the region's formal education system. The knowledge, skills, and abilities of a region's residents are the most important factor in the long-run health of a regional economy and of its ability to adapt to changing economic circumstances and environments.

Appendix 1

TABLE A.1 List of chronically distressed regions (employment)

NUMBER OF CONSECUTIVE YEARS OF SLOW GROWTH	NUMBER OF PERIODS THAT MSAS MEET THE CRITERIA	MSAs
7	24	Allentown-Bethlehem-Easton, PA-NJ (1982–1988)
		Boston-Cambridge-Quincy, MA-NH (1991–1997)
		Bridgeport-Stamford-Norwalk, CT (1991–1997)
		Chicago-Naperville-Joliet, IL-IN-WI (1982–1987)
		Corpus Christi, TX (1987–1993)
		Dubuque, IA (1982–1988)
		Hickory-Lenoir-Morganton, NC (2001–2007)
		Houma-Bayou Cane-Thibodaux, LA (1986–1992)
		Johnstown, PA (1998–2004)
		Los Angeles-Long Beach-Santa Ana, CA (1993–1999)
		Midland, TX (1988–1994)
		New Orleans-Metairie-Kenner, LA (1986–1992)
		Parkersburg-Marietta, WV-OH (1984–1990)
		Peoria, IL (1982–1988)
		Pine Bluff, AR (1998–2004)
		Poughkeepsie-Newburgh-Middletown, NY (1993–1999)
		Rochester, NY (1997–2003)
		Saginaw-Saginaw Township North, MI (2001–2007)

(Continued)

NUMBER OF CONSECUTIVE YEARS OF SLOW GROWTH	NUMBER OF PERIODS THAT MSAS MEET THE CRITERIA	MSAs
		Sandusky, OH (1981–1987)
		Shreveport-Bossier City, LA (1987–1993)
		Utica-Rome, NY (1984–1990, 1996–2002)
		Vineland-Millville-Bridgeton, NJ (1994–2000)
		Williamsport, PA (1996–2002)
8	29	Abilene, TX (1987–1994)
		Bangor, ME (1991–1998)
		Beaumont-Port Arthur, TX (1984–1991)
		Cleveland-Elyria-Mentor, OH (1981–1988)
		Columbus, IN (1981–1988)
		Danville, VA (2000–2007)
		Davenport-Moline-Rock Island, IA-IL (1982–1989)
		Duluth, MN-WI (1982–1989)
		El Centro, CA (1982–1989)
		Florence-Muscle Shoals, AL (1999–2006)
		Great Falls MT (1983–1990)
		Honolulu, HI (1996–2003)
		Huntington-Ashland, WV-KY-OH (1982–1989)
		Kingston, NY (1992–1999)
		Kokomo, IN (1980–1987, 2000–2007)
		Muskegon-Norton Shores, MI (1980–1987)
		New Haven-Milford, CT (1991–1998)
		New York-Northern NJ-Long Island, NY-NJ-PA (1991–1998)
		Odessa, TX (1986–1993)
		Providence-New Bedford-Fall River, RI-MA (1991–1998)
		Pueblo, CO (1982–1989)
		Sioux City, IA-NE-SD (1980–1987)
		Springfield, MA (1991–1998)
		Syracuse, NY (1995–2002)
		Terre Haute, IN (1982–1989)
		Weirton-Steubenville, WV-OH (2000–2007)
		Wichita Falls, TX (1986–1993)
		York-Hanover, PA (1988–1995)
9	24	Battle Creek, MI (1980–1988)
		Bay City, MI (1981–1989)
		Buffalo-Niagara Falls, NY (1995–2003)
		Canton-Massillon, OH (1981–1989)
		Charleston, WV (1983–1991)
		Cumberland, MD-WV (1982–1990)
		Dayton, OH (1999–2007)

NUMBER OF CONSECUTIVE YEARS OF SLOW GROWTH	NUMBER OF PERIODS THAT MSAS MEET THE CRITERIA	MSAs
		Flint, MI (1999–2007)
		Jackson, MI (1980–1988)
		Mansfield, OH (1978–1986, 1999–2007)
		Michigan City-La Porte, IN (1980–1988, 1999–2007)
		Muncie, IN (1999–2007)
		Pittsburgh, PA (1982–1990)
		Pittsfield, MA (1990–1998)
		Pocatello, ID (1983–1991)
		Rocky Mount, NC (1999–2007)
		Scranton–Wilkes-Barre, PA (1978–1986)
		Springfield, MA (1978–1986)
		Terre Haute, IN (1999–2007)
		Waterloo-Cedar Falls, IA (1982–1990)
		Williamsport, PA (1979–1987)
		Youngstown-Warren-Boardman, OH-PA (1999–2007)
10	11	Anderson, IN (1978–1987)
		Buffalo-Niagara Falls, NY (1978–1987)
		Casper, WY (1985–1994)
		Danville, VA (1982–1991)
		Elmira, NY (1978–1987)
		Erie, PA (1980–1989)
		Hartford-West Hartford-East Hartford, CT (1992–2001)
		Kankakee-Bradley, IL (1980–1989)
		Niles-Benton Harbor, MI (1978–1987)
		Springfield, IL (1998–2007)
		Springfield, OH (1978–1987)
11	8	Akron, OH (1978–1988)
		Altoona, PA (1978–1988)
		Anniston-Oxford, AL (1995–2005)
		Muncie, IN (1978–1988)
		Niles-Benton Harbor, MI (1997–2007)
		Pascagoula, MS (1980–1990)
		Pittsfield, MA (1978–1988)
		Vineland-Millville-Bridgeton, NJ (1978–1988)
12	6	Binghamton, NY (1990–2001)
		Decatur, IL (1979–1990)
		Flint, MI (1983–1994)
		Lebanon, PA (1978–1989)
		Springfield, OH (1996–2007)
		Youngstown-Warren-Boardman, OH-PA (1978–1989)

(Continued)

TABLE A.1 (Continued)

NUMBER OF CONSECUTIVE YEARS OF SLOW GROWTH	NUMBER OF PERIODS THAT MSAS MEET THE CRITERIA	MSAs
13	2	Johnstown, PA (1978–1990)
		Wheeling, WV-OH (1980–1992)
15	1	Weirton-Steubenville, WV-OH (1978–1992)
16	2	Anderson, IN (1992–2007)
		Lawton, OK (1988–2003)
29	1	Danville, IL (1978–2007)

TABLE A.2 List of chronically distressed regions (GMP)

NUMBER OF CONSECUTIVE YEARS OF SLOW GROWTH	NUMBER OF MSAS THAT MEET THE CRITERIA	MSAs
7	29	Albany, GA (2001–2007)
		Bangor, ME (1994–2000)
		Baton Rouge, LA (1987–1993)
		Bay City, MI (2001–2007)
		Beaumont-Port Arthur, TX (1986–1992)
		Canton-Massillon, OH (2001–2007)
		Corpus Christi, TX (1986–1992)
		Elmira, NY (2001–2007)
		Farmington, NM (1986–1992)
		Grand Forks, ND-MN (1998–2004)
		Great Falls, MT (1986–1992)
		Huntington-Ashland, WV-KY-OH (1986–1992)
		Ithaca, NY (1993–1999)
		Jackson, MI (1986–1992)
		Kalamazoo-Portage, MI (2001–2007)
		Kankakee-Portage, MI (2000–2006)
		Kokomo, IN (2001–2007)
		Lebanon, PA (1994–2000)
		Lewiston, ID-WA (2001–2007)
		Lubbock, TX (1986–1992)
		Owensboro, KY (2000–2006)
		Pascagoula, MS (2000–2006)
		Poughkeepsie-Newburgh-Middletown, NY (1994–2000)
		Saginaw-Saginaw Township North, MI (2001–2007)
		San Angelo, TX (1987–1993)

NUMBER OF CONSECUTIVE YEARS OF SLOW GROWTH	NUMBER OF MSAS THAT MEET THE CRITERIA	MSAs
		Sandusky, OH (2001–2007)
		Terre Haute, IN (1986–1992)
		Tulsa, OK (1987–1993)
		Victoria, TX (1986–1992)
8	26	Amarillo, TX (1987–1994)
		Bay City, MI (1986–1993)
		Billings, MT (1986–1993)
		Bismarck, ND (1986–1993)
		Canton-Massillon, OH (1986–1993)
		Charleston, WV (1986–1993)
		Danville, VA (2000–2007)
		Davenport-Moline-Rock Island, IA-IL (1986–1993)
		Erie, PA (2000–2007)
		Florence-Muscle Shoals, AL (1999–2006)
		Grand Forks, ND-MN (1986–1993)
		Kingsport-Bristol-Bristol, TN-VA (1998–2005)
		Lafayette, LA (1987–1994)
		Lake Charles, LA (1986–1993)
		Mansfield, OH (2000–2007)
		Muncie, IN (2000–2007)
		Niles-Benton Harbor, MI (2000–2007)
		Oklahoma City, OK (1987–1994)
		Owensboro, KY (1986–1993)
		Parkersburg-Marietta, WV-OH (1986–1993, 2000–2007)
		Pittsfield, MA (1992–1999)
		Pocatello, ID (1986–1993)
		St. Joseph, MO-KS (1986–1993)
		Vineland-Millville-Bridgeton, NJ (1995–2002)
		Youngstown-Warren-Boardman, OH-PA (1986–1993)
9	12	Atlantic City, NJ (1995–2003)
		Battle Creek, MI (1999–2007)
		Flint, MI (1986–1994, 1999–2007)
		Gadsden, AL (1999–2007)
		Great Falls, MT (1997–2005)
		Honolulu, HI (1996–2004)
		Kingston, NY (1993–2001)
		Longview, TX (1987–1995)
		Monroe, LA (1987–1995)
		Utica-Rome, NY (1995–2003)
		Youngstown-Warren-Boardman, OH-PA (1999–2007)

(Continued)

TABLE A.2 (Continued)

NUMBER OF CONSECUTIVE YEARS OF SLOW GROWTH	NUMBER OF MSAS THAT MEET THE CRITERIA	MSAs
10	10	Abilene, TX (1987–1996)
		Alexandria, LA (1988–1997)
		Glens Falls, NY (1994–2003)
		Houma-Bayou Cane-Thibodaux, LA (1986–1995)
		Huntington-Ashland, WV-KY-OH (1996–2005)
		Longview, WA (1996–2005)
		Mansfield, OH (1989–1998)
		Saginaw-Saginaw Township North, MI (1986–1995)
		Sherman-Denison, TX (1987–1996)
		Shreveport-Bossier City, LA (1987–1996)
11	4	Gadsden, AL (1986–1996)
		Lima, OH (1991–2001)
		Muskegon-Norton Shores, MI (1986–1996)
		Wichita Falls, TX (1986–1996)
12	4	Decatur, IL (1986–1997)
		Fairbanks, AK (1987–1998)
		New Orleans-Metairie-Kenner, LA (1987–1998)
		Odessa, TX (1986–1997)
13	2	Johnstown, PA (1995–2007)
		Syracuse, NY (1995–2007)
14	4	Binghamton, NY (1994–2007)
		Casper, WY (1986–1999)
		Rochester, NY (1994–2007)
		Williamsport, PA (1994–2007)
15	3	Anchorage, AK (1988–2002)
		Anniston-Oxford, AL (1990–2004)
		Cheyenne, WY (1987–2001)
16	2	Lawton, OK (1988–2003)
		Midland, TX (1987–2002)
17	2	Anderson, IN (1991–2007)
		Cumberland, MD-WV (1986–2002)
19	1	Wheeling, WV-OH (1986–2004)
22	3	Danville, IL (1986–2007)
		Pine Bluff, AR (1986–2007)
		Weirton-Steubenville, WV-OH (1986–2007)

TABLE A.3 List of regions that recovered from chronic slow-growth (employment)

YEARS OF CONSECUTIVE SLOW GROWTH BEFORE RECOVERY	MSA	YEARS OF CONSECUTIVE RECOVERY
1978–1988	Akron, OH	1989–2000
1982–1988	Allentown-Bethlehem-Easton, PA-NJ	2001–2007
1978–1988	Altoona, PA	1990–1997
1991–1998	Bangor, ME	2001–2007
1980–1988	Battle Creek, MI	1989–2000
1981–1989	Bay City, MI	1992–2001
1981–1989	Canton-Massillon, OH	1991–1998
1985–1994	Casper, WY	2001–2007
1983–1991	Charleston, WV	1993–2007
1981–1987	Chicago-Naperville-Joliet, IL-IN-WI	1988–2001
1981–1988	Columbus, IN	1990–2000
1987–1993	Corpus Christi, TX	1994–2007
1982–1989	Davenport-Moline-Rock Island, IA-IL	1991–1997
1982–1988	Dubuque, IA	1990–1998
1982–1989	Duluth, MN-WI	1991–2007
1982–1989	El Centro, CA	1991–2000
1980–1989	Erie, PA	1991–1997
1986–1992	Houma-Bayou Cane-Thibodaux, LA	1994–2007
1982–1989	Huntington-Ashland, WV-KY-OH	1991–1997
1980–1988	Jackson, MI	1990–2000
1980–1989	Kankakee-Bradley, IL	1990–2000
1993–1999	Los Angeles-Long Beach-Santa Ana, CA	2001–2007
1980–1988	Michigan City-La Porte, IN	1989–1996
1988–1994	Midland, TX	1995–2001
1978–1988	Muncie, IN	1990–1997
1980–1987	Muskegon-Norton Shores, MI	1996–2007
1991–1998	New York-Northern New Jersey-Long Island, NY-NJ-PA	2001–2007
1986–1993	Odessa, TX	1994–2007
1984–1990	Parkersburg-Marietta, WV-OH	1992–1998
1980–1990	Pascagoula, MS	1991–1999
1982–1988	Peoria, IL	1990–2001
1983–1991	Pocatello, ID	1992–2007
1993–1999	Poughkeepsie-Newburgh-Middletown, NY	2001–2007
1982–1989	Pueblo, CO	1991–2007
1981–1987	Sandusky, OH	1989–1997
1978–1986	Scranton–Wilkes-Barre, PA	1989–1995
1987–1993	Shreveport-Bossier City, LA	1994–2001

(Continued)

TABLE A.3 (Continued)

YEARS OF CONSECUTIVE SLOW GROWTH BEFORE RECOVERY	MSA	YEARS OF CONSECUTIVE RECOVERY
1980–1987	Sioux City, IA-NE-SD	1989–2000
1991–1998	Springfield, MA	2001–2007
1982–1989	Terre Haute, IN	1991–1997
1982–1990	Waterloo-Cedar Falls, IA	1992–2007
1986–1993	Wichita Falls, TX	1995–2001

TABLE A.4 List of regions that recovered from chronic slow-growth (GMP)

YEARS OF CONSECUTIVE SLOW GROWTH BEFORE RECOVERY	MSA	YEARS OF CONSECUTIVE RECOVERY
1988–1997	Alexandria, LA	1999–2007
1987–1993	Baton Rouge, LA	1994–2001
1986–1999	Casper, WY	2001–2007
1986–1992	Farmington, NM	1993–1999
1986–1995	Houma-Bayou Cane-Thibodaux, LA	1997–2007
1987–1994	Lafayette, LA	1995–2007
1986–1993	Lake Charles, LA	1994–2001
1987–1995	Longview, TX	1997–2007
1987–1994	Oklahoma City, OK	1997–2007
1986–1993	Pocatello, ID	1994–2000
1987–1993	Tulsa, OK	1997–2007

TABLE A.5 List of regions that did not recover from chronic slow growth (employment)

LAST YEAR OF CONSECUTIVE SLOW-GROWTH	MSA
1994	Abilene, TX
1987	Anderson, IN
1991	Beaumont-Port Arthur, TX
1997	Boston-Cambridge-Quincy, MA-NH
1997	Bridgeport-Stamford-Norwalk, CT
1987	Buffalo-Niagara Falls, NY
1988	Cleveland-Elyria-Mentor, OH
1990	Cumberland, MD-WV
1991	Danville, VA

LAST YEAR OF CONSECUTIVE SLOW-GROWTH	MSA
1990	Decatur, IL
1987	Elmira, NY
1994	Flint, MI
1990	Great Falls, MT
1990	Johnstown, PA
1999	Kingston, NY
1987	Kokomo, IN
1989	Lebanon, PA
1986	Mansfield, OH
1998	New Haven-Milford, CT
1992	New Orleans-Metairie-Kenner, LA
1987	Niles-Benton Harbor, MI
1990	Pittsburgh, PA
1998	Pittsfield, MA
1998	Providence-New Bedford-Fall River, RI-MA
1987	Springfield, OH
1984	Utica-Rome, NY
2000	Vineland-Millville-Bridgeton, NJ
1992	Weirton-Steubenville, WV-OH
1992	Wheeling, WV-OH
1987	Williamsport, PA
1995	York-Hanover, PA
1989	Youngstown-Warren-Boardman, OH-PA

Note: Does not include regions still enduring chronic slow-growth as of 2001.

TABLE A.6 List of regions that did not recover from chronic slow growth (GMP)

LAST YEAR OF CONSECUTIVE SLOW-GROWTH	MSA
1996	Abilene, TX
1994	Amarillo, TX
2000	Bangor, ME
1993	Bay City, MI
1992	Beaumont-Port Arthur, TX
1993	Billings, MT
1993	Bismarck, ND
1993	Canton-Massillon, OH
1993	Charleston, WV
1992	Corpus Christi, TX
1993	Davenport-Moline-Rock Island, IA-IL

(Continued)

TABLE A.6 (Continued)

LAST YEAR OF CONSECUTIVE SLOW-GROWTH	MSA
1997	Decatur, IL
1998	Fairbanks, AK
1994	Flint, MI
1996	Gadsden, AL
1993	Grand Forks, ND
1992	Great Falls, MT
1992	Huntington-Ashland, WV-KY-OH
1999	Ithaca, NY
1992	Jackson, MI
2000	Lebanon, PA
1992	Lubbock, TX
1998	Mansfield, OH
1995	Monroe, LA
1996	Muskegon-Norton Shores, MI
1998	New Orleans-Metairie-Kenner, LA
1997	Odessa, TX
1993	Owensboro, KY
1993	Parkersburg-Marietta, WV-OH
1999·	Pittsfield, MA
2000	Poughkeepsie-Newburgh-Middletown, NY
1995	Saginaw-Saginaw Township North, MI
1993	San Angelo, TX
1996	Sherman-Denison, TX
1996	Shreveport-Bossier City, LA
1993	St. Joseph, MO-KS
1992	Terre Haute, IN
1992	Victoria, TX
1996	Wichita Falls, TX
1993	Youngstown-Warren-Boardman, OH-PA

Note: Does not include regions still enduring chronic slow-growth as of 2001.

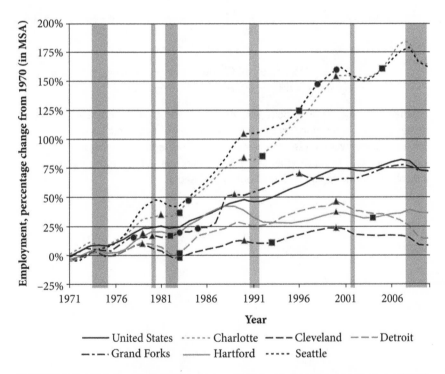

FIGURE A.1 Employment shocks and resilience. Vertical bars indicate national recessions, as determined by the National Bureau for Economic Research. Circles indicate when a region experienced a shock and was resistant. Triangles indicate when a region experienced a shock and was not resistant; squares indicate when the region was resilient to that shock.

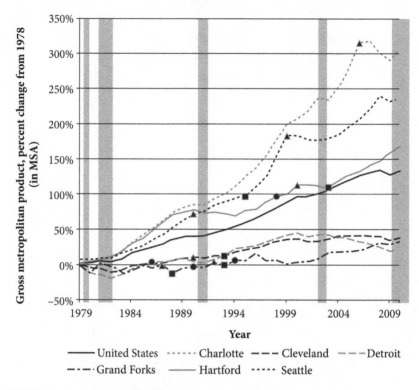

FIGURE A.2 Real GMP shocks and resilience. Vertical bars indicate national recessions, as determined by the National Bureau of Economic Research. Circles indicate when a region experienced a shock and was resistant. Triangles indicate when a region experienced a shock and was not resistant; squares indicate when the region was resilient to that shock.

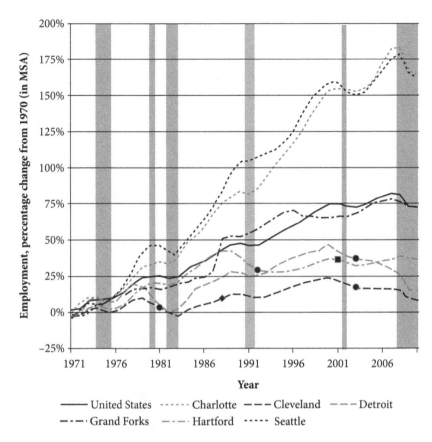

FIGURE A.3 Chronic distress—Employment. Vertical bars indicate national recessions, as determined by the National Bureau of Economic Research. Circles indicate when a region experienced chronic distress in employment. Squares indicate when the region recovered from that distress, while diamonds indicate when the period of chronic distress ended but the region never recovered. Because we do not know whether Cleveland or Detroit recovered from their 2003–2010 chronic distress, they do not have endpoints marked.

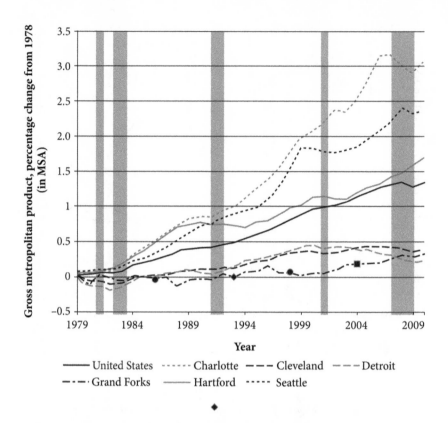

FIGURE A.4 Chronic distress—Real GMP. Vertical bars indicate national recessions, as determined by the National Bureau of Economic Research. Circles indicate when a region experienced chronic distress in GMP. Squares indicate when the region recovered from that distress, while diamonds indicate when the period of chronic distress ended but the region never recovered.

Notes

INTRODUCTION

1. Such shock results are a form of hysteresis, a situation where a one-time disturbance affects the path of the economy even after the disturbance has long passed. See, for example, Martin 2012 and Romer 2001.

2. For an excellent review of causes of long-term decline, see Boschma and Lambooy 1999.

3. The term "resilience" has achieved widespread use as a means of characterizing successful responses to an increasing number of systemic shocks in a variety of fields. (See the Community and Regional Resilience Institute 2013 for a compendium of uses.) Many writers on the subject date the interest in the idea of resilience to Holling (1973, 17), who defined resilience as "a measure of the ability of these systems to absorb changes of state variables, driving variables, and parameters, and still persist. In this definition, resilience is the property of the system."

This idea has now been applied to such phenomena as ecological systems (Hollings 1973; Peterson, Allen, and Hollings 1998); natural disasters (Adger et al. 2005; Bruneau et al. 2003; Campanella 2006; Colton, Kates, and Laska 2008; Norris et al. 2008; Vale and Campanella 2005a, 2005b); terrorism (Coaffee 2006); human response to trauma (Bonanno 2004; Bonanno and Mancini 2008); community response to trauma (Ganor and Ben-Levy 2003); population declines (Lin 2012); housing market foreclosures (Swanstrom, Chapple, and Immergluck 2009); human development (Rutter 1993; Werner 1993); organizational systems (U.S. Government Accountability Office 2009); urban development (Burby et al. 2000; Godschalk 2003); social justice (Morrow 2008); and businesses (Sheffi 2005). The literature draws on three separate, though sometimes related, concepts of resilience: resilience as *bounce-back* to a prior equilibrium (this is sometimes termed "engineering resilience"; see, for example, Peterson, Allen, and Hollings 1998), resilience as *adaptation* (the ability of a system to reorganize or restructure when faced with a sudden shock or with long-term stress), and *ecological resilience*, which refers to the "scale of shock or disturbance a system can absorb before it is destabilized and moved to another stable state or configuration" (Martin 2012, 6).

Most analyses of resilience have focused on the ability of a system to recover or bounce back from a disruption or perturbation. Sheffi (2005, ix) provides an example of bounce-back equilibrium when he states, "For companies, [resilience] measures their ability to, and the speed at which they can, return to their normal performance level following a high-impact/low-probability disruption." However, the concept of adaptive resilience has also been widely employed. For example, the Community and Regional Resilience Institute (CARRI) defines community resilience as "The capability to anticipate risk, limit impact, and bounce back rapidly through survival, adaptability, evolution and growth in the face of turbulent change" (2013, 13).

4. See, for example, Blanchard and Katz 1992; Rose and Liao 2005; Briguglio et al. 2006; Feyrer, Sacerdote, and Stern 2007; Fingleton, Garretsen, and Martin 2012; Ormerod 2012. Although these macroeconomic indicators are commonly used, it is also possible to apply this and other resilience concepts to other measures of regional economic performance, such as wage inequality or measures of environmental sustainability.

5. For a review of conceptual and operational definitions of economic resilience, see Modica and Reggiani 2014.

6. There is a challenge operationalizing this concept because the North American Industrial Classification (NAICS) system of accounts is a combination of products and production processes grouped into industry aggregates. By necessity the more aggregated the level of analysis, the more heterogeneous the products are within the industry grouping. This leads analysts to treat NAICS industries as if they produce and sell either a singular product or products that are close substitutes for each other. (See U.S. Bureau of the Census, Economic Classification Policy Committee, Issue Paper No. 1, "Conceptual Issues," and Issue Paper No. 2, "Aggregation Structures and Hierarchies," www.census.gov/eos/www/naics/history/history.html.)

1. SHOCKS AND REGIONAL ECONOMIC RESILIENCE

1. The previous eight-year growth rate is measured by the slope of the regression line of the natural logarithm of employment on a time trend for the previous eight years. If the prior eight-year growth rate is 4.0 % or higher, then the growth rate in the base year must decline by the number of percentage points equal to more than half of the prior eight-year growth rate. Our use of a decline in the growth rate to measure shocks is analogous to Hausmann, Pritchett, and Rodrik's (2004) use of an increase in the growth rate to measure growth accelerations.

2. In this chapter, we follow common usage in regional economics and use the term "export," at the regional level, to refer to goods and services that are produced in a region but consumed mainly by people who live in other regions. Those other regions may be located in either the United States or other countries.

3. In regional economics, location quotients (LQ) are often used to identify industries that are likely to export their goods and services outside of the region. The location quotient is the ratio of an industry's share of employment (or GMP) in a regional economy divided by that same industry's share of employment (or GMP) in a reference region. The reference region is typically the nation. Many studies use a LQ of 1.2 as the minimum necessary for an industry to qualify as part of the export sector, meaning that the industry's share of employment in the region is 20 basis points higher than it is in the nation. To ensure that the industry is truly part of the region's export sector, the standard employed in this work is 80 basis points higher than the national share.

4. An industry is considered to be in shock at the national level if it meets the same criteria as a national *downturn* shock: the industry's annual employment growth rate declines by more than 2.0 percentage points from its eight-year growth rate.

5. In the case that two separate industry shocks occur in the years preceding and concurrent with a downturn, one a national industry shock and one a regional industry shock, we look at the first year of the shock to determine whether the shock was local or national in nature.

6. Note that our definition of an economic downturn is thus similar to our definition of an economic shock. The difference is that an economic downturn results from a decline in the growth rate of the metropolitan area's economy. Shocks reflect declines in either the national economy or specific industries.

7. If a new "secondary" downturn begins before a region has been deemed resilient or non-resilient to the previous downturn, the region will have four years from the *end* of the secondary downturn in which to return to its eight-year growth rate from prior to the *original* downturn year.

8. We also ran separate models in which regions had five years in which to recover from a downturn. This had almost no impact on our quantitative findings.

9. Our definition of an economic downturn requires eight prior years of data so our analytical time period begins in 1978 for employment data and 1986 for GMP data.

Moody's Analytics employment data are based on Bureau of Labor Statistics data, while its GMP data are based on Bureau of Economic Analysis data. Moody's data extends back to 1978. Thus, except for the 1970–1977 period, we use Moody's Analytics data, rather than the federal data sources on which it is based, because Moody's Analytics estimates data that the federal sources suppress to preserve employer confidentiality and because it provides estimates that use current NAIC industry categories consistently for the entire 1970–2007 time period. For 1970–1977, we use data from the Bureau of Economic analysis. For GMP data, we utilize Moody's Analytics data from 1978 to 2007. Since GMP data are not available from federal sources for 1970–1977, and we need eight years of data prior to a shock to determine the annual average eight-year growth rate, our period for analysis of GMP data is truncated and covers only 1986–2007.

10. Given that there were three national economic shocks during the 1978–2007 period (1981, 1990, and 2000–2001) and 361 metropolitan areas, one might expect that there were more than 1,000 shock instances. However, we have not counted as shock instances those shocks that occurred while a region was still being affected by a prior shock. As a result, the total number of national economic shocks amounted to 661 instances.

11. We consider only the national economic downturn of 2007–2009 as a shock; we do not count regional or national industry shocks.

12. The "official" determination of when a recession begins and ends is made by the National Bureau of Economic Research (NBER). It is often stated that the definition is two consecutive quarters of real decline in the GDP, but the actual determination by NBER is more nuanced. NBER's Business Cycle Dating Committee states that, "The committee's procedure for identifying turning points differs from the two-quarter rule in a number of ways. First, we do not identify economic activity solely with real GDP and real GDI, but use a range of other indicators as well. Second, we place considerable emphasis on monthly indicators in arriving at a monthly chronology. Third, we consider the depth of the decline in economic activity. Recall that our definition includes the phrase, 'a significant decline in activity.' Fourth, in examining the behavior of domestic production, we consider not only the conventional product-side GDP estimates, but also the conceptually equivalent income-side GDI estimates." With respect to the Great Recession, the Committee notes that, "real GDP declined in the first, third, and fourth quarters of 2008 and in the first quarter of 2009. The committee places real Gross Domestic Income on an equal footing with real GDP; real GDI declined for six consecutive quarters in the recent recession." (See http://www.nber.org/cycles/recessions_faq.html.)

13. The calculations that include 2006 and 2007 risk being upward biased, since we do not know whether the metropolitan area economic effects may have been caused by factors such as national or regional industrial declines or unique circumstances such as earthquakes, floods, and so on. rather than by precursors of the Great Recession. To get some sense of this, we compared the average annual incidence of metropolitan area economic downturns caused by something other than national economic downturns from 1978 to 2007 to the overall incidence of downturns from all sources in 2006 and in 2007. If the 2006 and 2007 annual incidence was substantially greater than that from 1978 to 2007, we can conclude that the 2006 and 2007 downturns were mostly a result of the recession's pre-cursor. The average annual incidence for 1978–2007 was thirty-five, while the average for 2006–2007 was ninety-seven, thus clearly suggesting that the 2006 and 2007 downturns were very likely to have been precursors of the Great Recession.

14. As a result, the calculation of the number of adversely affected metropolitan areas risks being biased slightly upward, since it assumes that none of the downturns that began in 2006 through 2009 achieved resilience status in the year or years after its initial downturn and then experienced an additional downturn in 2010 or prior to that.

15. Of these, 113 suffered were already in the midst of an existing downturn.

16. See Ficenec (2010) for a review of the literature.

17. Olmerod (2010) also finds that the larger the proportion of coal mining in an area, the lower was subsequent total employment growth.

18. For a survey of recent studies, see Nunn (2009).

19. Because the Office of Management and Budget has changed its definition of metropolitan areas over time, we aggregated our data from the county level where necessary to ensure consistency. The metropolitan area definitions that we use are from 2003.

20. Health care is combined with social assistance at the two-digit NAICS level. We originally included professional, scientific, and technical services as another category of employment, but removed it from the model when it was found to be highly correlated with other variables and not statistically significant.

21. For those demographic variables that we obtained from Census data, we applied linear interpolation to gather estimates for noncensus years. See table 1.5 for summary statistics.

22. It is, of course, possible to model each of the shocks separately to assess whether the relationship of the independent to the dependent variables differs by type of shock. Initial efforts to do so suggest that this may well be the case.

23. We also collected data on average July temperature. We discarded the temperature variable as we found it to be highly correlated with the regional dummies.

24. We apply the conditional gap time correction to the standard Cox model as recommended by Box-Steffensmeier and Zorn (2002) for sequential repeated events, using the Efron method to account for coterminous event occurrences or "ties." The model stratifies by the order in which the event (in this case, a downturn) occurs and uses robust variance estimates. Standard errors are clustered by metropolitan area.

2. CHRONIC DISTRESS AND REGIONAL ECONOMIC RESILIENCE

1. See Baumol 1986; Barro and Sala-I-Martin 1991; and James and Moeller 2013.

2. Markusen (1985) develops a profit life cycle theory that consists of five steps that are related to each of the four steps of the product life cycle theory. Markusen's five profit cycle steps are: 1) zero profit (the initial birth and design stage of an industry; 2) super profit (reflecting temporary monopoly and innovative edge); 3) normal profit (open entry, competition, and movement toward market saturation); 4) normal-plus or normal-minus profit (post-saturation stage where successful oligopolization boosts profit or excessive competition squeezes profit); and 5) negative profit (obsolescence). For a discussion of the historical development of product cycle theory, see Storper 1985.

3. Some accounts of the revitalization of New England in the 1980s posit that low relative wages for skilled workers were necessary to restart the region's growth (Flynn 1984; Harrison 1984).

4. Blumenthal, Wolman, and Hill (2009) find a positive relationship between percentage manufacturing in 1990 and regional economic growth between 1990 and 2000.

5. We note that Glaeser and Shapiro (2001) found no statistically significant relationship between initial population and economic growth at the metropolitan level.

6. A research literature on the evaluation of regional policy exists and has been widely applied in European countries in a variety of forms. The earliest and most persistent type of regional policy has consisted of grants and subsidized loans to firms to stimulate investment in lagging regions. (In the United States, the primary manifestation of regional policy at the national level has been the effort to economically jump-start the Appalachian region through infrastructure improvement.) The burden of this evaluative literature is that these regional policy approaches have shown little success (Pack 2002).

7. We account for this in our longitudinal regressions by removing 2002–2007 as years of observation.

8. We use the same data as in the previous chapter.

9. In the ensuing discussion, all results discussed are statistically significant at the 0.10 level or below.

3. REGIONS THAT LACKED RESILIENCE

1. In addition to the authors, the team involved in the interviewing and/or write-ups of the six regions included Patricia Atkins (Charlotte), Pamela Blumenthal (Cleveland, Grand Forks), Sarah Ficenec (Detroit), Alec Friedhoff (Charlotte, Cleveland, Hartford, Seattle), Alex Gold (Seattle), Tara Kotagal (Hartford), Rosa Lee (Hartford, Seattle), Howard Lempel (Hartford), Chad Shearer (Hartford, Seattle), and Fran Stewart (Cleveland). Atkins, Blumenthal, Ficenec, and Lee were staff members of the George Washington Institute of Public Policy. Friedhoff, Gold, Kotagal, Lempel, and Shearer were staff members at the Brookings Institution, and Stewart was at Cleveland State University.

2. The "Cleveland region" refers to the Cleveland-Elyria-Mentor metropolitan statistical area, which consists of five counties: Cuyahoga, Geauga, Lake, Lorain, and Medina.

3. It is important to note that the first eight-year average employment growth rate in our study, in 1979, was just under 1% for the Cleveland region. By 1979, Cleveland's growth trajectory had already slowed; at no time during our study did it reach 2%.

4. The Cleveland region was incorporated into a larger region of counties in Northeast Ohio. Called "NEO," this region includes sixteen Ohio counties: Ashland, Ashtabula, Carroll, Columbiana, Cuyahoga, Geauga, Lake, Lorain, Mahoning, Medina, Portage, Richland, Stark, Summit, Trumbull, and Wayne.

5. Lee and Rudick (2006) studied employment growth in Ohio between 1989 and 2001 and find that the state had lower than average job creation rates as well as a low job destruction rate. The authors find that slowly growing states are not falling behind because they are losing more existing jobs, but because their labor market is stagnant; both job creation and destruction are relatively low.

6. TeamNEO is a regional economic development organization that focuses on attraction. Housed within it is the region's press and advocacy effort Cleveland+. TeamNEO's geography consists of eighteen counties in Northeast Ohio: the same sixteen counties as the NEO region except it omits Carroll County, and includes Erie County, Huron County, and Tuscarawas County. The counties in TeamNEO's footprint include the central cities of Akron, Youngstown, Canton, Lorain, and Elyria.

7. The "Detroit region" consists of the, Detroit-Warren-Livonia metropolitan statistical area, which represents six counties: Wayne, Lapeer, Livingston, Macomb, Oakland, and St. Clair. However, during the interviews with policy makers, Washtenaw County, home of Ann Arbor and the University of Michigan but a separate metropolitan area, was often referenced as part of the Detroit region and, thus, is part of the narrative discussion of the region but is not included in the data provided.

8. BMW in South Carolina, Daimler (Mercedes) in Alabama and South Carolina, Honda in Ohio, Indiana, and Alabama, Hyundai in Alabama, Kia in Georgia, Mitsubishi in Illinois, Nissan in Tennessee and Mississippi, Toyota in Kentucky, Indiana, Mississippi, and Texas, Subaru (Fuji) in Indiana, and Volkswagen in Tennessee.

9. The heavy influence of the labor unions on automobile production costs is often cited as a factor in the movement or opening of new plants in the Southern U.S. Ford has assembly plants in Michigan, Ohio, Illinois, Kentucky and Missouri as well as in Mexico The new General Motors has plants in Michigan, Ohio, Indiana, Kentucky, Tennessee, Missouri, Kansas, and Texas. It was also one of the impetuses behind Michigan's implementation of a right-to-work law in 2013. For more information on right-to-work laws in connection with our analysis of resilience, see the discussion in chapter 1.

10. This includes the New International Trade Crossing, a new bridge between Detroit and Windsor, Ontario, that is projected to begin construction in 2015. While we were conducting our interviews in the region, the proposal for a new crossing was still under discussion, without any concrete plans developed, but we did hear from several individuals about the importance of the current bridge and the border to the region.

11. The city of Detroit declared bankruptcy in July 2013, less than six months after the state took financial control of the city and appointed an emergency financial manager for it. It is unknown at the time of publication what the effects of the bankruptcy would be on the city and the region.

12. The "Hartford region" refers to the Hartford-West Hartford-East Hartford, Connecticut, metropolitan statistical area, which consists of Hartford, Middlesex, and Tolland counties.

13. Sikorsky is headquartered in Stratford, Connecticut, just outside the Hartford metropolitan area.

14. Hartford actually lost jobs from 2000 to 2001, but that decline did not mark a large enough departure from its prior growth trend to qualify as the beginning of an employment shock by our definition.

15. The state also supports clusters related to bioscience, software and information technology, metal manufacturing, maritime, plastics, and agriculture industries.

4. RESILIENT REGIONS

1. The "Charlotte region" refers to the Charlotte-Gastonia-Concord MSA, which includes York County in South Carolina and five counties in North Carolina: Anson, Cabarrus, Gaston, Mecklenburg, and Union counties.

2. These policies included funding for existing businesses to improve the skills of current workers in order to increase existing workforce productivity, support for an extensive community college system with a focus on customized training to meet specific employer needs, and more detailed programs such as a provision permitting motorsports racing teams or motorsports sanctioning bodies (which are important economic export activities in the region) to receive a refund of sales taxes on certain purchases. Moreover, in the mid-1990s, the University of North Carolina-Charlotte became the first institution of higher education in the region to offer doctoral degrees (although, as some interviewees noted, it still has no public law school, is the largest city in the nation without a medical school, and is not recognized as a major research university).

3. The "Seattle region" refers to the Seattle-Tacoma-Bellevue, WA, metropolitan statistical area, which includes King, Snohomish, and Pierce counties.

4. On January 11, 2013, the organization decided to return to its former name, Economic Development Council of Seattle and King County. It was known as Enterprise Seattle from 2005 to January 2013.

5. The Grand Forks metropolitan statistical area consists of Polk County, MN, and Grand Forks County, ND.

6. We interviewed a journalist in the region, who noted that the region's agricultural competitiveness (particularly with regard to wheat) depends in part on the strength of the Canadian dollar, such that, when the Canadian dollar is strong, the region is more competitive.

7. GFAFB's initial mission was as home to bombers and tankers. It also served as the home to 150 Minuteman III intercontinental ballistic missiles, which were removed as part of the 1995 BRAC Commission. It suffered further reductions as a result of the 2005 BRAC. See 319th Air Refueling Wing 2007.

8. Another factor mentioned by some interviewees was reduced retail sales from the rise of the U.S. dollar in relation to the Canadian dollar. The U.S. dollar, which had an

exchange rate of 1.17 Canadian dollars in 1990, strengthened to 1.36 CAD in 1996, 1.38 in 1997, and 1.48 in 1998. In 2008, the exchange rate was 1.07 (Oanda Corporation 2013). According to one person we talked with, once the exchange rate exceeds 1.33, the Canadians "quit coming." However, the funds flowing into the region to help households recover and rebuild after the flood would likely offset lost retail sales to Canadians.

9. Funding included $357,000,000 from the Federal Emergency Management Agency; $142,000,000 in Community Development Block Grants, and $66,000,000 from the U.S. Economic Development Administration.

10. In 1987, the state enabled home rule cities to levy local option sales tax of up to 1% for economic development, infrastructure improvement, property tax relief, and other community uses. Between Grand Forks' adoption of the tax in 1988 and 1995, it raised $7,000,000, of which 10% was spent outside the central city and 8% was spent outside the county; the funds examined preclude assisting business located outside of North Dakota (Leistritz and Bangsund 1998).

11. The remainder of the $8.75 million to build REAC was funded in part by the State Center of Excellence (CoE) program ($3.5 million for a CoE in life sciences and advanced technologies), U.S. Economic Development Administration ($1.5 million), and the North Dakota Development Fund ($1 million). The Knight Foundation provided a $550,000 grant for operational expenses. See http://sayanythingblog.com/entry/und-research-foundation-reac/.

12. University of North Dakota, Center for Innovation, http://www.innovators.net/innovators/public_html/.

13. The local airport was also cited as a "major liability" by many of our interviewees due to its lack of flights and connections. One said that businesses and investors "get excited, then look at [the] airport and say they can't do that, can't sit in Minneapolis for four hours."

5. ASSESSING THE EFFECT OF RESILIENCE POLICIES DIRECTED TOWARD BUSINESS AND INDIVIDUALS

This chapter was coauthored by Sarah Ficenec. Sarah was also the primary coauthor of the human capital section and the entrepreneurship section (with research assistance on the latter from Diana Hincapie). Pamela Blumenthal was the principal coauthor of the leadership section; and Sarah Ficenec, Diana Hincapie, Claire Thomison, and Kelly Kinahan contributed to the cluster and targeting section.

1. This has been confirmed in surveys of executives (see, e.g., Goldstein 1985; Hill 2004; Kieschnick 1981; Malpezzi 2001 Schmenner 1982; Milward and Newman 1989; Musil 2001). See also Fisher and Peters (1998), who came to the same conclusion utilizing a hypothetical firm approach that compared location specific profit estimates for sixteen hypothetical firm located in twenty-four different states.

2. With respect to what are appropriate public services, Mofidi and Stone (1990) find that state and local expenditures for education, health, and public infrastructure have a positive effect on manufacturing investment and employment, while those for transfer payment programs have a negative effect. See also Helms (1985), whose research comes to the same conclusion.

3. As Bartik (2007, 107) points out, "under the assumption that a 'dollar is a dollar,' tax incentives for a large business should have similar effects on its location decisions to an equal dollar-sized business tax cut."

4. In an earlier review of the literature, Wasylenko (1997, 49) remarks, "taxes have a small, statistically significant effect on interregional location behavior."

5. Phillips and Goss (1995, 329) conduct a meta-analysis of studies on the effects of taxes on inter-regional and intraregional firm location and conclude, "The results generally support the conclusions reached earlier by Bartik."

6. Even if tax incentives do increase job growth, it is not always the case that the social benefits will exceed the social costs. Bartik (2007, 108–111) provides an extended discussion of the conditions under which benefits are likely to be positive.

7. Shift/share analysis corrects for some of these problems. Shift/share analysis is a decomposition technique that takes the observed change in the economy—typically employment, but at times gross product is used—and allocates the change in the observed variable to three sources. The decomposition is based on the numerical answers to three "what if" questions. Although this discussion is framed in terms of employment many studies used gross product as well, as was done in the RECS process in Cleveland. (For more on this, see chapter 3.)

The first "what if" question is: "What would the change in the outcome variable have been if the industry in the region changed at the same rate as the national economy?" If these calculations were done for employment then the national average growth rate in jobs would be multiplied by base year employment in the region's industry. This is called the national growth effect.

The second "what if" question is: "What would have been the industry's change in employment in the region if employment grew at the same rate as the industry nationally?" Here the national average employment growth rate is subtracted from the industry's national industry growth rate. (The national average growth rate has to be subtracted so that the national effect is not double counted in the decomposition.) This net national industry growth rate is then multiplied by base-year employment for the industry in the region. This is termed the industry effect. When these net industry effects are added together across all industries in the region the impact of the region's industrial structure on employment becomes apparent.

The last step is to calculate the region's local competitive effect. The most intuitive way to do this is to take the observed regional change in employment in the industry over the time period studied and subtract the employment change attributed to the national effect and the employment change attributed to the industry effect. The residual, the result from this double subtraction, is termed the "local competitive effect." It is the observed change in the regional industry's employment that is not allocated to the average change in the national economy and not allocated to the average performance of the industry nationally. When the local competitive effect is added up across all industries in the region the sum is termed the change in the local economy that is due to the regional economy's local competitive factors.

8. Shift/share is also extremely sensitive both to the time period used and to the level of aggregation. Thus, a shift/share analysis of the period 1990–2010 will likely yield much different results than a shift/share analysis of 2000–2010. A shift/share analysis conducted at the two-digit NAICS code level may show, for example, that manufacturing does not have a competitive advantage in the region. However, the same analysis conducted at the three-digit level might show that there are some specific manufacturing sectors for which the regional employment is indeed growing at a faster rate than nationally and which might productively be the subject of area policy efforts.

9. More generally, Cortright (2006) argues that it is futile to try to measure the impact of clusters on economic development because clusters are only a loosely defined concept that provides a useful way of thinking about economic development and general lessons for economic development policy.

10. For a discussion of this problem, see Duranton (2009).

11. Klepper (2010), for example, looks at two of the best-known clusters in the country—the automobile and integrated circuit clusters in Detroit and Silicon Valley, respectively—to find out how they developed. His results demonstrate the important role of spinoff companies in developing clusters.

12. Small businesses also make important contributions to regional economies (and are the foundations of tomorrow's future large firms). We discuss policies focused on supporting small and new businesses in the next section.

13. Replicating Jarmin's methodology, Ordowich et al. (2012) find that MEP services had a significant and effect on productivity (6%) from 1997 to 2002, as compared to firms not using MEP services. Utilizing a different (lagged dependent variable) model, they find a positive and significant, though modest (2% increase over the five-year period), increase in productivity for MEP clients as opposed to similar firms that did not use MEP services. When the results are viewed by establishment size, MEP services to small establishments (less than twenty employees) have a positive and significant increase on labor productivity (in the range of 5–6% over the five-year period); mixed effects (depending on model specification) for firms with between twenty to forty-nine employees; and no significant effect on firms with more than fifty employees. The MEP impacts found in this study, however, may be underestimated because the non-MEP-using firms in their study are not closely matched to the MEP-using firms.

14. Baumol (2002, 57) discusses how both "independent inventors" and firms are important to the innovation cycle: "In this process there is no reason to expect independent inventors or innovators to become obsolete any time in the foreseeable future. It is more plausible that the division of the work of technical progress will continue, with the independent entrepreneur providing many if not most of the revolutionary and heterodox contributions, while the routine innovation activities of the oligopoly corporations take those contributions and improve and extend them." An example of this innovation process is the development of the first personal computers, which was driven by independent actors (e.g., Microsoft, Dell Computers, Hewlett-Packard, Apple) but most of the innovation occurs today within the resulting firms.

15. In a study for the RAND Institute for Civil Justice, Gu, Karoly, and Zissimopoulos (2008) found sixteen large-scale direct service programs for start-ups and expanding small businesses. There is no complete count of all entrepreneurship assistance programs nationally, considering that multiple providers in an individual region may offer separate entrepreneurship programs, while others may offer services in multiple regions.

16. For a review on educational programs on entrepreneurism, see Solomon (2007).

17. GAO (2012) reviews federal programs for economic development and entrepreneur assistance and finds that there was a significant amount of overlap in fifty-three programs in three departments and the SBA, especially with regard to the types of entrepreneurs and businesses targeted.

18. According to the SBIR website, any agency with an external R&D budget over $100,000,000 must allocate 2.5% of that budget to this program. SBA serves as the federal coordinator of the SBIR program, even though the individual agencies make their own grant solicitations and decisions.

19. Fairlie (2011) notes the findings of other studies that there is a relationship between the new business owner's personal wealth and access to capital for the business and that most loans to small businesses are backed by personal commitments by the entrepreneur.

6. ASSESSING THE EFFECT OF RESILIENCE POLICIES DIRECTED TOWARD PUBLIC GOODS, INSTITUTIONS, AND LEADERSHIP

1. While the focus of this chapter is on public programs, it should be noted that public funding for training programs is dwarfed by the amount that private companies spend on training employees. GAO (2011, 5) estimates that federal agencies "spent approximately $18 billion on employment and training services in fiscal year 2009." The inclusion of other federal programs with an education component (e.g., Pell Grants) would of course increase that total. But it would probably still be less than the $59.7 billion

spent on training by private companies and educational organizations with more than one hundred employees in 2011 (*Training* 2011), although some of this private training might be funded through state or federal programs. (For another breakdown of public versus private spending on training, see King and Heinrich 2011.) Formal evaluations of the effects of publicly sponsored on-the-job training are generally positive. For example, Holzer et al. (1993) find that a one-time training grant to firms in Michigan resulted in more employee training during the year the firm received the grant and small, positive effect on employment at those firms, while Hollenbeck (2008) observes the generally positive survey responses by firms participating in a state-funded program in Massachusetts.

2. GAO (2011) notes that fourteen of these programs received additional funding as part of the ARRA. Three of the programs were created through the ARRA legislation, which also changed the target populations or eligibility criteria of other programs.

3. One useful reference on WIA is the Department of Labor's "plain English" version of the act, http://www.doleta.gov/usworkforce/wia/plaintext.pdf.

4. Although not the focus of this section, workforce programs for youth (which typically provide services for high school dropouts or students at risk of dropping out) usually do not show any effects, with the exception of the Job Corps program, which included a residential component.

5. Friedlander, Greenberg, and Robins (1997) note that earnings gain due to these and other programs likely resulted in a decrease in transfer benefits to the worker and her family and also that the gains probably were not enough to raise most families from poverty.

6. The application of different evaluation methodologies also makes it difficult to compare results of WIA with those of JTPA and CETA.

7. For more information on CETA or JTPA, see Barnow (1993).

8. The important role of community colleges was recognized by the Obama administration, which in February 2012 proposed a Community College to Career Fund of $8 billion to bolster training for two million workers to prepare them for jobs in well-paying, high-demand industries (Lewin 2012). This is on top of $2 billion that community colleges received through the 2009 American Graduation Initiative (Lewin 2012). For a review of the history and role of community colleges in education and economic development, see Grubb (2009a) or Kane and Rouse (1999).

9. They found that women generally received $8,000 more in annual earnings and had a 17–18% increase in probability of employment when they earned an associate degree, while men earned $7,000 and had an increased probability of employment of 20%. At least in the case of earnings, though, they note that the higher returns to women may be since women in their sample generally had lower earnings.

10. Some of these findings were not statistically significant.

11. A national survey cited by O'Leary, Straits, and Wandner (2004, 298) finds that "95 percent of businesses that contract out training for their workers preferred using community colleges."

12. Bartik (2007) estimates that in the long run, eight out of ten new jobs created in a metropolitan area are captured by new in-migrants. Despite this, he concludes (2011) that local residents will benefit from the creation of these jobs. For every 1% increase in employment, he estimates that the income of original local residents will increase by 0.28%. Goodman (2003) uses a general equilibrium analysis and found that economic development incentives in Pueblo, Colorado, in the 1990s resulted in new jobs and businesses, but these jobs went to new residents, rather than existing residents who had voted for the subsidy funding the incentives. In addition, these new businesses changed the sectoral mix of businesses, pulling capital away from pre-existing businesses toward more export-focused industries.

13. See also Summers and Linneman (1993), who find that metropolitan employment growth was significantly related to an MSA's 1981 rating in the *Places Rated Almanac.*

14. Even under these "no effect" circumstances, there may still be a net fiscal loss for the region if the economic activity is just shifted in the region. This is because the jurisdictions are competing by offering new attraction incentives to businesses that switch jurisdictions but stay in the region or simply because the resources expended on recruiting businesses from other jurisdictions in the region could have been used for other more useful purposes.

15. It is important to note, however, that other market failures that need to be addressed are extremely local and reside with local government—this is the nitty-gritty detail of commercial and industrial real estate development. Plans have to be approved, permits have to be issued, buildings have to be inspected, and access has to be guaranteed. All of this means that local government has to be a participant as well.

16. Agranoff and McGuire (2003), in a 1994 survey of local governments about their collaborative economic development activities, find that cities work most frequently as a cluster with their county government, local development corporations, and chamber (22% of all linkages with other horizontal actors). They also find that most of the city's collaborative horizontal activities (which include working with actors in the city, not just the region) were focused on policy- or strategy-making, including inter-local agreements between cities in the region.

17. This viewpoint is often traced back to Tiebout's (1956) theory of local expenditures, in which he argued that multiple competing local governmental units allowed "consumer-voters" (presumably including businesses) to select the communities that best satisfied their preference patterns. The greater the number of communities, the more likely the "consumer-voter" will be able to locate in a place that meets his/her ideal preferences. Further, the need to compete for "consumer-voters" provides an incentive for local governments to operate efficiently. In addition, some argue that tax competition among many local governments will result in driving down the cost of doing business throughout the region by reducing the tendency of local governments to use taxes on businesses (who are nonvoters) to cross-subsidize taxes on households (who are voters).

18. COGs are voluntary organizations whose members are local government officials. In most cases COGs play a data collection, planning, and coordinating role within the region and serve as a useful venue for discussion of regional concerns, but they do not have governmental powers. However, COGs may play a more important role when, as is sometimes the case, the COG is colocated with or serves as the MPO, a federally mandated and funded regional transportation agency that also includes local public officials.

19. For purposes of this discussion, we exclude leadership of an individual firm or organization. While corporate or institutional leadership are demonstrably important for the vitality of the respective company or organization—which can be important for the region's economic growth and resiliency—this type of leadership is distinct from the leadership related to regional economic development.

20. There has been some work on quantifying the skills of leaders and changes to those skill levels due to leadership training programs (e.g., Brown and Detterman 1987; Earnest 1996). In addition to often being calculated as self-assessments and thus affected by the subjects' perceptions and biases and difficult compare across studies, they are not being collected for analysis related to regional economic outcomes.

References

319th Air Refueling Wing. 2007. "History of Grand Forks Air Force Base and the 319th Air Refueling Wing." Grand Forks Air Force Base, ND: Office of History, 319th Air Refueling Wing.

Aasheim, Ryan. 2014. "Rise of Drones in Grand Forks." Red River Valley Research Corridor, October 16. http://www.theresearchcorridor.com/content/00475-rise-drones-grand-forks.

Acs, Zoltan, Ed Glaeser, Robert Litan, Lee Fleming, Stephan Goetz, William Kerr, Steven Klepper, Stuart Rosenthal, Olav Sorenson, and William Strange. 2008. "Entrepreneurship and Urban Success: Toward a Policy Consensus." Ewing Marion Kauffman Foundation, Kansas City, MO. http://papers.ssrn.com/sol3/papers.cfm?abstract_id=1092493.

Adger, W. Neil, Terry P. Hughes, Carl Folke, Stephen R. Carpenter, and Johan Rockström. 2005. "Social-Ecological Resistance to Coastal Disasters." *Science* 309 (5737): 1036–1039.

Ady, Robert. 1997. "Discussion." *New England Economic Review* (March/April): 77–82.

Aerospace Futures Alliance of Washington. 2008. "Report to the Governor and Legislature: Governor's Council on Aerospace." http://www.afa-wa.com/downloads/AFA_SummitReport_Summit2008.pdf.

Agranoff, Robert, and Michael McGuire. 2003. *Collaborative Public Management: New Strategies for Local Governments*. Washington, DC: Georgetown University Press.

Anderson, John, and Robert Wassmer. 2000. *Bidding for Business: The Efficacy of Local Economic Development Incentives in a Metropolitan Area*. Kalamazoo, MI: W.E. Upjohn Institute for Employment Research.

Andreason, Stuart. 2014. "Will Talent Attraction and Retention Improve Metropolitan Labor Markets?" Ph.D. diss., University of Pennsylvania.

Andrews, Rhys, and George Boyne. 2012. "Structural Change and Public Service Performance: The Impact of the Reorganization Process in English Local Government." *Public Administration* 90 (2): 297–312.

Armstrong, Harvey, and Jim Taylor. 2000. *Regional Economics and Policy*. 3rd ed. Oxford: Blackwell.

Aschauer, David A. 1989. "Is Public Expenditure Productive?" *Journal of Monetary Economics* 23 (2): 177–200.

Atkins, Patricia, Pamela Blumenthal, Leah Curran, Adrienne Edisis, Alec Friedhoff, Lisa Lowry, Travis St. Clair, Howard Wial, and Harold Wolman. 2011. "Responding to Manufacturing Job Loss: What Can Economic Development Policy Do?" Discussion Paper, Brookings Institution, Washington, DC. https://www.brookings.edu/research/responding-to-manufacturing-job-loss-what-can-economic-development-policy-do/.

Bacheller, John M. 2000. "Commentary on State-Level Economic Development in New York." *Economic Development Quarterly* 14 (1): 5–10.

Barnes, William, and Larry Ledebur. 1998. *The New Regional Economies*. Thousand Oaks, CA: Sage.

Barnow, Burt. 1993. "Thirty Years of Changing Federal, State, and Local Relationships in Employment and Training Programs." *Publius* 23 (3): 75–94.

Barro, Robert J. 1992. "Human Capital and Economic Growth." Paper presented at Policies for Long-Run Economic Growth symposium sponsored by the Federal Reserve Bank of Kansas City, Jackson Hole. http://www.kc.frb.org/publications/research/escp/escp-1992.cfm.

Barro, Robert J., and Xavier Sala-i-Martin. 1991. "Convergence across States and Regions." Brookings Papers on Economic Activity, no. 1, 107–182. Brookings Institution, Washington, DC.

Bartik, Timothy J. 1991. *Who Benefits from State and Local Economic Development Policies.* Kalamazoo, MI: W.E. Upjohn Institute.

———. 1992. "The Effects of State and Local Taxes on Economic Development: A Review of Recent Research." *Economic Development Quarterly* 6 (1): 102–111.

———. 1994. "Jobs, Productivity, and Local Economic Development: What Implications Does Economic Research Have for the Role of Government?" *National Tax Journal* 47 (4): 847–861.

———. 1996. "Eight Issues for Policy toward Economic Development Incentives." *Region* 10 (2): 43–46.

———. 2003. "Local Economic Development Policies." Upjohn Institute Staff Working Paper No. 03-91, W.E. Upjohn Institute for Employment Research, Kalamazoo, MI. http://research.upjohn.org/up_workingpapers/91/.

———. 2005. "Solving the Problems of Economic Development Incentives." *Growth and Change* 36 (2): 139–166.

———. 2007. "Solving the Problems of Economic Development Incentives." In *Reining in the Competition for Capital,* edited by Ann Markusen, 103–140. Kalamazoo, MI: W.E. Upjohn Institute for Employment Research.

———. 2009. "What Proportion of Children Stay in the Same Location as Adults, and How Does This Vary across Location and Groups?" Upjohn Institute Staff Working Paper No. 09-145. W.E. Upjohn Institute for Employment, Kalamazoo, MI. http://research.upjohn.org/up_workingpapers/145/.

———. 2010. "Bringing Jobs to People: How Federal Policy Can Target Job Creation for Economically Distressed Areas." The Hamilton Project, Discussion Paper, Brookings Institution, Washington, DC.

———. 2011. *Investing in Kids: Early Childhood Programs and Local Economic Development.* Kalamazoo, MI: W.E. Upjohn Institute for Employment Research.

Bartik, Timothy J., and Randall W. Eberts. 2006. "Urban Labor Markets." In *A Companion to Urban Economics,* edited by Richard J. Arnott and Daniel P. McMillen, 389–403. Malden, MA: Blackwell.

Baumol, William J. 1986. "Productivity, Growth, Convergence, and Welfare: What the Long-Run Data Show." *American Economic Review* 78 (5): 1072–1085.

———. 2002. *The Free-Market Innovation Machine: Analyzing the Growth Miracle of Capitalism.* Princeton: Princeton University Press.

Bearse, Peter. 1998. "A Question of Evaluation: NBIA's Impact Assessment of Business Incubators." *Economic Development Quarterly* 12 (4): 322–333.

Beason, Richard, and David E. Weinstein. 1996. "Growth, Economies of Scale, and Targeting in Japan (1955–1990)." *Review of Economics and Statistics* 78 (2): 286–300.

Beatty, Christina, Stephen Fothergill, and Ryan Powell. 2007. "Twenty Years On: Has the Economy of the UK Coalfields Recovered?" *Environment and Planning A* 39 (7): 1654–1675.

Beeson, Patricia E. 1992. "Agglomeration Economies and Productivity Growth." *Sources of Metropolitan Growth*, edited by Edwin Mills and John McDonald, 19–35. New Brunswick, NJ: Center for Urban Policy Research.

Beeson, Patricia E., and Randall Eberts. 1989. "Identifying Productivity and Amenity Effects in Interurban Wage Differentials." *Review of Economics and Statistics* 71 (3): 443–452.

Bell, Michael, David Brunori, Richard Green, Hal Wolman, Joe Cordes, and Tanya Qadir. 2005. "State and Local Fiscal Policy and Economic Growth and Development." George Washington Institute of Public Policy Working Paper 026, George Washington Institute of Public Policy, Washington, DC.

Belman, Dale, Richard Block, and Karen Roberts. 2009. "The Economic Impact of State Differences in Labor Standards in the United States, 1998–2000." *Employment Policy Research Network* (blog), February. http://www.employmentpolicy.org.

Bennett, Robert J. 2007. "Expectations-Based Evaluation of SME Advice and Consultancy: An Example of Business Link Services." *Journal of Small Business and Enterprise Development* 14 (3): 435–457.

Bennett, Robert J., and Paul Robson. 2005. "The Advisor-SME Client Relationship: Impact, Satisfaction and Commitment." *Small Business Economics* 25 (3): 255–271.

Benus, Jacob, Theodore Shen, Sisi Zhang, Marc Chan, and Benjamin Hansen. 2009. "Growing America through Entrepreneurship: Final Evaluation of Project GATE." Columbia, MC: IMPAQ International. http://www.impaqint.com/files/4-Content/1-6-publications/1-6-2-project-reports/GATEFinal1209.pdf.

Berglund, Dan, and Marianne Clarke. 2000. *Using Research and Development to Grow State Economies*. Washington, DC: NGA Center for Best Practices.

Berry, Christopher R., and Edward L. Glaeser. 2005. "The Divergence of Human Capital Levels across Cities." NBER Working Paper No. 11617, National Bureau of Economic Research, Cambridge, MA. http://www.nber.org/papers/w11617.

Bingham, Richard, and Randall Eberts, eds. 1988. *Economic Restructuring of the American Midwest*. Boston: Kluwer Academic.

Blanchard, Olivier, and Lawrence F. Katz. 1992. "Regional Evolutions." Brookings Papers on Economic Activity, no. 1: 1–75. Brookings Institution, Washington, DC.

Bloom, Howard S., Larry L. Orr, Stephen H. Bell, George Cave, Fred Doolittle, Winston Lin, and Johannes M. Bos. 1997. "The Benefits and Costs of JTPA Title II-A Programs: Key Findings from the National Job Training Partnership Act Study." *Journal of Human Resources* 32 (2): 549–576.

Bloom, Nicholas Dagen. 2004. *Merchant of Illusion: James Rouse: America's Salesman of the Businessman's Utopia*. Columbus: Ohio State University Press.

Bluestone, Barry, and Mary Huff Stevenson. 2010. *The Boston Renaissance: Race, Space, and Economic Change in an American Metropolis*. New York: Russell Sage Foundation.

Blumenthal, Pamela, Harold Wolman, and Edward Hill. 2009. "Understanding the Economic Performance of Metropolitan Areas in the United States." *Urban Studies* 46 (3): 605–627.

Bonanno, George A. 2004. "Loss, Trauma, and Human Resilience: Have We Underestimated the Human Capacity to Thrive After Extremely Aversive Events?" *American Psychologist* 59 (1): 20–28.

Bonanno, George A., and Anthony D. Mancini. 2008. "The Human Capacity to Thrive in the Face of Potential Trauma." *Pediatrics* 121 (2): 369–375.

Boschma, Ron, and Jan Lambooy. 1999. "The Prospects of an Adjustment Policy Based On Collective Learning in Old Industrial Regions." *GeoJournal* 49 (4): 391–399.

Box-Steffensmeier, Janet, and Bradford Jones. 2004. *Event History Modeling.* New York: Cambridge University Press.

Box-Steffensmeier, Janet, and Christopher Zorn. 2002. "Duration Models for Repeated Events." *Journal of Politics* 64 (4): 1069–1094.

Briguglio, Lino, Gordon Cordina, Nadia Farrugia, and Stephanie Vella. 2006. "Conceptualising and Measuring Economic Resilience." In *Building the Economic Resilience of Small States,* edited by Lino Briguglio, Gordon Cardigan, and Eliawony J. Kisanga, 265–287. Malta: Islands and Small States Institute.

Brown, L. David, and Lynda B. Detterman. 1987. "Small Interventions for Large Problems: Reshaping Urban Leadership Networks." *Journal of Applied Behavioral Science* 23 (2): 151–168.

Bruneau, Michel, Stephanie E. Chang, Ronald T. Eguchi, George C. Lee, Thomas D. O'Rourke, Andrei M. Reinhorn, Masanobu Shinozuka, Kathleen Tierney, William A. Wallace, and Detlof von Winterfeldt. 2003. "A Framework to Quantitatively Assess and Enhance the Seismic Resilience of Communities." *Earthquake Spectra* 19 (4): 733–752.

Burby, Raymond J., Robert E. Deyle, David R. Godschalk, and Robert B. Olshansky. 2000. "Creating Hazard Resilient Communities through Land-Use Planning." *National Hazards Review* 1 (2): 99–106.

Burns, Peter. 2002. "The Intergovernmental Regime and Public Policy in Hartford, Connecticut." *Journal of Urban Affairs* 24 (1): 55–73.

Burtless, Gary, ed. 1996. *Does Money Matter? The Effect of School Resources on School Achievement and Adult Success.* Washington, DC: Brookings Institution Press.

Buss, Terry F. 1995. "Assessing the Accuracy of BLS ES202 Files." *Journal of Government Information* 22: 389–402.

———. 1999. "The Case against Targeted Industry Strategies." *Economic Development Quarterly* 13 (4): 339–356.

Calman, Leslie J., and Linda Tarr-Whelan. 2005. Early Childhood Education for All: A Wise Investment. New York: Legal Momentum. web.mit.edu/workplacecenter/docs/Full%20Report.pdf.

Campanella, Thomas J. 2006. "Urban Resilience and the Recovery of New Orleans." *Journal of the American Planning Association* 72 (2): 141–146.

Campbell, Candice, and David N. Allen. 1987. "The Small Business Incubator Industry: Micro-Level Economic Development." *Economic Development Quarterly* 1 (2): 178–191.

Card, David, Jochen Kluve, and Andrea Weber. 2010. "Active Labor Market Policy Evaluations: A Meta-Analysis." NBER Working Paper No. 16173, National Bureau of Economic Research, Cambridge, MA.

Carlino, Gerald, and Robert Inman. 2013. "Local Deficits and Local Jobs: Can US States Stabilize Their Own Economies?" NBER Working Paper No. 18930, National Bureau of Economic Research, Cambridge, MA.

Carlino, Gerald, and Albert Saiz. 2008. "City Beautiful." Working Paper No. 08-22, Federal Reserve Bank of Philadelphia, Philadelphia.

Carr, Jered B., and Richard C. Feiock. 1999. "Metropolitan Government and Economic Development." *Urban Affairs Review* 34 (3): 476–488.

Castilla, Emilio J. 2003. "Networks of Venture Capital Firms in Silicon Valley." *International Journal of Technology Management* 25 (1/2): 113–135.

Chapple, Karen, and T. William Lester. 2007. "Emerging Patterns of Regional Resilience." Working Paper 2007-13, Institute of Urban and Regional Development, Berkeley, CA.

——. 2010. "The Resilient Regional Labour Market? The U.S. Case." *Cambridge Journal of Regions, Economy and Society* 3 (1): 85–104.

Chapple, Karen, Ann Markusen, Greg Schrock, Daisaku Yamamoto, and Pingkang Yu. 2004. "Gauging Metropolitan 'High-Tech' and 'I-Tech' Activity." *Economic Development Quarterly* 18 (1): 10–29.

Chinitz, Benjamin. 1961. "Contrasts in Agglomeration: New York and Pittsburgh." *American Economic Review* 51 (2): 279–289.

Chrisman, James J. 2011. "Economic Impact of Small Business Development Center Counseling Activities in the United States: 2009–2010." http://www.apsu.edu/sites/apsu.edu/files/ext-ed/SBDC_National_Impact_Study_2009-10.pdf.

Christensen, Clayton. 1997. *The Innovator's Dilemma: The Revolutionary Book that Will Change the Way You Do Business.* Cambridge: Harvard Business School Press.

Christopherson, Susan, and Jennifer Clark. 2007. "Power in Firm Networks: What It Means for Regional Innovation Systems." *Regional Studies* 41 (9): 1223–1236.

Christopherson, Susan, Jonathan Michie, and Peter Tyler. 2010. "Regional Resilience: Theoretical and Empirical Perspectives." *Cambridge Journal of Regions, Economy, and Society* 3 (1): 3–10.

Cigler, Beverly. 2008. "Economic Development in Metropolitan Areas." In *Urban and Regional Policies for Metropolitan Livability,* edited by David Hamilton and Patricia Atkins, 296–323. Armonk, NY: M.E. Sharpe.

Clark, Jennifer. 2013. *Working Regions: Reconnecting Innovation and Production in the Knowledge Economy.* London: Routledge.

ClevelandPlusBusiness.com. 2013. "One Team + One Mission." http://www.cleve landplusbusiness.com/About-Team-NEO.aspx.

Coaffee, Jon. 2006. "From Counterterrorism to Resilience." *European Legacy* 11 (4): 389–403.

Cohen, Natalie. 2000. "Business Location Decision-Making and the Cities: Bringing Companies Back." Center on Urban and Metropolitan Policy Discussion Paper, Brookings Institution, Washington, DC. http://www.brookings.edu/research/reports/2000/05/business-location-cohen.

Cohen, Wesley M., and Daniel A. Levinthal. 1989. "Innovation and Learning: The Two Faces of R & D." *Economic Journal* 99 (397): 569–596.

Coleman, Morton, David Houston, and Edward K. Muller. 2000. "Pittsburgh's Failed Industry Targeting Strategy of the 1960s." Center for Industry Studies Working Paper, University of Pittsburgh. http://www.industrystudies.pitt.edu/_files/papers/skybus.pdf.

Colten, C. E, R. W. Kates, and S. B. Laska. 2008. "Community Resilience: Lessons from New Orleans and Hurricane Katrina." CARRI Research Report 3, Community and Regional Resilience Initiative, Oak Ridge National Laboratory.

Community and Regional Resilience Institute. 2013. "Definition of Community Resilience." CARRI Report. http://www.resilientus.org/wp-content/uploads/2013/08/definitions-of-community-resilience.pdf.

Connecticut Department of Labor. 2013. "Office of Workforce Competitiveness/Connecticut's Workforce Investment System." http://www.ctdol.state.ct.us/rwdb/workforce.htm.

Conway, Patrick, Robert Connolly, Alfred Field, and Douglas Longman. 2003. "The North Carolina Textiles Project: An Initial Report." *Journal of Textile and*

Apparel, Technology, and Management 3 (3). http://www.unc.edu/~pconway/
Textiles/nctp_tatm_rev.pdf.

Cortright, Joseph. 2006. "Making Sense of Clusters: Regional Competitiveness and
Economic Development." Discussion Paper, Brookings Institution, Washington,
DC. https://www.brookings.edu/research/making-sense-of-clusters-regional-
competitiveness-and-economic-development/.

Cumbers, Andy, and Danny MacKinnon. 2004. "Introduction: Clusters in Urban and
Regional Development." *Urban Studies* 41 (5/6): 959–970.

David, Paul A. 2000. "Path Dependence, Its Critics and the Quest for Historical
Economics." In *Evolution and Path Dependence in Economics Ideas: Past and
Present*, edited by Pierre Garrouste and Stavros Iōannidēs, 15–40. Cheltenham,
UK: Edward Elgar.

Davies, Sara. 2011. "Regional Resilience in the 2008–2010 Downturn: Comparative
Evidence from European Countries." *Cambridge Journal of Regions, Economy
and Society* 4 (3): 369–382.

Dawley, Stuart, Andy Pike, and John Tomaney. 2010. "Towards the Resilient Region?"
Local Economy 25 (8): 650–667.

Delgado, Mercedes, Christian Ketels, and Samantha Zyontz. 2012. "Clusters and
Economic Performance: Levering the Cluster Mapping Database." Paper
presented at the Symposium on Use of Innovative Data Sets for Regional
Economic Research, Washington, DC.

Delgado, Mercedes, Michael E. Porter, and Scott Stern. 2010. "Clusters and
Entrepreneurship." *Journal of Economic Geography* 10 (4): 495–518.

——. 2012. "Clusters, Convergence and Economic Performance." NBER Working
Paper No. 18250, National Bureau of Economic Research, Cambridge, MA.
http://www.nber.org/papers/w18250.

Deller, Steven. 2012. "Targeting Industrial Gaps and Disconnects for Community
Economic Development." *Choices: The Magazine of Food, Farm and Resource
Issues* 27 (2): 14.

Deryugina, Tatyana, Laura Dawano, and Steven Levitt. 2014. "The Economic Impact
of Hurricane Katrina on Its Victims." NBER Working Paper No. 20713, National
Bureau of Economic Research, Cambridge, MA.

DeSantis, Mark, and Roger R. Stough. 1999. "Fast Adjusting Urban Regions,
Leadership and Regional Economic Development." *Revue Région et
Développement* 10: 37–57.

Desmet, Klaus, and Esteban Rossi-Hansberg. 2009. "Spatial Growth and Industry Age."
Journal of Economic Theory 144 (6): 2477–2502.

Dhawan, Rajeev, and Karsten Jeske. 2006. "How Resilient is the Modern Economy to
Energy Price Shocks?" *Economic Review* 91 (3): 21–32.

Drucker, Joshua, and Harvey Goldstein. 2007. "Assessing the Regional Economic
Development Impacts of Universities: A Review of Current Approaches."
International Regional Science Review 30 (1): 20–46.

Dudensing, Rebekka M., and David L. Barkley. 2010. "Competitiveness of Southern
Metropolitan Areas: The Role of New Economy Policies." *Review of Regional
Studies* 40 (2): 197–226.

Duranton, Gilles. 2009. "California Dreamin': The Feeble Case for Cluster Policies."
Unpublished paper, Department of Economics, University of Toronto.

Duranton, Gille, and Diego Puga. 2001. "Nursery Cities: Urban Diversity, Process
Innovation, and the Life Cycle of Products." *American Economic Review* 91 (5):
1454–1477.

Duscha, Steve, and Wanda Lee Graves. 2006. "The Employer as the Client: State-financed Customized Training 2006." Washington, D.C: U.S. Department of Labor, Employment and Training Administration.

Duval, Romain, Jorgen Elmeskov, and Lukas Vogel. 2007. "Structural Policies and Economic Resilience to Shocks." Economics Department Working Paper 567, Organisation for Economic Cooperation and Development, Paris.

Dziczek, Kristin, Daniel Luria, and Edith Wiarda. 1998. "Assessing the Impact of a Manufacturing Extension Center." *Journal of Technology Transfer* 23 (1): 29–36.

Earnest, Garee W. 1996. "Evaluating Community Leadership Programs." *Journal of Extension* 34 (1). http://www.joe.org/joe/1996february/rb1.php.

Eberts, Randall W. 1986. "Estimating the Contribution of Urban Public Infrastructure to Regional Growth." Working Paper No. 8610, Federal Reserve Bank of Cleveland, Cleveland.

———. 1990. "Public Infrastructure and Regional Economic Development." *Economic Review* 26 (1): 15–27.

Eberts, Randall W., and Duffy-Deno, Kevin T. 1991. "Public Infrastructure and Regional Economic Development: A Simultaneous Equations Approach." *Journal of Urban Economics* 30 (3): 329–343.

Eberts, Randall W., and George A. Erickcek. 2009. "Where Have All the Michigan Auto Jobs Gone?" *Employment Research* 16 (4): 1–3.

Eberts, Randall W., and Michael Fogarty. 1987. "Estimating the Relationship between Local Public and Private Investment." Working Paper 8703, Federal Reserve Bank of Cleveland, Cleveland.

Eberts, Randall W., George Erickcek, and Jack Kleinhenz. 2006. "Dashboard Indicators for the Northeast Ohio Economy: Prepared for the Fund for Our Economic Future." Working Paper 06-05, Federal Reserve Bank of Cleveland, Cleveland.

Economic Development Council of Seattle and King County. n.d. "2013–2018 Business Plan." Seattle.

Ehlen, Mark A. 2001. "The Economic Impact of Manufacturing Extension Centers." *Economic Development Quarterly* 15 (1): 36–44.

Ellef, Peter N. 1997. "Industry Clusters Shape New CT Economy." *Connecticut Economy* 5 (Summer).

Entrepreneur. 1995, August 30. "Economic Incentives Pivotal in Relocation Decisions." http://www.entrepreneur.com/tradejournals/article/17778158.html.

Erickcek, George A., Jason M. Preuss, Brad R. Watts, Kevin O'Brien, Claudette Robey, Daila Shimek, Jim Robey, and Jacob Duritsky. 2008. "Comprehensive Study of Regionalism: Tools for Comparison and Evaluation." Report prepared for the Economic Development Administration, W.E. Upjohn Institute for Employment Research, Kalamazoo, MI. http://research.upjohn.org/reports/20/.

European Social Planning Observation Network. 2014. *Economic Crisis: Resilience of Regions.* Brussels: European Regional Development Fund. http://www.espon.eu/main/Menu_Projects/Menu_AppliedResearch/ECR2.html.

Ewing Marion Kauffman Foundation. 2011. "The Startup Act." Kansas City: Ewing Marion Kauffman Foundation.

Fairlie, Robert W. 2011. "The Great Recession and Entrepreneurship." Working Paper WR-822-EMKF, RAND Institute for Civil Justice, Santa Monica, CA.

———. 2012. "Kauffman Index of Entrepreneurial Activity 1996–2011." Ewing Marion Kauffman Foundation, Kansas City, MO. http://www.kauffman.org/uploadedFiles/KIEA_2012_report.pdf.

Fee, Kyle, and Robert Sadowksi. 2007. "Economic Trends: The Cleveland Metropolitan Statistical Area." Federal Reserve Bank of Cleveland, Cleveland, OH. https://www.clevelandfed.org/en/newsroom-and-events/publications/economic-trends/economic-trends-archives/2007-economic-trends/et-20070806-the-cleveland-metropolitan-statistical-area.aspx.

Feiock, Richard, Annette Steinacker, and Hyung Jun Park. 2009. "Institutional Collective Action and Economic Development Joint Ventures." *Public Administration Review* 69 (2): 256–269.

Feiock, Richard C., Jill Tao, and Linda Johnson. 2004. "Institutional Collective Action: Social Capital and the Formation of Regional Partnerships." In *Metropolitan Governance: Conflict, Competition, and Cooperation*, edited by Richard C. Feiock, Richard C, 147–158. Washington, DC: Georgetown University Press.

Feldman, Maryann P., and Maryellen R. Kelley. 2006. "The *Ex Ante* Assessment of Knowledge Spillovers: Government R&D Policy, Economic Incentives and Private Firm Behavior." *Research Policy* 35 (10): 1509–1521.

Feldman, Maryann P., and Dieter F. Kogler. 2008. "The Contribution of Public Entities to Innovation and Technological, Change." In *The Handbook of Technology and Innovation Management*, edited by Scott Shane, 431–460. Chichester, UK: Wiley.

Felsenstein, Daniel. 1996. "The University in the Metropolitan Area: Impacts and Public Policy Prescriptions." *Urban Studies* 33 (9): 1565–1580.

Feser, Edward, Henry Renski, and Harvey Goldstein. 2008. "Clusters and Economic Development Outcomes: An Analysis of the Link between Clustering and Industry Growth." *Economic Development Quarterly* 22 (4): 324–344.

Feyrer, James Bruce Sacerdote. 2011. "Did the Stimulus Stimulate? Real Time Estimates of the Effects of the American Recovery and Reinvestment Act." NBER Working Paper Series Working Paper No. 16759, National Bureau of Economic Research, Cambridge, MA.

Feyrer, James Bruce Sacerdote, and Ariel Dora Stern. 2007. "Did the Rust Belt Become Shiny? A Study of Cities and Counties That Lost Steel and Auto Jobs in the 1980s." In *Brookings-Wharton Papers on Urban Affairs 2007*, edited by Gary Burtless and Janet Rothenberg Pack, 41–102. Washington, DC: Brookings Institution Press.

Ficenec, Sarah, 2010. "Building Regional Economic Resilience: What We Can Learn from Other Fields," Working Paper 043, George Washington Institute of Public Policy, Washington, DC. http://www.gwu.edu/~gwipp/Ficenec%20factors%20related%20to%20resilience.pdf.

Fingleton, Bernard, Henry Garretsen, and Ron Martin. 2012. "Recessionary Shocks and Regional Employment: Evidence on the Resilience of the U.K. Regions." *Journal of Regional Science* 52 (1): 109–133.

Fisher, Peter, and Alan Peters. 1998. *Industrial Incentives: Competition among American States and Cities*. Kalamazoo, MI: W.E. Upjohn Institute.

Florida, Richard. 2002. *The Rise of the Creative Class: And How It's Transforming Work, Leisure, Community, and Everyday Life*. New York: Basic Books.

Flynn, Patricia M. 1984. "Lowell: A High Technology Success Story." *New England Economic Review* (September–October): 39–49.

Foster, Kathryn A. 1999. *The Political Economy of Special-Purpose Government*. Washington, DC: Georgetown University Press.

———. 2001. "Regionalism on Purpose." Cambridge: Lincoln Institute of Land Policy.

Frieder, Larry A. 1988. "The Interstate Banking Landscape: Legislative Policies and Rationale." *Contemporary Economic Policy* 6 (2): 41–66.

Friedland, Daniel, David H. Greenberg, and Philip K. Robins. 1997. "Evaluating Government Training Programs for the Economically Disadvantaged." *Journal of Economic Literature* 35: 1809–1855.

Fulford, Amy. 2013 *Northeast Ohio Regional Economic Competitiveness Strategy: Report to the Team NEO Board.* Shaker Heights, Ohio: enlight advisors

Fund for Our Economic Future. 2012. "About the Fund." http://www.futurefundneo. org/en/About.

Gabe, Todd M., and David S. Kraybill. 2002. "The Effect of State Economic Development Incentives on Employment Growth of Establishments." *Journal of Regional Science* 42 (4): 703–730.

Gabriel Stuart, Joe Mattey, and William Wascher. 1999. "Compensating Differentials and Evolution of Quality of Life among U.S. States." Working Paper # 2001-1009, Lusk Center for Real Estate, Los Angeles.

Galster, George. 2012. *Driving Detroit: The Quest for Respect in the Motor City.* Philadelphia: University of Pennsylvania Press.

Ganor, Michael, and Yuli Ben-Levy. 2003. "Community Resilience: Lessons derived from Gilo Under Fire." *Journal of Jewish Communal Service* 79 (2–3): 105–108.

Garcia-Mila, Teresa, Therese McGuire, and Robert Porter. 1996. "The Effect of Public Capital in State-level Production Functions Re-considered." *Review of Economics and Statistics* 78 (1): 177–180.

Garmise, Shari. 2009. "Building a Workforce Development System as an Economic Development Strategy: Lessons from US Programs." *Local Economy* 24 (3): 211–223.

Gerber, Elisabeth R., and Carolyn G. Loh. 2010. "Prospects for Expanding Regional Planning Efforts." CLOSUP Working Paper Series Number 24, Center for Local, State, and Urban Policy, Gerald R. Ford School of Public Policy, Ann Arbor, MI.

Gill, Andrew M., and Duane E. Leigh. 2003. "Do the Returns to Community Colleges Differ between Academic and Vocational Programs?" *Journal of Human Resources* 38 (1): 134–155.

Giloth, Robert P. 2000. "Learning from the Field: Economic Growth and Workforce Development in the 1990s." *Economic Development Quarterly* 14 (4): 340–359.

Glaeser, Edward L. 2005a. "Reinventing Boston: 1630–2003." *Journal of Economic Geography.* 5 (2): 119–153.

——. 2005b. "Review of Richard Florida's *The Rise of the Creative Class.*" *Regional Science and Urban Economics* 35 (5): 593–596.

——. 2009. "The Wealth of Cities: Agglomeration Economies and Spatial Equilibrium in the United States." *Journal of Economic Literature* 47 (4): 983–1028.

Glaeser, Edward L., and Joshua Gottlieb. 2006. "Urban Resurgence and the Consumer City." *Urban Studies.* 43 (8): 1275–1299.

Glaeser, Edward L., Hedi D. Kallal, José A. Scheinkman, and Andrei Shleifer. 1992. "Growth in Cities." *Journal of Political Economy* 100 (6): 1126–1152.

Glaeser, Edward L., and William R. Kerr. 2009. "Local Industrial Conditions and Entrepreneurship: How Much of the Spatial Distribution Can We Explain?" *Journal of Economics & Management Strategy* 18 (3): 623–663.

Glaeser, Edward L., Jed Kolko, and Albert Saiz. 2001. "Consumer City." *Journal of Economic Geography* 1 (10): 27–50.

Glaeser, Edward L., Sari Pekkala Kerr, and William R. Kerr. 2012. Entrepreneurship and Urban Growth: An Empirical Assessment with Historical Mines. NBER Working Paper No. 18333, National Bureau of Economic Research, Cambridge, MA. http://www.nber.org/papers/w18333.

Glaeser, Edward L., Matt Resseger, and Kristina Tobio. 2009. "Inequality in Cities." *Journal of Regional Science* 49 (4): 617–646.

Glaeser, Edward L., Stuart S. Rosenthal, and William C. Strange. 2010. "Urban Economics and Entrepreneurship." *Journal of Urban Economics* 67 (1): 1–14.

Glaeser, Edward L., and Albert Saiz. 2004. "The Rise of the Skilled City." In *Brookings-Wharton Papers on Urban Affairs 2004*, edited by William G. Gale and Janet Rothenberg Pack, 47–94. Washington, DC: Brookings Institution Press.

Glaeser, Edward L., Jose A Scheinkman, and Andrei Shleifer. 1995. "Economic Growth in a Cross-Section of Cities." *Journal of Monetary Economics* 36 (1): 117–143.

Glaeser, Edward L., and Jesse Shapiro. 2001. "Is There a New Urbanism? The Growth of U.S. Cities in the 1990s." NBER Working Paper No. 8357, National Bureau of Economic Research, Cambridge, MA.

Glasmeier, Amy. 2000. "Economic Geography in Practice: Local Economic Development Policy." In *The Oxford Handbook of Economic Geography*, edited by Gordon L. Clark, Maryann P. Feldman, and Meric S. Gertler, 567–568. Oxford: Oxford University Press.

Glazer, Lou, and Donald Grimes, Donald. 2008. *Michigan's Transition to a Knowledge-Based Economy: First Annual Progress Report*. Ann Arbor: Michigan Future.

Godschalk, David R. 2003. "Urban Hazard Mitigation: Creating Resilient Cities." *Natural Hazards Review* 4 (3): 136–143.

Goetz, Edward G., and Terrence Kayser. 1993. "Cooperation and Competition in Economic Development: A Study of the Twin Cities Metropolitan Area." *Economic Development Quarterly* 7 (1): 63–78.

Goldstein, Harvey A. 2009a. "Theory and Practice of Technology-Based Economic Development." In *Theories of Local Economic Development: Linking Theory to Practice*, edited by James Edward Rowe, 237–264. Farnham, UK: Ashgate.

Goldstein, Harvey A. 2009b. "What We Know and What We Don't Know about the Regional Economic Impacts of Universities." In *Universities, Knowledge Transfer and Regional Development: Geography, Entrepreneurship and Policy*, edited by Attila Varga, 11–25. Cheltenham, UK: Edward Elgar.

Goldstein, Harvey A. Maier, Gunther, and Michael Luger. 1995. "The University as an Instrument for Economic, and Business Development: U.S. and European Comparisons." In *Emerging Patterns of Social Demand and University Reform: Through a Glass Darkly*, edited by David D. Dill and Barbara Sporn, 105–133. Oxford: Pergamon.

Goldstein, Mark. 1985. "Choosing the Right Site." *Industry Week,* April 15, 57–60.

Gompers, Paul, Anna Kovner, Josh Lerner, and David Scharfstein. 2006. "Skill vs. Luck in Entrepreneurship and Venture Capital: Evidence from Serial Entrepreneurs." NBER Working Paper No. 12592, National Bureau of Economic Research, Cambridge, MA. http://www.nber.org/papers/w12592.

Goodman, D.J. 2003. "Are Economic Development Incentives Worth It? A Computable General Equilibrium Analysis of Pueblo, Colorado's Efforts to Attract Business." *Journal of Regional Analysis and Policy* 33 (1): 43–55.

Goss, Ernest, and Joseph Phillips. 2001. "The Impact of Tax Incentives: Do Initial Economic Conditions Matter?" *Growth and Change* 32 (2): 236–250.

Gottlieb, Paul. 1994. "Amenities as an Economic Development Tool." *Economic Development Quarterly.* 8 (3): 270–285.

Gottlieb, Paul, and Michael Fogarty. 2003. "Educational Attainment and Metropolitan Growth." *Economic Development Quarterly* 17 (4): 325–336.

Grand Forks Region Economic Development Corporation. 2012. "Grand Forks Region Economic Development, Workforce." http://www.grandforks.org/commdata/workforce.php.

——. 2013. "Support Programs Provide Ingredients for Success." http://www.grandforks.org/location_financing#.Umq1yPmw7_Y.

Grassmueck, Georg, and Martin Shields. 2010. "Does Government Fragmentation Enhance or Hinder Metropolitan Economic Growth?" *Papers in Regional Science* 89 (3): 641–657.

Graves, Phillip. 1980. "Migration and Climate." *Journal of Regional Science* 20 (2): 227–237.

Green, Richard. 2007. "Airports and Economic Development." *Real Estate Economics* 35 (1): 91–112.

Greenwood, Michael. 1985. "Human Migration: Theory, Models, and Empirical Studies." *Journal of Regional Science* 25 (4): 521–544.

Greenwood, Michael, and Gary Hunt. 1989. "Jobs Versus Amenities in the Analysis of Metropolitan Migration." *Journal of Urban Economics* 25 (1): 1–16.

Gregersen, B., and B. Johnson 1997. "Learning Economies, Innovation Systems and European Integration." *Regional Studies* 31 (5): 479–490.

Grimes, Paul W. and Margaret A. Ray. 1988. "Right to Work Legislation and Employment Growth in the 1980's: A Shift-Share Analysis." *Regional Science Perspectives* 18 (2): 78–93.

Grubb, W. Norton. 2002. "Learning and Earning in the Middle, Part I: National Studies of Pre-baccalaureate Education." *Economics of Education Review* 21 (4): 299–321.

——. 2009a. "The Education Gospel and the Metropolis: The Multiple Roles of Community Colleges in Workforce and Economic Development." In *Urban and Regional Policy and Its Effects,* edited by Nancy Pindus, Howard Wial, and Harold Wolman, vol. 2, 124–166. Washington, DC: Brookings Institution Press.

——. 2009b. *The Money Myth: School Resources, Outcomes, and Equity.* New York: Russell Sage Foundation.

Gu, Qian, Lynn A. Karoly, and Julie Zissimpoulos. 2008. "Small Business Assistance Programs in the United States: An Analysis of What They Are, How Well They Perform, and How We Can Learn More about Them." Working Paper WR-603-EMKF, RAND Institute for Civil Justice, Santa Monica, CA.

Ha, Hyunsang, Inwon Lee, and Richard C. Feiock. 2010. "Organizational Networks and Economic Performance in Local Economic Development." Paper presented at the Annual Meeting of the Southern Political Science Association, Atlanta.

Hackett, Sean M., and David M. Dilts. 2004. "A Systematic Review of Business Incubation Research." *Journal of Technology Transfer* 29 (1): 55–82.

Hageman, John. 2013. "FAA Names ND as UAS Test Site." *Prairie Business,* December 31.

Haltiwanger, John C., Ron S. Jarmin, and Javier Miranda. 2011. "Who Creates Jobs? Small vs. Large vs. Young." NBER Working Paper No. 16300, National Bureau of Economic Research, Cambridge, MA. http://www.nber.org/papers/w16300.

Hamilton, David K., David Y. Miller, and Jerry Paytas. 2004. "Exploring the Horizontal and Vertical Dimensions of the Governing of Metropolitan Regions." *Urban Affairs Review* 40 (2): 147–182.

Hanson, Royce, Harold Wolman, David Connolly, Katherine Pearson, and Robert McManmon. 2010. "Corporate Citizenship and Urban Problem Solving: The Changing Civic Role of Business Leaders in American Cities." *Journal of Urban Affairs* 32 (1): 1–23.

Hanushek, Eric. 1997. "Assessing the Effects of School Resources on Student Performance: An Update." *Education Evaluation and Policy Analysis* 19 (2): 141–164.

Hanushek, Eric, and Ludger Woessmann. 2007. "The Role of School Improvement in Economic Development." https://www.hks.harvard.edu/pepg/PDF/Papers/PEPG07-01_Hanushek_Woessmann.pdf.

Harr, Dan. 1997. "State Convenes Economic Board." *Hartford Courant*, February 26.

Harrison, Bennett. 1984. "Regional Restructuring and 'Good Business Climates': The Economic Transformation of New England since World War II." In *Sunbelt/ Snowbelt: Urban Development and Regional Restructuring*, edited by Larry Sawers and William K. Tabb, 48–96. New York: Oxford University Press.

Harrison, Bennett, Maryellen Kelley, and Jon Gant. 1996. "Specialization Versus Diversity in Local Economies: The Implications for Innovative Private-Sector Behavior." *Cityscape* 2: 61–93.

Harrison, Bennett, Ari Kuncoro, and Matt Turner. "Industrial Development in Cities." *Journal of Political Economy* 103 (5): 1067–1090.

Haughwout, A.F. 2002. "Public Infrastructure Investments, Productivity and Welfare in Fixed Geographic Areas." *Journal of Public Economics* 83 (3): 405–428.

Hausmann, Ricardo, Lant Pritchett, and Dani Rodrik. 2004. "Growth Accelerations." NBER Working Paper No. 10566, National Bureau of Economic Research, Cambridge, MA. http://www.nber.org/papers/w10566.

Heilbrun, James. 1987. *Urban Economics and Public Policy*. New York: St. Martin's Press.

Heinrich, Carolyn J., Peter R. Mueser, and Kenneth R. Troske. 2008. "Workforce Investment Act Non-Experimental Net Impact Evaluation: Final Report." Columbia, MD: IMPAQ International. http://wdr.doleta.gov/research/FullText_Documents/Workforce%20Investment%20Act%20Non-Experimental%20Net%20Impact%20Evaluation%20-%20Final%20Report.pdf.

Helms, Jay. 1985. "The Effect of State and Local Taxes on Economic Growth: A Times Series-Cross Section Approach." *Review of Economics and Statistics* 67 (4): 574–582.

Henderson, Daniel, and Subal Kumbhakar. 2006. "Public and Private Capital Productivity Puzzle: A Nonparametric Approach." *Southern Economic Journal* 73 (1): 219–232.

Henderson, Vernon. 2003. "Marshall's Scale Economies." *Journal of Urban Economics* 53 (1): 1–28.

Hewitt-Dundas, Nola. 2011. "The Role of Proximity in University-business Cooperation for Innovation." *Journal of Technology Transfer* 38 (2): 93–115.

Hicks, Jonathan. 1991. "United Technologies' Bumpy Ride." *New York Times*, 1 May.

Hill, Edward W. 1990. "Cleveland, Ohio: Manufacturing Matters, Services Strengthen, But Earnings Erode." In *Economic Restructuring in the American Midwest*, edited by Richard Bingham and Randall Eberts, 103–140. Boston: Kluwer,.

———. 1992. "Perspective: Contested Cleveland." *Urban Affairs Association Newsletter* (Winter).

———. 2004. "Manufacturing Pennsylvania's Future: Regional Strategies that Build from Current Strengths and Address Competitive Challenges." *Urban Publications*. Paper 6. http://works.bepress.com/edward_hill/10.

———. 2012. "Economic Performance of Northeast Ohio: 2000 to 2010. A Report to the Regional Economic Competitiveness Strategy." Levin College of Urban Affairs, Cleveland State University, July 27.

Hill, Edward W., and Iryna Lendel. 2007. "The Impact of the Reputation of Bio-Life Science and Engineering Doctoral Programs on Regional Economic Development." *Economic Development Quarterly* 21 (3): 223–243.

Hill, Edward W, Howard Wial, and Harold Wolman. 2008. "Exploring Regional Economic Resilience." Working Paper 2008-04, Building Resilient Regions Network, Berkeley, CA.

Hollenbeck, Kevin. 2008. "Is There a Role for Public Support of Incumbent Worker On-the-Job Training?" Upjohn Institute Working Paper No. 08-138, W.E. Upjohn Institute for Employment Research, Kalamazoo, MI. http://research. upjohn.org/up_workingpapers/138.

———. 2009a. "Does the Workforce Investment Act Work?" Paper presented at Annual Conference of the Association for Public Policy Analysis and Management, Washington, DC. http://research.upjohn.org/confpapers/39.

———. 2009b. "Workforce Investment Act (WIA) Net Impact Estimates and Rates of Return." Paper presented at What the European Social Fund Can Learn from the WIA Experience meeting sponsored by the European Commission, Washington, DC. http://research.upjohn.org/confpapers/2.

Holling, C.S. 1973. "Resilience and Stability of Ecological Systems." *Annual Review of Ecology & Systematics* 4 (1): 1–23.

Holmes, Thomas J. 1998. "The Effect of State Policies on the Location of Manufacturing: Evidence from State Borders." *Journal of Political Economy* 106 (4): 667–705.

Holtz-Eakin, Douglas. 1994. "Public-Sector Capital and the Productivity Puzzle. *Review of Economics and Statistics* 76 (1): 12–21.

Holzer, Harry J. 2008. "Workforce Development and the Disadvantaged: New Directions for 2009 and Beyond." Low-Income Working Families Project Brief 7, Urban Institute, Washington, DC. http://www.urban.org/ publications/411761.html.

———. 2009. "Workforce Development as an Antipoverty Strategy: What Do We Know? What Should We Do?" In *Changing Poverty, Changing Policies*, edited by Maria Cancian and Sheldon Danziger, 301–329. New York: Russell Sage Foundation.

Holzer, Harry J., Richard N. Block, Marcus Cheatham, and Jack H. Knott. 1993. "Are Training Subsidies for Firms Effective? The Michigan Experience." *Industrial and Labor Relations Review* 46 (4): 625–636.

Howland, Marie. 1984. "Age of Capital and Regional Business Cycles." *Growth and Change* 15 (2): 29–37.

Huag, P. 1995. "Formation of Biotechnology Firms in the Greater Seattle Region: An Empirical Investigation of Entrepreneurial, Financial, and Educational Perspectives." *Environment and Planning A* 27 (2): 249–267.

Hudson, Ray. 1999. "The Learning Economy, the Learning Firm and the Learning Region: A Sympathetic Critique of the Limits to Learning." *European Urban and Regional Studies* 6, 59–72.

Hula, Richard C., and Cynthia Jackson-Elmore. 2001. "Governing Nonprofits and Local Political Profits." *Urban Affairs Review* 36 (3): 324–358.

Hungerford, Thomas L., and Robert W. Wassmer. 2004. "K–12 Education in the U.S. Economy: Its Impact on Economic Development, Earnings, and Housing Values." NEA Research Working Paper, National Education Association, Washington, DC. www.nea.org/assets/docs/HE/economy.pdf.

Hurst, Erik and Benjamin Wild Pugsley. 2011. "What Do Small Businesses Do?" Brookings Working Paper No. 17041, Brookings Institution, Washington, DC. http://www.nber.org/papers/w17041.

Huxham, Chris, and Siv Vangen. 1996. "Working Together: Key Themes in the Management of Relationships between Public and Non-Profit Organizations." *International Journal of Public Sector Management* 9 (7): 5–17.

Jacob, Brian A., and Jens Ludwig. 2009. "Improving Educational Outcomes for Poor Children." In *Changing Poverty, Changing Policies*, edited by Maria Cancian and Sheldon Danziger, 266–300. New York: Russell Sage Foundation.

Jacobson, Louis, Robert LaLonde, and Daniel G. Sullivan. 2005a. "Estimating the Returns to Community College Schooling for Displaced Workers." *Journal of Econometrics* 125 (1–2): 271–304.

———. 2005b. "The Impact of Community College Retraining on Older Displaced Workers: Should We Teach Old Dogs New Tricks?" *Industrial and Labor Relations Review* 58 (3): 398–415.

James, Ryan, and Devin Moeller. 2013. "Income Convergence, Product Cycles, and Space: Explaining How Wages Influence Growth in the Spatial Economy." *Industrial Geographer* 10 (1): 1–29.

Jarmin, Ronald S. 1999. "Evaluating the Impact of Manufacturing Extension on Productivity Growth." *Journal of Policy Analysis and Management* 18 (1): 99–119.

Jepsen, Christopher, Kenneth Troske, and Paul Coomes. 2009. "The Labor-Market Returns to Community College Degrees, Diplomas, and Certificates." Discussion Paper 2009-08. University of Kentucky Center for Poverty Research, Lexington. http://www.ukcpr.org/Publications/DP2009-08.pdf.

Judd, Dennis, and Michael Parkinson, eds. 1990. *Leadership and Urban Regeneration: Cities in North America and Europe*. Newberry Park, CA: Sage.

Kane, Thomas J., and Cecilia Elena Rouse. 1995. "Labor-Market Returns to Two- and Four-Year College." *American Economic Review* 85 (3): 600–614.

———. 1999. "The Community College: Educating Students at the Margin between College and Work." *Journal of Economic Perspectives* 13 (1): 63–84.

Katz, Bruce, and Jennifer Bradley. 2013. *The Metropolitan Revolution: How Cities and Metros Are Fixing Our Broken Politics and Fragile Economy*. Washington, DC: Brookings Institution Press.

Kellerman, Barbara. 2012. *The End of Leadership*. New York: HarperCollins.

Kieshnick, Michael. 1981. *Taxes and Growth: Business Incentives and Economic Development*. Washington, DC: Council of State Planning Agencies.

Kilburn, M. Rebecca, and Lynn A. Karoly. 2008. "The Economics of Early Childhood Policy: What the Dismal Science Has to Say about Investing in Children." Occasional Paper, RAND Corporation, Santa Monica, CA. http://www.rand.org/pubs/occasional_papers/OP227.html.

King, Christopher T. 2004. "The Effectiveness of Publicly Financed Training in the United States: Implications for WIA and Related Programs." In *Job Training Policy in the United States*, edited by Christopher J. O'Leary, Robert A. Straits, and Stephen A. Wandner, 57–99. Kalamazoo, MI: W.E. Upjohn Institute.

King, Christopher T., and Carolyn J. Heinrich. 2011. "How Effective Are U.S. Workforce Development Programs? Implications for U.S. Workforce Development Policies." Paper presented at Association for Public Policy Analysis and Management Fall Research Conference, Washington, DC. http://www.naswa.org/assets/utilities/serve.cfm?GID=b7f36023-ff87-4b5f-a752-5d99b1d6afcf.

Kingsley, G. Thomas. 1982. *The Cleveland Metropolitan Economy*. Santa Monica CA: RAND Corporation, 1982.

Klepper, Steven. 2010. "The Origin and Growth of Industry Clusters: The Making of Silicon Valley and Detroit." *Journal of Urban Economics* 67 (1): 15–32.

Kolko, Jed, and David Neumark. 2010. "Does Local Business Ownership Insulate Cities from Economic Shocks?" *Journal of Urban Economics* 67 (1): 103–115.

Kortum, Samuel, and Josh Lerner. 1998. "Does Venture Capital Spur Innovation?" NBER Working Paper Series Working Paper 6846, National Bureau of Economic Research, Cambridge, MA. http://www.nber.org/papers/w6846.

Krugman, Paul. 1993. "The Lessons of Massachusetts for EMU." In *Adjustment and Growth in the European Monetary Union*, edited by F. Torres and F. Giavazzi, 241–269. Cambridge: Cambridge University Press.

Ladd, Helen F. 2012. "Education and Poverty: Confronting the Evidence." *Journal of Policy Analysis and Management* 31 (2): 203–227.

Lafer, Gordon. 2002. *The Job Training Charade*. Ithaca: Cornell University Press.

Lee, Yoonsoo, and Brian Rudick. 2006. "Employment Growth, Job Creation, and Job Destruction in Ohio." *Economic Commentary* (April): 1–4.

Leigh, Duane E., and Andrew M. Gill. 1997. "Labor Market Returns to Community Colleges: Evidence for Returning Adults." *Journal of Human Relations* 32 (2): 334–353.

Leistritz, F. Larry, and Dean Bangsund. 1998. "Regional Economic Development: Evaluation of a Local Initiative in North Dakota." *Great Plains Research: A Journal of Natural and Social Sciences* 8 (2): 281–298.

Lendel, Iryna. 2010. "The Impact of Research Universities on Regional Economies: The Concept of University Products." *Economic Development Quarterly* 24 (3): 210–230.

Lewin, Tamar. 2012. "Money Urged for Colleges to Perform Job Training." *New York Times*, February 13.

Lewis, David A. 2001. "Does Technology Incubation Work? A Critical Review." Reviews of Economic Development Literature and Practice, no. 11.

Lin, Jeffrey. 2012. "Regional Resilience." Working Paper No. 13-1, Federal Reserve Bank of Philadelphia, Philadelphia, PA.

Liu, Ben-chieh. 1975. "Net Migration Rates and the Quality of Life." *Review of Economics and Statistics* 57 (3): 329–337.

Lochner, Lance. 2011. "Non-Production Benefits of Education: Crime, Health, and Good Citizenship." NBER Working Paper No. 16722, National Bureau of Economic Research, Cambridge, MA. http://www.nber.org/papers/w16722.

Loveless, Tom, and Frederick M. Hess. 2007. "What Do We Know about School Size and Class Size." In *Brookings Papers on Education Policy*, 205–272. Washington, DC: Brookings Institution Press.

Lowe, Nichola, Harvey Goldstein, and Mary Donegan. 2011. "Patchwork Intermediation: Challenges and Opportunities for Regionally Coordinated Workforce Development." *Economic Development Quarterly* 25 (2): 158–171.

Luria, Daniel. 2011. *Evaluating MEP Evaluation*. Presentation at "Strengthening American Manufacturing: The Role of the Manufacturing Extension Partnership" for National Academy of Sciences, November 14. http://sites.nationalacademies.org/PGA/step/PGA_066048.

Luria, Dan, and Edith Wiarda. 1996. "Performance Benchmarking and Measuring Programme Impacts on Customers: Lessons from the Midwest Manufacturing Technology Center." *Research Policy* 25: 233–246.

Lynch, Robert G. 2004. *Rethinking Growth Strategies: How State and Local Taxes and Services Affect Economic Development*. Washington, DC: Economic Policy Institute.

Lynde, Catherine, and James Richmond. 1992. "The Role of Public Capital in Production." *Review of Economics and Statistics* 74 (1): 37–44.

MacEwan, Arthur. 2013. *Early Childhood Education as an Essential Component of Economic Development: With Reference to the New England States.* Amherst: Political Economy Institute, University of Massachusetts.

Malizia, Emil, and Edward Feser. 1999. *Understanding Local Economic Development.* New Brunswick, NJ: Center for Urban Policy Research.

Malpezzi, Stephen. 2001. "What Do We Know about Economic Development? What Does It Mean for Wisconsin's State and Local Governments?" Working Paper, Center for Urban Land Economics Research, University of Wisconsin, Madison.

Marcotte, Dave E., Thomas Bailey, Carey Borkoski, and Greg S. Kienzl. 2005. "The Returns of a Community College Education: Evidence from the National Education Longitudinal Survey." *Educational Evaluation and Policy Analysis* 27 (2): 157–175.

Markley, Deborah M., and Kevin T. McNamara. 1996. "Local Economic and State Fiscal Impacts of Business Incubators." *State & Local Government Review* 28 (1): 17–27.

Markusen, Ann. 1985. *Profit Cycles, Oligopoly, and Regional Development.* Cambridge: MIT Press.

———. 2004. "Targeting Occupations in Regional and Community Economic Development." *Journal of the American Planning Association* 70 (3): 253–268.

———. 2006. "Urban Development and the Politics of a Creative Class: Evidence from the Study of Artists." *Environment and Planning A* 38 (10): 1921–1940.

Markusen, Ann, Peter Hall, and Amy Glasmeier. 1986. *High Tech America: The What How, When, and Why of Sunrise Industries.* Boston: Allen and Unwin.

Martin, Ron. 2012. "Regional Economic Resilience, Hysterisis and Revolutionary Shock." *Journal of Economic Geography* 12 (1): 1–32.

Martin, Ron, and Peter Sunley. 1996. "Paul Krugman's Geographical Economics and Its Implications for Regional Development Theory: A Critical Assessment." *Economic Geography* 72 (3): 259–292.

———. 2003. "Deconstructing Clusters: Chaotic Concept or Policy Panacea?" *Journal of Economic Geography* 3 (1): 5–35.

Mathur, Vijay K. 1999. "Human Capital-Based Strategy for Regional Economic Development." *Economic Development Quarterly* 13 (3): 203–216.

Mayer, Heike. 2006. "What Is the Role of Universities in High-Tech Economic Development? The Case of Portland, Oregon, and Washington, DC." *Local Economy* 21 (3): 292–315.

Mian, Sarfraz A. 1996. "Assessing Value-Added Contributions of University Technology Business Incubators to Tenant Firms." *Research Policy* 25 (3): 325–335.

Michigan Future, Inc. 2006. *A New Agenda for a New Michigan.* Ann Arbor: Michigan Future, Inc.

Miller, Carol Poh, and Robert A. Wheeler. 1997. *Cleveland: A Concise History, 1796–1996.* Bloomington: Indiana University Press.

Milward, H. Brinton, and Heidi Hosbach Newman. 1989. "State Incentive Packages and the Industrial Location Decision." *Economic Development Quarterly* 3 (3): 203–222.

Modica, Marco, and Aura Reggiani. 2014. "Spatial Economic Resilience: Overview and Perspectives. *Networks and Spatial Economics* 15 (2): 211–233.

Mofidi, Alaeddin, and Joe Stone. 1990. "Do State and Local Taxes Affect Economic Growth?" *Review of Economics and Statistics* 72 (4): 686–691.

Mole, Kevin F., Mark Hart, Stephen Roper, and David S. Saal. 2008. "Assessing the Effectiveness of Business Support Services in England: Evidence from a Theory-Based Evaluation." *International Small Business Journal* 27 (5): 557–582.

———. 2011. "Broader or Deeper? Exploring the Most Effective Intervention Profile for Public Small Business Support." *Environment and Planning A* 43 (1): 87–105.

Molnar, L.A. et al. 1997. *Business Incubation Works.* Athens, OH: National Business Incubation Association.

Morgan, Kevin. 1997. "The Learning Region: Institutions, Innovation and Regional Renewal." *Regional Studies* 31 (5): 491–503.

Moretti, Enrico. 2003. "Human Capital Externalities in Cities." NBER Working Paper No. 9641, National Bureau of Economic Research, Cambridge, MA.

———. 2004. "Estimating the Social Return to Higher Education: Evidence from Longitudinal and Repeated Cross-sectional Data." *Journal of Econometrics* 121 (1–2): 175–212.

Morrow, Betty. 2008. "Community Resilience: A Social Justice Perspective." CARRI Research Report 4, Community and Regional Resilience Initiative, Oak Ridge National Laboratory.

Munnell, Alicia H. 1990a. "How Does Public Infrastructure Affect Regional Economic Performance?" *New England Economic Review* (September/October): 11–32.

———. 1990b. "Why Has Productivity Growth Declined? Productivity and Public Investment." *New England Economic Review* (January/February): 3–22.

———. 1992. "Infrastructure Investment and Economic Growth." *Journal of Economic Perspectives* 6 (4): 189–198.

Murname, Richard. 2009. "Education: Educating Urban Children." In *Making Cities Work: Prospects and Policies for Urban America*, edited by Robert P. Inman, 269–296. Princeton: Princeton University Press.

Musil, Tom. 2001. "Project Impact Analysis: Insights for Developers." *Site Selection* 46 (2): 146–151.

Myrdal, Gunnar. 1957. *Economic Theory and Underdeveloped Regions.* London: Duckworth.

National Business Incubation Association. 2011. "Business Incubation FAQs." http://www.nbia.org/resource_library/faq/index.

National Institute of Standards and Technology. 2012. "Manufacturing Extension Partnership Homepage." http://www.nist.gov/mep/.

Nelson, Arthur C., and Kathryn A. Foster. 1999. "Metropolitan Governance Structure and Income Growth." *Journal of Urban Affairs* 21 (3): 309–324.

Newman, Robert, and Dennis Sullivan. 1988. "Econometric Analysis of Business Tax Impacts on Industrial Location: What Do We Know and How Do We Know It?" *Journal of Urban Economics* 53 (2): 215–234.

NEXUS Associates, Inc. 2003. "Assessing the Poverty Impact of Small Enterprise Initiatives." Prepared for Working Group for Impact Measurement and Performance Committee of Donor Agencies for Small Enterprise Development.

NEXUS Associates, Inc., Jack Russell & Associates, Inc., and Michigan Manufacturing Technology Center. 1999. *The Pennsylvania Industrial Resource Centers: Assessing the Record and Charting the Future: Final Report.* Belmont: NEXUS Associates.

Norris, Fran H., Susan P. Stevens, Betty Pfefferbaum, Karen F. Wyche, and Rose L. Pfefferbaum. 2008. "Community Resilience as a Metaphor, Theory, Set of Capacities, and Strategy for Disaster Readiness." *American Journal of Community Psychology* 41 (1/2): 127–150.

North Dakota Mill & Elevator. 2012. "NDM History." https://www.ndmill.com/history.cfm.

Norton, R.D., and J. Rees. 1979. "The Product Cycle and the Spatial Decentralization of American Manufacturing." *Regional Studies* 13 (2): 141–151.

Nunn, Nathan. 2009. "The Importance of History for Economic Development." NBER Working Paper No. 14899, National Bureau of Economic Research, Cambridge, MA. http://www.nber.org/papers/w14899.

Oanda Corporation. 2013. "Historical Exchange Rates." http://www.oanda.com/currency/historical-rates.

Oates, Wallace E., and Robert M. Schwab. 1991. "The Allocative and Distributive Implications of Local Fiscal Competition." In *Competition among States and Local Governments*, edited by Daphne A. Kenyon and John Kincaid, 127–146. Washington, DC: Urban Institute Press.

O'Huallachain, Breandan. 1992. "Economic Structure and Growth of Metropolitan Areas." In *Sources of Metropolitan Growth*, edited by Edwin S. Mills and John F. McDonald, 51–85. New Brunswick, NJ: Center for Urban Policy Research.

Olberding, Julia. 2002a. "Diving into the 'Third Waves' of Regional Governance and Economic Development Strategies: A Study of Regional Partnerships for Economic Development in U.S. Metropolitan Areas." *Economic Development Quarterly* 16 (3): 251–272.

———. 2002b. "Does Regionalism Beget Regionalism: The Relationship between Norms and Regional Partnerships for Economic Development." *Public Administration Review* 62 (4): 480–491.

———. 2009. "Toward Evaluating the Effectiveness of Regional Partnerships for Economic Development in U.S. Metropolitan Areas." *International Journal of Public Administration* 32 (5): 393–414.

Oldsman, Eric. 1996. "Does Manufacturing Extension Matter? An Evaluation of the Industrial Technology Extension Service in New York." *Research Policy* 25 (2): 215–232.

O'Leary, Christopher J., Robert A. Straits, and Stephen A. Wandner. 2004. "Public Job Training: Experience and Prospects." In *Job Training Policy in the United States*, edited by Christopher J. O'Leary, Robert A. Straits, and Stephen A. Wandner, 289–309. Kalamazoo, MI: W.E. Upjohn Institute.

Ordowich, Christopher, David Cheney, Jan Youtie, Andrea Fernández-Ribas, and Philip Shapira. 2012. "Evaluating the Impact of MEP Services on Establishment Performance: A Preliminary Empirical Investigation." Center for Economic Studies Discussion Paper CES-12-15, U.S. Census Bureau, Washington, DC.

Ormerod, Paul. 2010. "Resilience after Local Economic Shocks." *Applied Economic Letters* 17 (5): 503–507.

O'Toole, Laurence J., Jr. 1997. "Treating Networks Seriously: Practical and Research-Based Agendas in Public Administration." *Public Administration Review* 57 (1): 45–52.

Pack, Janet Rothberger. 2002. *Growth and Convergence in Metropolitan America*. Washington, DC: Brookings Institution Press.

———, ed. 2005. *Sunbelt/Frostbelt: Public Policies and Market Forces in Metropolitan Development*. Washington, DC: Brookings Institution Press.

Parker, Robert E., and Joe R. Feagin. 1990. "A 'Better Business Climate' in Houston." In *Leadership and Urban Regeneration: Cities in North America and Europe*, edited by Dennis Judd and Michael Parkinson, 216–238. Newbury Park, CA: Sage.

Pastor, Manuel, and Chris Benner. 2008. "Been Down so Long: Weak-Market Cities and Regional Equity." In *Retooling for Growth*, edited by Richard M. McGahey and Jennifer S. Vey, 89–118. Washington, DC: Brookings Institution Press.

Pastor, Manuel, Peter Dreier, J. Eugene Grigsby, and Marta Lopez-Garza. 2000. *Regions That Work: How Cities and Suburbs Can Grow Together*. Minneapolis: University of Minnesota Press.

Paton, Douglas, and David Johnston. 2001. "Disaster and Communities: Vulnerability, Resilience, and Preparedness." *Disaster Prevention and Management* 10 (4): 270–277.

Paytas, Jerry. 2001. Does Governance Matter? The Dynamics of Metropolitan Governance and Competitiveness. Pittsburgh: Carnegie Mellon Center for Economic Development.

Peck, Jamie. 2005. "Struggling with the Creative Class." *International Journal of Urban and Regional Research* 29 (4): 740–770.

Peirce, Neal. 1993. *Citistates*. Washington, DC: Seven Locks Press.

Pendall, Rolf, Kathryn Foster, and Margaret Cowell. 2010. "Resilience and Regions: Building Understanding of the Metaphor." *Cambridge Journal of Regions, Economy and Society* 3 (1): 1–14.

Perry, David C. 1990. "Recasting Urban Leadership in Buffalo." In *Leadership and Urban Regeneration: Cities in North America and Europe*, edited by Dennis R. Judd and Michael Parkinson, 258–276. Newbury Park, CA: Sage.

Persky, Joseph, Daniel Felsenstein, and Virginia Carlson. 2004. *Does "Trickle Down" Work? Economic Development Strategies and Job Chains in Local Labor Markets*. Kalamazoo, MI: W.E. Upjohn Institute for Employment Research.

Peters, Alan, and Fisher, Peter. 2004. "The Failures of Economic Development Incentives." *Journal of the American Planning Association* 70 (1): 27–37.

Peterson, Garry, Craig Allen, and C. S. Holling. 1998. "Ecological Resilience, Biodiversity, and Scale." *Ecosystems* 1 (1): 6–18.

Phillips, Joseph M., and Ernest P. Goss. 1995. "The Effect of State and Local Taxes on Economic Development: A Meta-Analysis." *Southern Economic Journal* 62 (2): 297–316.

Pittman, Kirsten Valle. 2012. "Question Remains for BofA: Are Charlotte Ties Fading?" *Charlotte Observer*, May 13.

Plosila, Walter H. 2004. "State Science- and Technology-Based Economic Development Policy: History, Trends and Developments, and Future Directions." *Economic Development Quarterly* 18 (2): 113–126.

Porter, Michael. 1998. *Competitive Advantage: Creating and Sustaining Superior Performance*. New York: Free Press.

——. 2003. "The Economic Performance of Regions." *Regional Studies* 37 (6): 545–578.

——. 2009. "Clusters and Economic Policy: Aligning Public Policy with the New Economics of Competition." Institute for Strategy and Competitiveness White Paper, Harvard Business School, Boston.

Prosperity Partnership. 2012. *Regional Economic Strategy for the Central Puget Sound Region: Strategy*. Seattle: Puget Sound Regional Council.

Puget Sound Regional Council. 2013. "History." http://www.psrc.org/assets/3305/timeline.pdf.

Rappa, John. 2007. "Legislative History of the Economic Development and Manufacturing Assistance Act." OLR Research Report 2007-R-0447, Office of Legislative Research, Hartford, CT. http://www.cga.ct.gov/2007/rpt/2007-R-0447.htm.

Rauch, James E. 1993. "Productivity Gains from Geographic Concentration of Human Capital: Evidence from the Cities." *Journal of Urban Economics* 34 (3): 380–400.

Renski, Henry. 2009. "A New Era of Federal Involvement in Regional Economic Development? The Case of the WIRED Initiative." *Environment and Planning C: Government and Policy* 27 (4): 593–611.

Roback, Jennifer. 1982. "Wages, Rents, and Quality of Life." *Journal of Political Economy* 90 (6): 1257–1278.

Robson, Paul J.A., and Robert J. Bennett. 2010. "Paying Fees for Government Business Advice: An Assessment of Business Link Experience." *Applied Economics* 42 (1): 37–48.

Romer, David. 2001. *Advanced Macroeconomics*. New York: McGraw-Hill.

Romer, Paul M. 1986. "Increasing Returns and Long-run Growth." *Journal of Political Economy* 94 (5): 1002–1037.

Romp, Ward, and Jakob de Haan. 2007. "Public Capital and Economic Growth: A Critical Survey." *Perspektiven der Wirtschaftspolitik* 8: 6–52.

Rose, Adam. 2004. "Defining and Measuring Economic Resilience to Disasters." *Disaster Prevention and Management* 13 (4): 307–314.

———. 2009. "Economic Resilience to Disasters." CARRI Research Report 8, Community and Regional Resilience Initiative, Oak Ridge National Laboratory.

Rose, Adam, and Shu-Yi Liao. 2005. "Modeling Regional Economic Resilience to Disasters: A Computable General Equilibrium Analysis of Water Service Disruptions." *Journal of Regional Science* 45 (1): 75–112.

Rosenfeld, Stuart. 2000. "Community College/Cluster Connections: Specialization and Competitiveness in the United States and Europe." *Economic Development Quarterly* 14 (1): 51–62.

———. 2002. "Creating Smart Systems. A Guide to Cluster Strategies in Less Favoured Regions." A report to the European Union-Regional Innovation Strategies, Regional Technology Strategies, Carrboro.

Rosenthal, Stuart S., and William C. Strange. 2004. "Evidence of the Nature and Sources of Agglomeration Economies." In *Handbook of Regional and Urban Economics,* edited by J. Vernon Henderson and Jacques-François Thisse, vol. 4, 2119–2171. Amsterdam: Elsevier.

Roussakis, Emmanuel N. 1997. *Commercial Banking in an Era of Deregulation.* 3rd ed. Westport, CT: Praeger.

Rozario, Kevin. 2005. "Making Progress: Disaster Narratives and the Art of Optimism in Modern America." In *The Resilient City*, edited by Lawrence J. Vale and Thomas J. Campanella, 27–54. New York: Oxford University Press.

RTI International. 2007. *Maryland Incubator Impact Analysis and Evaluation of Additional Incubator Capacity*. Research Triangle Park: RTI International.

Rubel, Thom, and Scott Palladino. 2000. Nurturing Entrepreneurial Growth in State Economies. Washington, DC: National Governors' Association. nga.org/files/live/sites/NGA/files/pdf/ENTREPRENEUR.PDF.

Rusk, David. 1993. *Cities without Suburbs*. Washington, DC: Woodrow Wilson Center Press.

Rutter, Michael. 1993. "Resilience: Some Conceptual Considerations." *Journal of Adolescent Health* 14 (8): 626–631.

Safford, Sean. 2009. *Why the Garden Club Couldn't Save Youngstown: The Transformation of the Rust Belt*. Cambridge: Harvard University Press.

Salter, Ammon J., and Ben R. Martin. 2001. "The Economic Benefits of Publicly
Funded Basic Research: A Critical Review." *Research Policy* 30 (3): 509–532.

Samila, Sampsa, and Olav Sorenson. 2011. "Venture Capital, Entrepreneurship, and
Economic Growth." *Review of Economics and Statistics* 93 (1): 338–349.

Saxenian, AnnaLee. 1990. "Regional Networks and the Resurgence of Silicon Valley."
California Management Review 33 (1): 89–112.

———. 1994. *Regional Advantage: Culture and Competition in Silicon Valley and Route
128.* Cambridge: Harvard University Press.

Schanzenbach, Diane Whitmore. 2006/2007. "What Have Researchers Learned from
Project STAR?" in *Brookings Papers on Education Policy*, 205–228. Washington,
DC: Brookings Institution Press.

Schmenner, Roger. 1982. *Making Location Decisions.* Englewood Cliffs, NK: Prentice
Hall.

Scott, Allen J. 2006. "Creative Cities: Conceptual Issues and Policy Questions." *Journal
of Urban Affairs* 28 (1): 1–17.

Shane, Scott. 2009. "Why Encouraging More People to Become Entrepreneurs Is Bad
Public Policy." *Small Business Economics* 33 (2): 141–149.

Shapira, Philip, Jan Youtie, and Luciano Kay. 2011. "Building Capabilities for
Innovation in SMEs: A Cross-country Comparison of Technology Extension
Policies and Programmes." *International Journal of Innovation and Regional
Development* 3 (3/4): 254–272.

Shapiro, Jesse M. 2005. "Smart Cities: Quality of Life, Productivity, and the Growth
Effects of Human Capital." NBER Working Paper No. 11615, National Bureau of
Economic Research, Cambridge, MA.

Sheffi, Yossi. 2005. *The Resilient Enterprise: Overcoming Vulnerability for Competitive
Advantage.* Cambridge: MIT Press.

Small Business Innovation Research. 2012. "SBIR." http://www.sbir.gov/about/
about-sbir.

Smith-Doerr, Laurel, and Powell, Walter W. 2005. "Networks and Economic Life." In
The Handbook of Economic Sociology, edited by Neil J. Smelser and Richard
Swedberg, 379–402. 2nd ed. Princeton: Princeton University Press.

Solomon, George. 2007. "An Examination of Entrepreneurship Education in the
United States." *Journal of Small Business and Enterprise Development* 14 (2):
168–182.

SSTI. 2006. "A Resource Guide for Technology-based Economic Development:
Positioning Universities as Drivers, Fostering Entrepreneurship, Increasing
Access to Capital." Report prepared for the U.S. Department of Commerce,
Economic Development Administration. http://ssti.org/Publications/
Onlinepubs/resource_guide.pdf.

Stangler, Dane, and Robert E. Litan. 2009. "Where Will the Jobs Come From?"
Kauffman Foundation Research Series: Firm Formation and Economic Growth,
Ewing Marion Kauffman Foundation, Kansas City, MO.

Stanley, Marcus, Lawrence Katz, and Alan Krueger. 1998. "Developing Skills: What We
Know About the Impacts of American Employment and Training Programs on
Employment, Earnings, and Educational Outcomes." http://scholar.harvard.
edu/lkatz/publications/developing-skills-what-we-know-about-impact-
american-educational-and-training-pro.

Stansel, Dean. "Local Decentralization and Local Economic Growth: A Cross-Sectional
Examination of US Metropolitan Areas." *Journal of Urban Economics* 57 (1):
55–72.

State of Connecticut. 1998. "Governor Rowland Offers Plan to Promote the Redevelopment of Downtown Hartford." Press Release, March 19. http://www.ct.gov/governorrowland/cwp/view.asp?A=1331&Q=256160.

Stevans, Lonnie K. 2009. "The Effect of Endogenous Right-to-Work Laws on Business and Economic Conditions in the United States: A Multivariate Approach." *Review of Law and Economics* 5 (1): 595–612.

Stimson, Robert, Roger R. Stough, and Maria Salazar. 2009. *Leadership and Institutions in Regional Endogenous Development*. Northhampton, MA: Edward Elgar.

Stokan, Eric, Lyke Thompson, and Robert J. Mahu. 2015. "Testing the Differential Effect of Business Incubators on Firm Growth." *Economic Development Quarterly* 29 (4): 317–327.

Stone, Clarence N. 1989. *Regime Politics: Governing Atlanta, 1946–1988*. Lawrence: University of Kansas Press.

Storper, Michael. 1985. "Oligopoly and the Product cycle: Essentialism in Economic Geography." *Economic Geography* 61 (3): 260–282.

———. 2013. *Keys to the City*. Princeton: Princeton University Press.

Sturm, Jan Egbert, and Jakob de Haan. 1995. "Is Public Expenditure Really Productive? New Evidence for the US and the Netherlands." *Economic Modelling* 12 (1): 60–72.

Summers, Anita and Peter Linneman. 1993. "Patterns and Processes of Employment and Population Decentralization in the United States." In *Urban Change in the United States and Western Europe*, edited by Anita Summers, Paul Cheshire, and Lanfranco Senn, 89–147. Washington, DC: Urban Institute Press.

Swanstrom, Todd. 2002. "What We Argue about When We Argue about Regionalism." *Journal of Urban Affairs* 23 (5): 479–496.

———. 2008. "Regional Resilience: A Critical Examination of the Ecological Framework." Working Paper 2008-07, Building Resilient Regions Network, Berkeley, CA.

Swanstrom, Todd, Karen Chapple, and Dan Immergluck. 2009. "Regional Resilience in the Face of Foreclosures: Evidence from Six Metropolitan Areas." Working Paper 2009-05, Building Resilient Regions Network, Berkeley, CA.

Tannenwald, Robert. 1997. "State Regulatory Policy and Economic Development." *New England Economic Review* (March/April): 83–108.

Tatom, J.A. 1991. "Public Capital and Private Sector Performance." *Federal Reserve Bank of St. Louis Review* 73 (3): 3–15.

Taylor, Jill S. 2006. "What Makes a Region Entrepreneurial? A Review of the Literature." Levin College of Urban Affairs, Cleveland State University.

Thompson, Jeffrey. 2010. "Prioritizing Approaches to Economic Development in New England: Skills, Infrastructure and Tax Incentives." Political Economy Research Institute, University of Massachusetts, Amherst.

Tiebout, Charles M. 1956. "A Pure Theory of Local Expenditures." *Journal of Political Economy* 64 (5): 416–424.

Training. 2011. "2011 Training Industry Report." http://www.trainingmag.com/content/digital-archives.

Udell, Gerald G. 1990. "Are Business Incubators Really Creating New Jobs by Creating New Businesses and New Products." *Journal of Product Innovation Management* 7 (2): 108–122.

University of North Dakota. "Annual Financial Report, 2010." Grand Forks: University of North Dakota. http://und.edu/finance-operations/_files/docs/und-fy-2010-financial-report.pdf.

U.S. Bureau of Labor Statistics. 2013. "Databases, Tables & Calculators by Subject." http://data.bls.gov/timeseries/LAUMT38242203?data_tool=XGtable.

U.S. Government Accountability Office. 2009. "IRS Practices Contribute to Its Resilience, But It Would Benefit from Additional Emergency Planning Efforts." GAO-09-418, Government Printing Office, Washington, DC. http://www.gao.gov/products/GAO-09-418.

———. 2011. "Multiple Employment and Training Programs: Providing Information on Colocating Services and Consolidating Administrative Structures Could Promote Efficiencies." GAO-11-92, Government Printing Office, Washington, DC. http://www.gao.gov/products/GAO-11-92.

———. 2012. "Efficiency and Effectiveness of Fragmented Economic Development Programs Are Unclear." GAO-12-553T, Government Printing Office, Washington, DC. http://www.gao.gov/products/GAO-12-553T.

U.S. Small Business Administration. 2012. "Small Business Development Centers (SBDCs)." http://www.sba.gov/content/small-business-development-centers-sbdcs.

Vale, Lawrence J., and Thomas J. Campanella. 2005a. "Conclusion: Axioms of Resilience." In *The Resilient City*, edited by Lawrence J. Vale and Thomas J. Campanella, 335–355. New York: Oxford University Press.

———. 2005b. "Introduction: The Cities Rise Again." In *The Resilient City*, edited by Lawrence J. Vale and Thomas J. Campanella, 3–23. New York: Oxford University Press.

Van Vugt, Mark, Robert Hogan, and Robert B. Kaiser. 2008. "Leadership, Followership, and Evolution: Some Lessons from the Past." *American Psychologist* 63 (3): 182–196.

Varaiya, Pravin, and Michael Wiseman. 1978. "The Age of Cities and the Movement of Manufacturing Employment: 1947–1972." *Papers in Regional Science* 41 (1): 127–140.

Vernon, Raymond. 1966. "International Investment and International Trade in the Product Cycle." *Quarterly Journal of Economics* 80 (2): 190–207.

———. 1979. "The Product Cycle Hypothesis in a New International Environment." *Oxford Bulletin of Economics and Statistics* 41 (4): 255–267.

Voytek, Kenneth P., Karen L. Lellock, and Mark A. Schmit. 2004. "Developing Performance Metrics for Science and Technology Programs: The Case of the Manufacturing Extension Partnership Program." *Economic Development Quarterly* 18 (2): 174–185.

Waits, Mary Jo. 2002. "The Added Value of the Industry Cluster Approach to Economic Analysis, Strategy Development, and Service Delivery." *Economic Development Quarterly* 14 (1): 35–50.

Wallace, Sally. 2008. "Interjurisdictional Competition under U.S. Fiscal Federalism." In *Fiscal Decentralization and Land Policies*, edited by Gregory K. Ingram and Yu-Hung Hong, 219–237. Cambridge: Lincoln Institute of Land Policy.

Wasylenko, Michael. 1997. "Taxation and Economic Development: The State of the Economic Literature." *New England Economic Review* (March/April): 37–52.

Weiss, Jonathan D. 2004. "Public Schools and Economic Development: What the Research Shows." Cincinnati: KnowledgeWorks Foundation. www.mea.org/tef/pdf/public_schools_development.pdf.

Werner, Emmy E. 1993. "Risk, Resilience, and Recovery: Perspectives from the Kauai Longitudinal Study." *Development and Psychopathology* 5 (4): 503–515.

Wiewel, Wim. 1999. "Policy Research in an Imperfect World: Response to Terry F. Buss, 'The Case against Targeted Industry Strategies.'" *Economic Development Quarterly* 13 (4): 357–360.

Wolman, Harold, and Diana Hincapie. 2015. "Clusters and Cluster-Based Development Policy." *Economic Development Quarterly* 29 (2): 135–149.

Wolman, Harold, Alice Levy, Garry Young, and Pam Blumenthal. 2008. "Economic Competitiveness and the Determinants of Sub-National Economic Activity." Working Paper 34, George Washington Institute of Public Policy, Washington, DC. http://www.gwu.edu/~gwipp/Competitiveness%20lit%20rev%20final%20. word.pdf.

Wu, Yonghong. 2008. "State R&D Tax Credits and High-Technology Establishments." *Economic Development Quarterly* 22 (2): 136–148.

Yusuf, Juita-Elena. 2010. "Research Note: Meeting Entrepreneurs' Support Needs: Are Assistance Programs Effective?" *Journal of Small Business and Enterprise Development* 17 (2): 294–307.

Index

Page numbers followed by *f* or *t* refer to figures or tables. Page numbers followed by n or nn refer to notes.

CPSIA information can be obtained
at www.ICGtesting.com
Printed in the USA
LVHW02s2223180818
587393LV00004B/415/P